D1125023

21 TEXAS *Short Stories*

21 TEXAS *Short Stories*

Edited by WILLIAM PEERY

UNIVERSITY OF TEXAS PRESS ⌥ AUSTIN

013205

NORTHEAST TEXAS COMMUNITY COLLEGE
LEARNING
MT. PLEASANT, TEXAS

For Beverley

International Standard Book Number 0–292–73452–2
Library of Congress Catalog Card Number 54–7339
Introduction and biographical sketches copyright © 1954 by William
Peery; stories copyright by respective authors and/or publishers
and used by permission.
All rights reserved
Printed in the United States of America

Fifth Paperback Printing, 1985

Requests for permission to reproduce material from this work should
be sent to Permissions, University of Texas Press, Box 7819, Austin,
Texas 78713.

Acknowledgments

ACKNOWLEDGMENTS to the authors and other copyright owners of the stories herein are offered on the first page of each story. Here I want to thank them for allowing the use of their work and for revising the introductory sketches. For helpful suggestions and assistance I am grateful also to Miss Edleen Begg, Mr. Elroy Bode, and Professors Mody C. Boatright, J. Frank Dobie, Robert A. Law, and Walter P. Webb.

WILLIAM PEERY

Austin, Texas
March 21, 1954

Contents

Contents

21 **TEXAS** *Short Stories*

*You shall hear how we fared
In Texas, down by the Rio Grande*
—FRANK DESPREZ, "Lasca"

Texas in the Short Story

THE EARLIEST CONNECTION I know of between Texas and the short story was the publication, April 3, 1830, of a translation of Prosper Mérimée's world-famous "Mateo Falcone" in *The Texas Gazette*. During the state's first fifty or more years, Texans were so busy living life that few of them had much time to write about it. Karl Postl, it is true, wrote *The Cabin Book, or Sketches of Life in Texas* (1844), and Charles W. Webber wrote *Tales of the Southern Border* (1852), but these works contain what their titles say they contain, sketches and tales, comparatively formless episodic narratives not at all in the Poe–De Maupassant–Hemingway–Joyce tradition. To have included in this anthology selections from these historically important Texas books would have been to include narratives that properly lie outside even the broadest definition of the short story.

The definition used to determine what went into this book is, indeed, broad enough. I have not confined myself to selections from little magazines and books, to works of "Art" that will please such critics and writers as speak of the short story only in tones of religious awe. Those who make a cult of the short story may find fiction of the sort they admire in the selections by Goyen, Katherine Anne Porter, O'Donnell, and Thompson. Others, however, may hold the view, not very respectable in some artistic and critical circles, that *Collier's, Saturday Evening Post*, and certain woman's magazines sometimes print good fiction. They may enjoy more the selections by Benefield, Carver, Cousins, and Perry. By their first appearances you may know them—whether in the slicks, or in a book or a little or quality-group magazine. I omit the pulps, though Texans have, as might be expected, done well in these magazines that, with remarkable simplification, stress guns, tall lean good cowboys, and short heavy bad men. I omit also autobiographies, such as

3

Texas in the Short Story

Davy Crockett's (the *Exploits and Adventures in Texas* was not, however, written by Crockett), and tall and other folk tales, such as Professor Mody C. Boatright tells in *Tall Tales from Texas Cow Camps* and he and others recount in the publications of the Texas Folklore Society. Even if it appears in a large-circulation magazine, the short story proper is a self-conscious form wrought by a conscious artist. Folk material, when collected and assimilated, may of course be transmuted into fiction, as the best work of J. Frank Dobie shows.

To present in one volume all the good short stories or even all the good writers of short stories that have interpreted Texas is not possible. The present selection is my effort to represent this body of writing faithfully and with what I think is proper emphasis. One possible departure from ideal proportion is the arbitrary limitation I have felt myself forced to impose, of one story to an author. In the final reckoning, which this book does not attempt to make, it may be that such a writer as Katherine Anne Porter or William Goyen will prove to have deserved two or ten of the twenty-one places that have here been filled.

So far as possible, I present these stories in the chronological order of their time settings. According to her short-story writers, the history of Texas begins, not with the Indians, the conquistadores, or the missions, not with Ysleta or with Austin's colony, but with the settlers of the 1850's. The locales of these stories involve all parts of the state—and much of its fauna and flora—from Amarillo to the Border, from El Paso to the Louisiana line. If Central, North, and East Texas are more often represented than other regions, they are more heavily populated.

Here are stories of Indians, Mexicans, Negroes, Europeans, and just plain Texans. The principal interests of Texans are represented: cattle, horses, farming, oil, railroads, politics, religion, industry, money, love, and the weather. The characters include adventurers, cowboys, clerks, legislators, oilmen, preachers, rangers, trainmen, and union organizers. Here are a cotton planter, cow-catcher, horse trader, hunter, landlord, scavenger, sheriff, and watchman at a rice barn. The women are resourceful housewives and wise mothers, but they include also a café hash-slinger, a self-sacrificing daughter and sister, a music teacher, and a rooster-raiser and church builder. The men are men and the women are memorable.

And like the real Texans they are, these Texans of fiction have many

4

children, from infants in arms to a tomboy first awakening into young womanhood. A five-year-old gets a pony; a six-year-old takes her first solo train ride and learns about Santa Claus. But the younger generation is predominantly male. Boys of varying ages are central characters and effectively chosen narrators of six stories, grappling with some rather adult problems, such as where they stand on the Negro question, and that universal and perennially baffling question, how to live the good life.

Two common errors of regional anthologists I have taken some pains to avoid. In an effort to achieve quantity, the makers of state books have too often forgotten quality. Regional writing is worth collecting, I think, only if by other standards it is good writing—if, transcending the regional, it reveals the universal. All the stories in this collection, I believe, are successful as *stories* (of the sort their authors were trying to write). I have put in nothing just because of the author's residence address.

I have tried, in the second place, not to claim more for Texas than her stories justify. Few would doubt that a land and people so rich in racial heritages, of so romantic a past and fabulous a present, ought to be able to evoke worthy writing. Only in our own century have they begun to do so. Despite the *Southwest Review* (to which this book is heavily indebted) and the Southern Methodist University Press and the University of Texas Press, despite the writers' conferences and the courses in writing everywhere, and despite the huge Poetry Society of Texas and all the city symphonies, we are not necessarily undergoing any great cultural awakening. Texas is in its cultural young manhood, and that makes its short stories exciting. We should and will leave the ultimate appraisal of them to time, the best of literary critics.

Yet we may, I think, be proud of our contribution to the short story and of the Texans who have practiced the form. The Texas output of short stories has been tremendous. I have not attempted to estimate it, but to choose the stories here collected I have read nearly four hundred, by eighty-one different Texas authors. Fourteen of the twenty-one writers here represented are native Texans. The seven who are not natives, like your editor, did what they could to remedy that deficiency, came here to stay for some years. They all write of Texas with authority and understanding. Some, moreover, write of it with critical acumen. Critics of Texas writing have sometimes said that it lacked this quality of mature literature. There is self-examination, however, in Crowell's "The Stoic," Sanford's "Windfall," and Thompson's "A Shore for the Sinking." Even O. Henry, most of whose stories in *Heart of the West* are sentimental and deal in type characters, is not uncritical in "Art and the Bronco."

A hopeful sign, too, is the tendency of the more recent writers of Texas short stories to concern themselves with the real present rather than with the imaginary past. The barrenness of our industrialized life is indicted in Goyen's "Her Breath upon the Windowpane" and Karchmer's "A Fistful of Alamo Heroes," which chronicles also a postwar readjustment. Both racial friction and the exploited farm hand are treated in Kidd's "Low Road Go Down." The workings of the legislature are satirized, though mildly, in the O. Henry story. Although some writers still dwell on the romantic past, we now welcome other treatments of the stock themes. George Sessions Perry evidently thinks that the time is ripe for spoofing about our "predilection for Western ways of a century ago." Fred Gipson in "My Kind of a Man" and Mr. Dobie in "Midas on a Goatskin" ask questions that give pause to the apologists for modern progress. To keep his bearings in mid-century urban life, with its professional, civic, and social responsibilities, Dillon Anderson invents those charming irresponsibles, "I and Claudie." "Grass Grow Again" treats the current rural scene honestly and incisively, and with that sympathetic discernment which characterizes the best fiction today.

Throughout my reading for this book I have been impressed by the large number of Texans who year by year for half a century have kept the large-circulation magazines supplied with stories of professional journalistic quality. From this group some of the men who might well have been included here are George W. Barrington, J. Frank Davis, Joseph Hall Ransom, and Andrew W. Somerville; of the women—who seem to be in the majority—Anna Brand, Claudia Cranston, Ruth Cross, Margaret Bell Houston, Olive McClintic Johnson, Grace Sothcote Leake, Helen Topping Miller, and Norma Patterson. Some interesting writers of the "serious" story, too, have been omitted. This would be a more definitive book if it contained work by Karle Wilson Baker, Sigman Byrd, Edwin Lanham, Vernon Loggins, Thelma Maxey, Dorothy Scarborough, Weldon Stone, and Owen P. White. Stephen Crane, Conrad Richter, and Stark Young have written excellent stories about Texas and might thus have been claimed, but they are better known for their other work and Crane's stay here was only brief. Contemporary Texas writers of the short story whom I find it difficult to leave out are Thomas Edward Barlow, Henry Exall, Frank Goodwyn, F. A. Hardman, Gerald Langford, and William A. Owens.

JOHN W. THOMASON, JR.

JOHN W. THOMASON, JR., was born on February 28, 1893, in Huntsville, whose Old South way of life he celebrated in a gracious essay. He was educated at Southwestern University, Sam Houston Normal Institute, the University of Texas, and the Art Students' League of New York City.

The lifelong experience as a professional soldier which was to give Thomason much of his material began when, after short turns as school-teacher and reporter, he joined the Marines on the day the United States entered World War I. Lieutenant, Captain, and Major Thomason served his country in France, the West Indies, Central America, China, and at sea. He was cited for gallantry in action at Soissons, where with an enlisted man he captured a nest of two German heavy machine guns that had stopped his company, and "killed the crew of thirteen." For this act he was awarded both the Army's Silver Star and the Navy Cross. For his service in mapping new airways in Central and South America, Lieutenant Colonel Thomason received the Air Medal. Colonel Thomason served on the staff of Admiral Nimitz, commander in chief of the United States Pacific Fleet. He died March 12, 1944, in San Diego, and is buried in Huntsville. The Navy promptly honored his memory by naming a new destroyer the U.S.S. *John W. Thomason;* his state, by hanging his portrait in the Gallery of Famous Texans in the Capitol.

But fighting all over the world was not enough for this distinguished gentleman. In 1938, Georgetown University awarded him a D.Litt. degree for his writings—in the short story, novel, and biography. Thomason used his pen, moreover, to report war in more than words, sketching front-line battle scenes on maps or whatever else he could pick up. Another famous recorder of World War I saw some of these drawings and took them to *Scribner's,* whose editors wanted some text to go with them. Thomason had it already completed: the manuscript of *Fix Bayonets!* Thus his self-illustrated stories and sketches were published, and he never had to submit an unsolicited manuscript in his life. Thomason's works in line and word were well received and have attained sufficient importance to have been solemnly studied in a recent

8

John W. Thomason, Jr.

doctoral dissertation, Raymond Past's "Illustrated by the Author." Between three and four thousand manuscripts, drawings, letters, and books by the "Fighting, Writing Marine" are on loan to the University of Texas, whose Rare Books Rooms in 1950 held an important Thomason exhibit.

Thomason's most significant books are *Fix Bayonets!* (1926), *Red Pants and Other Stories* (1927), *Jeb Stuart* (1930), *Gone to Texas* (1937), and *Lone Star Preacher* (1941). "A Preacher Goes to Texas" is from the last-named book, which J. Frank Dobie called the "most moving . . . the most heart-lightening book that Texas users of English have endowed the land with." Like *Gone to Texas,* it may be regarded as a by-product in fiction of the research in Confederate history which the author undertook for his biography of Stuart. This story gives a vivid, authentic picture of life at Washington on the Brazos in the 1850's. Praxiteles Swan, who Thomason tells us is "a combination of two distinguished early Methodist saints in Texas," is one of the author's most successful and appealing characters.

9

A Preacher Goes to Texas

IT IS ONE OF THOSE STORIES Uncle Jimmy Farrow used to tell, at Mr. Lee Rodgers' place on Patterson Lake in Houston County, when we sat, after supper, on the porch through summer evenings: How the Rev. Praxiteles Swan appeared in Texas and preached his first sermon at Washington on the Brazos, to the notable confusion of the devil in those parts. In his years of achievement, they called Praxiteles Swan "the Hurricane of God." He was superannuated before my time, but all my old folks had trembled under his thunders, and he loomed vast and legendary, even in the country where Sam Houston and Davy Crockett were remembered.

Uncle Jimmy, a dried-up little fox squirrel of a man who claimed to have served with Quantrell, and who, for sixty years after the war, never sat in line with a window, day or night, was a shirttail boy in Washington County in the 1850's, and saw the preacher arrive. But the actual beginnings of that career I found myself, years after Uncle Jimmy told the tale, in an old thick book dealing with the saints of early Texas Methodism. In it is preserved, besides other edifying material, Praxiteles Swan's own journal of his life and acts.

Uncle Jimmy's narrative style was of the leisurely contemplative type, best enjoyed by persons having no other engagements. It owed much of its effectiveness, I think, to the setting—the deep and timeless peace of the Trinity River bottom, the noises of the night and the woods, and the dark shimmer of the lake under the stars. And the journal, although it recorded immense and laborious travels in a wilderness, and fiery contests for immortal souls, is also the chronicle of an elder and un-hurried time—it is, in fact, long-winded. Therefore, I abridge the one and paraphrase the other.

Reprinted from *Lone Star Preacher*, by John W. Thomason, Jr.; copyright 1941 by John W. Thomason, Jr.; used by permission of the publishers, Charles Scribner's Sons, and Mrs. John W. Thomason, Jr.

10

Of Praxiteles' beginnings, it is enough to know that he came of a regretted *mésalliance* between a Yankee schoolteacher named Swan, and Miss Cassandra Pelham, a lady of imperious Virginia blood. He was orphaned early. His uncle, Col. Marius Pelham, raised him, as they say, on his place in the pleasant Piedmont country outside of Charlottesville, where the Colonel lived, withdrawn and feudal, among his Negroes, his fighting cocks and his blood horses; drinking brandy juleps before dinner, port after, and Madeira between meals, and reading the more outrageous of the Augustan poets in the original Latin. An Army officer until it bored him, a member of the Congress until, he said, the tone of the lower house became too degraded for a refined person's stomach, and a duelist always, he instructed his nephew in the accomplishments and prejudices of the Virginia gentry; and through Praxiteles' adult life, the violent old autocrat stood sneering over the shoulder of the man of God—although I am sure Praxiteles would never have admitted this.

His uncle sent him to Princeton College for his education, because he regarded Mr. Jefferson as a nauseous demagogue, and could not abide his works; and after that he designed the young man for the law. But, unaccountably, the nephew came under other influences. In his twenty-second year, the summer after his graduation—he being then six feet and upward of lank red-headed youth—he faced his uncle in his own garden, and told him plainly he was called to the Methodist ministry.

Praxiteles records the interview at length, and it must have been of a nature to make the house servants turn gray under their dark skins and seek places of safety. He quotes his own remarks, which are elevated and improving, but his uncle's statements he barely suggests, with the explanation that they were horrid blasphemies, and he feared his aged relative to be already in Satan's waistcoat pocket. He comments sadly that Colonel Pelham was a man of honor, infatuated in the delusion that a man of honor could live a decent life according to his personal standards, without dependence on higher guidance. "In such there is no hope; they are worse than the most dissolute and hardened sinners, for whom there is at least repentance and salvation. 'Drunk with wine, as Ephraim in his fat valleys—'"

The upshot of it was, his uncle threw him out, and they never saw each other again; they came of the same violent blood. But you identify

11

John W. Thomason, Jr.

Colonel Pelham as the unrepentant sinner; a figure at once moving and repellent and somehow glamorous, which Praxiteles thereafter used effectively through fifty years of sermons. The same afternoon he departed from his home, taking some gold pieces left out of his quarterly allowance, his riding cloak, and a change of linen in his saddlebags, astride the big, hammer-headed, three-quarter-bred mare given him when a colt. He went to Baltimore.

Baltimore was the outpost of Southern Methodism, lately split away from the Northern brethren on the vexatious question of Negro slavery. I abridge his account of what he did there, and how he was ordained; and how old Bishop Andrew, a shrewd prince of the church, had him in for an interview and detailed him to the Texas mission. Because, nowhere else, the bishop said, indicating the letters and memorials on the episcopal desk, were the shepherds so sorely tried as in the Texas missions; nowhere else were the sheep so black and the wolves so bold. You conceive him appraising Praxiteles' lean length of bone and sinew, his shock of red hair, his purposeful green eyes, aggressive nose, and the thin firm mouth over the long jaw and the pointed chin, and considering that such a young soldier belonged in the forefront of the battle. Perhaps he thought of King David, who was also white and ruddy. No bishop would have wanted to be responsible for King David's discipline, and Texas was a long way off. He cautioned Praxiteles about Texas. The people were sensitive in unexpected spots, he warned, and it would be better not to refer to his calling as missionary work, or to his colleagues as missionaries. Up here, of course; but down there "be ye therefore wise as serpents, and harmless as doves." Praxiteles, he ordered, would proceed forthwith to the settlement called Washington on the Brazos, in the Rutersville District, pending the yearly assembly of the Texas Conference and a permanent assignment. The pastor of that flock, he explained, had succumbed to a lung fever induced by his toils. In Texas, the bishop warned him, a minister's body needed to be as robust as his soul. His honorarium, he thought, would be a hundred and sixty dollars a year, the years his congregation made a crop. When they didn't, the Lord would provide. At the end, he blessed Praxiteles and sent him forth, quoting the appropriate scriptures.

Praxiteles neglected his journal for two months; he states, merely, that he rode down to Texas after Christmas. And he resumed his entries in early March, 1852, the day he crossed into the state by Gaines' Ferry on the Sabine. A cold rain drove on a northeast wind, he mentions, and the roads were trying to his mare, who was not now up into her bridle as when they left Virginia. He refers to great discomfort from his breeches, which were worn through inside the knees—"Mem. . . . get some good woman to patch them for me."

Texas was excessively well-watered that year. He listed the creeks between the Sabine and the Neches rivers, all of them high and some of them overflowing from the rains, and never a bridge in the country, and no bottom to the roads. He discovered that his mare could swim, which was probably a surprise to both of them when the ford went out from under in an innocent-looking brown creek east of the Trinity, and they all but drowned. He pressed on, as only circuit riders and fugitives did in those parts, resting where darkness overtook him; one night in a verminous tavern, another in a loft above a barn full of horned cattle, and once in the attic of a poor man's house—man who received him hospitably enough, fed him bacon and greens and corn bread, showed a readiness to discuss spiritual affairs, and then, when Praxiteles disclosed his denomination, tried to eject him into the wet and stormy wilderness. The journal briefly states that Praxiteles declined to be ejected, but it contains this entry: "I had rather associate with howling savages than with Campbellites."

By Swartout he came to the Trinity, booming along at flood stage, and found a ferry, and had directions to Washington. "Just keep goin' west," they told him helpfully. "Don't turn neither north nor south. There ain't but one road goin' west."

He passed Cold Spring and Montgomery, climbed the watershed between the Trinity and the San Jacinto, with its solemn pine forests, and plunged again into bottom land, smothered under pin oak, walnut, pecan, hickory and sweet gum, every tree trailing Spanish moss, mournful in the rain as dripping beards on hanged men. Miles of the road were under water, and the occasional higher stretches marched, rutted, between rain-dappled lagoons that carried a current, more often than not. Houses were a day's ride apart, and there were no settlements, and nobody on the road beyond occasional glum mud-plastered mail riders. He spent a night in the bottom, huddled under a tree, his mare trembling and the water making noises all around. There was a panther— the first he had encountered—hunting in the neighborhood, and its squalls were dreadful in his ears. He took comfort, he recorded, from singing hymns, and felt that the Lord's hand was over him. He forded the East Fork, which was not bad, and swam Winter's Creek and Peach Creek, and late on a gray March evening he approached the Middle Fork of the San Jacinto; two days' ride, he calculated, from the Brazos. It was still raining.

The Middle Fork ran banks full, foul with floating brush. Where it lapped into the road, one stood with a sodden quilt on his shoulders and a shotgun under his arm, gazing downstream into the last of the light. That man was, in fact, our Uncle Jimmy Farrow; then a sort of roustabout for the cook on Old Man Locke's wagon train, that did hauling between Cincinnati on the Trinity and Brenham. The cook had given him a ten-gauge double gun, and told him to go get a mess of ducks, because the teamsters were promising to fry him over his own fire if he fed them any more side meat and corn pone; the high water had detained the wagon train for days and they were in the worst possible humor.

Uncle Jimmy, telling us the story, says he was watching so sharp down the river for the evening flight that he let the fellow get right up on him before he noticed. Long-legged fellow on a big gaunted mare; all he could see was a white face between a hat brim and a turned-up cloak collar, stopping to speak to him. As he turned his head, Uncle Jimmy saw ducks from the corner of his eye, and he told the man, blast his bowels, if he moved he'd kill him.

The fellow sat there, frozen—it's not what a duck sees that scares him, Uncle Jimmy claims; it's what moves—and five hundred mallards came along the river about as high as the treetops. Right at the ford they flared out over the bank, making for a stubble field back in the woods, and Uncle Jimmy picked his correct second of time and let them have both barrels, knocking down a dozen or so. Those old ten-gauges, with thirty-inch, cylinder-bored barrels, scattered fine. The ducks fell on the land, but some were crippled, and he had to be mighty spry to beat them to the water and twist their necks; and this man dismounted and helped; had legs like a sandhill crane, Uncle Jimmy says, and a reach like a hayrake. When they collected the ducks—nice mallards in prime condition from the winter on the Gulf Coast—Uncle Jimmy saw the stranger was just a youngster—little older than he was—and he took him to the wagon camp on some higher ground a quarter of a mile upstream.

14

A *Preacher Goes to Texas*

The boys—half a dozen teamsters—were playing brag under the lean-to shelter they had knocked up and covered with a wagon sheet, and they were sullen and ugly, and down to ten gallons of whisky, which Old Man Locke was sitting on with his pistol in his waistband, and dealing out just a tin cupful at a time, before meals. Old Man Locke told the stranger he reckoned he was welcome to what grub there was, and he could sleep under a wagon; and if he was stayin', he could turn to and help the cook. Old Man Locke was rough-talkin', they said, in those days.

Well, there was nothing finicky about the stranger; first he unsaddled and scraped the mud off his mare, then he helped with the ducks. The cook had boiling water ready to scald them, and Uncle Jimmy and this man snatched the feathers right off of them, all in no time.

Here Uncle Jimmy digressed to describe at length the way they broiled the ducks; something we all knew and did in those parts, and liked to talk about, but need not here repeat. Uncle Jimmy recalls, the teamsters were in a better humor after supper. Nobody really paid any attention to the stranger until he declined the slug of bitters that Old Man Locke courteously offered him. Then they wanted to know who he was and where he came from.

He stood up, as tall as a tree, Uncle Jimmy remembers, and told them he was a preacher of the gospel, a-bound for Washington on the Brazos.

"Well," says Old Man Locke, who was strong on religion himself, "you must be a Methodist. Either they're Methodists over thar, or they ain't anything."

"I am," says the preacher, "an unworthy servant of the Methodist Episcopal Church, South. The name is Swan."

"Well," Old Man Locke answered, "I'm a man that takes my religion serious. I'm a blue-light Presbyterian, I am, and so is all my folks. Young man—Reverend, I should say, though you look mighty young and mighty redheaded to be a shepherd—even a Methody shepherd—it—mought turn out your luck, one of these days, to sit under ouah preacher, down in Victoria—the Elder Calvin Knox Singletree. When he talks, you can smell hell, brother—that's what you can! And the way Elder Singletree puts it, I like a religion that's a religion, not spoon vittles, or sugar-tits fer babes, but strong meat fer men! A religion, as Elder Singletree says, a man kain get his tushes into. No, young man, you're a foreigner here, and far from home, and you're welcome to yo' share of

15

John W. Thomason, Jr.

my grub an' campfire, but you're unfortunate. So are a lot of folks. Elder Singletree's religion is the only religion fer grown folks. No other kind will be preached in my wagon train. But if you want to read us a Psa'm before we turn in, I'm agreeable and the boys will listen."

Uncle Jimmy says they sat quiet while the Reverend Swan read them a scripture and prayed them a prayer; and I found the story briefed in Praxiteles' journal.

Next morning, the rain blew off and the Middle Fork went down, and they got across in good shape; and Old Man Locke sent Uncle Jimmy ahead on a mule to make some arrangements for him in Washington. He rode with Praxiteles, who, Uncle Jimmy remembers, asked all sorts of questions about everything, and they made good time, for before dark they came out on the river, and the ferryman set them across, of a Saturday afternoon.

There was not a great deal to Washington, although the orators referred to it freely as the cradle of Texas independence, the town on the great river the Spaniards call *Brazos de Dios*—Arms of God.

There were some log cabins and barns, and a few clapboarded houses, the wide whipsawed boards cleated on over the original logs and whitewashed. Some stores were ranked out of alignment; the most elaborate building in sight, a rambling unpainted structure behind a false front, was Gadsen's Saloon and Billiard Parlors. Patient horses stood on three legs in front of it; elsewhere, dejected mules and phlegmatic oxen labored through the mud, drawing high-slung wagons. There was a cotton shed and a platform handy to the river, but the steelyards over the weighing stand hung rusty on a rusty wire, and the dull yellow sky lowered over all. Razorback hogs moved importantly across the road, or stood to scratch their ticks against the corner posts of the buildings. Everywhere there was mud; all the men wore their trousers inside their boots.

Praxiteles came up from the ferry with Uncle Jimmy and rode toward the saloon, from which proceeded loud shouts of laughter and considerable swearing in bad-tempered, drawling voices. Elsewhere, sallow men lounged in front of stores, whittled and chewed tobacco; only around the saloon was there life and movement. As Praxiteles drew in his horse and sat, undecided, looking about him, a man came with great dignity from the saloon, caromed off the hitch rail, and walked

16

into Praxiteles' mare. He leaned against her shoulder, his hand going uncertainly to the rider's knee.

"Well, I declar'," he said, amiably—"I declar'. Gettin' to be so many people in town, a man can't make his way thoo 'em, noways." He got his chin up, beamed at the preacher, and said, with interest, "I never seed you befo'. You strangeh hyar? My name's Medary; ev'ybody knows me."

Praxiteles confirmed him. Yes. A pilgrim and a stranger. The Reverend Swan. Would he be so good as to point out the tavern?

The other brought his eyes into coincidence and studied him gravely. Tallest preacher, he remarked, he ever did see. But there wasn't no tavern. Could get a shakedown, now, in Goat Gadsen's place, but nothing fitten for a preacher. He, the man continued, always slept the preachers—that is, the Methodist preachers. He wasn't a Methodist, himself—reckoned he was a kind of backslidden sinner—but his wife was the all-fired out-prayingest Methodist between the Sabine and the Colorado rivers; had a preacher in the house right now. "Come on, preacher," he added hospitably. "Come on. Come on out to my place. I'll show you."

He cast his weight against the mare and paid no attention to Praxiteles' courteous protest. He would walk, he stated. Little walk do him good. He feared he was sort of overtaken. If he'd knowed the preacher was comin', he wouldn't—this he swore roundly—have smoked so many seegyars. He then recognized Uncle Jimmy, and told him to come along, too, and lead his horse for him.

He was a very persuasive man, and Praxiteles was tired, and they went willingly, Mr. Medary hanging to a stirrup leather, and recovering an admirable equilibrium as the heavy walking brought the sweat out on him. They plodded a mile down the road, plunged into the woods, then proceeded between new-cleared land where raw furrows ran under trees, girdled and dead, to a sprawling house in a grove of moss-draped oaks. It was as good a house as Praxiteles had seen in Texas. Its original logs had been sheathed in weatherboarding; it was roofed with cypress shingles and had a huge stone chimney at each end. All around it ran a deep porch, and the kitchen and outbuildings and barn, as well as the house itself, were smartly whitewashed. Chickens and turkeys scratched in the yard, and a whole congregation of potlikker hounds boiled out noisily to greet the master. Hard behind the dogs came two

17

little Negroes; then a couple of towheaded children, very bashful, and a brisk, neat lady with a humorous dark eye and a firm mouth, evidently mistress of herself and others. An older girl appeared at the door, looked out, and withdrew hastily.

"'Light down, rev'rend, 'light down!" cried Mr. Medary, now perfectly steady on his legs. "Gimme those saddlebags. Walk right in, seh; you' in yo' own house! . . . Nigger, take the rev'rend's mar'. Rub her down with a snatch of hay befo' you water her, and give her a feed of cawn in the corner stall. . . . She stand quiet in the stable, rev'rend? . . . Nigger, I'll be out to look at her, an' if she ain't bedded right, I'll cut yo' years off and make you eat 'em!" He led the way to the house and did the honors: "Mrs. Medary, hyar's the Rev'rend Swan—him that the presidin' elder was tellin' us was coming. . . . Rev'rend, this is Nick, an' this is Bubber, and this is Lucindy. Chillun air the po' man's blessin', rev'rend! . . . Mrs. Medary, whar's Jinny?"

They hustled him into the house. A fine fire snapped and crackled in a deep fireplace, taking the chill out of the wet March air.

By the fire in a rocking chair, with a shawl over his shoulders, sat a lean man in a rusty black store suit which was weather-stained and mottled with age. He got painfully to his feet, extending a limp hand; he had a sad sallow face, thinly bearded, and hot-tempered dyspeptic eyes.

"Hyar's Brother Grebs—Rev'rend Brother Grebs," continued Mr. Medary cordially. "He's passin' thoo, goin' up to Marshall. He was took sick."

"I'm mighty po'ly," agreed the Rev. Elkanah Grebs. "I'm mighty po'ly. The Lord's hand has been heavy on me, brother. Boils, even as Job, and a touch of the bloody flux."

The good man was vastly depressed; the ills of the spirit, he asserted, graveled him worse than the weaknesses of the flesh. He had proposed to conduct services for the little flock in Washington; they having been without spiritual food since the late Brother Haggers passed to his reward last November. He had sent the word ahead that he would preach tomorrow, and the good folks were making ready to come in, by buggy, oxcart and wagon, from Dan even to Beersheba—that is, from as far west as Brenham, and from Anderson and Big Sandy, the other way. There would surely be young olive branches, born during the winter, for baptism, and probably couples to be church-married—

18

maybe things you wouldn't want to keep waiting. But the Methodist Church, called Gilgal Chapel, was struck by lightning last fall and burned. The cotton warehouse was full up to the rafters. About the only place a gathering might be held was Mr. Gadsen's Saloon and Billiard Parlors; and Reverend Grebs had approached Mr. Gadsen in the matter with confidence, for the faithful those days congregated in eccentric places when the weather was too bad to sit under the trees.

Mr. Gadsen, Praxiteles was informed, hardened his heart like Pharaoh and said he wasn't going to lose his Sunday-afternoon trade for a parcel of howling Methodists; he was a Campbellite himself, and his customers would be put out with him. No, seh. He wasn't even polite about it. And while they talked within, young sinners placed cockleburs under the saddle of the preacher's mule; so that when he came out and mounted, he was flung off into a mud puddle and further humiliated. Here Mr. Medary felt constrained to interrupt. It wasn't, he told Praxiteles, as though the community was down on preachers. They treated them right well—everybody did. That was just a bunch of young hellions who'd been heating their coppers with Goat Gadsen's forty-rod, and sort of hellin' around. They didn't mean anything by it—just boys, reely.

The sad feature, Brother Grebs concluded, was that the good folks would be coming along, and no way to stop them. They'd have that haul over heavy roads— His voice trailed off sadly. Praxiteles, listening with concern, recalled something of his furious uncle's conversation— philosophic reminiscences to the effect that, coming on a new scene, the superior man always does something impressive; something to command public attention—like the time, in Natchez, Colonel Pelham, on arrival, called Col. Marmaduke Astley out and shot him within an hour. Like the time, again, in his first term with the Federal Congress, he caned the congressman from Rhode Island.

Praxiteles announced, a cold fire behind his green eyes: "There'll be services, as God willeth, in this publican's place of business. I'll conduct them myself."

About that time, Uncle Jimmy says, Miss Jinny entered the room, having primped herself up for company; she was the oldest girl in the family, peart as a red heifer, and fat as a butterball—fine a gyu'l as you ever did see, Uncle Jimmy asserted, slapping his leg. It was time she was married off, everybody was saying in those parts; and it was her own fault she wasn't. The young bucks were around her thick as

WITHDRAWN NORTHEAST TEXAS COMMUNITY COLLEGE

flies in fly time, but she just couldn't seem to make up her mind. The Lord only knew, Uncle Jimmy recollected, how many gougings and kneeings and general ruckuses there had been over her in the settlement. The field was narrowed down to Bud Pike and Jim Pike, two cousins that farmed up the river a ways. They'd had their eye on her, and between them they whipped off the others—being, Uncle Jimmy says, as mean a pair of wildcats as ever came out of the Brazos Bottom —and now they were running each other for her, nip and tuck.

First one would be ahead, and then the other, said Uncle Jimmy; the whole community was watching it, and there were bets made every day in Goat Gadsen's Saloon and Billiard Parlors.

As for the Reverend Praxiteles, he wrote that night in his diary, how he was made acquainted, at Mr. Medary's house, with a most comely young lady, Miss Jael Medary; and he notes that, before retiring, he read from the Book of Judges the story of Jael, and the decisive steps Jael took in the case of the soldier Sisera, as celebrated by the great triumphant song Deborah the prophetess made about her on that occasion. It edified him considerably. And he added to his diary: "Genesis ii, 23 & 24. Mayhap the Lord sends me an helpmeet."

Meantime, they all went in to supper.

Never, anywhere, Praxiteles reflected, looking through half-shut lids as Brother Grebs delivered a comprehensive grace, had he seen so much, or such a variety, of food on a table. Whatever else Mr. Medary did with his talents, it was evident that he was a good provider; and when the grace was finished, Mr. Medary exhorted his guests to eat hearty. A man shouldn't let himself die in debt to his stomach, he stated, and he, for one, did not intend to.

"That's right. Plenty more in the kitchen!" cried Mrs. Medary.

Uncle Jimmy remembers that Miss Jinny—only her mother called her Jael—kept looking sideways at the preacher, and he looking back at her, in a way to make you sick. He never could see, Uncle Jimmy remarked, why the women in them days took on so over a preacher. And they still did, he was told.

The family possessed an organ capable of music. It was not in tune, and the dampness had done unfortunate things to its keys, but Miss Jinny was able to coax recognizable melody out of it, and after supper, her father, who, by frequent trips out to the smokehouse—from which he returned wiping his mouth and chewing a clove—maintained him-

self in a state of geniality, insisted that they sing. His wife reminded him that it was Saturday night, and too near Sunday for ballads and breakdowns, especially with preachers in the house.

Mr. Medary replied that, like nothing on earth, he honed and hankered for a hymn tune.

They placed the lamps and Miss Jinny sat herself to the organ. Praxiteles admired the bronze lights in her hair and the lines of her flat back. He came gallantly near to turn the music, and made bold to recommend a noble hymn of praise, Mount Zion—No. 36. She struck the chords with confident strong hands, and he led boldly:

> "O Love divine, how sweet thou art,
>   When shall I find my willing heart
>   All taken up by thee? . . ."

Mrs. Medary lifted a thin soprano, some beats behind the rest; Mr. Medary amiably contributed a growling bass, far from the key; and Miss Jinny, whose voice was untrained, but sweet and fresh, came along effectively with Praxiteles' baritone. The Reverend Elkanah, wrapped in a quilt by the fire, beat time with a slippered foot and hummed approvingly.

Somebody hollered outside, "Hello, the house!" and there entered Mr. Bud Pike and Mr. Jim Pike, two of the ugliest young men Praxiteles had ever seen; when their eyes fell on him, they bristled visibly. One was tall—not so tall as Praxiteles, but tall enough—and very solidly built; he had a broad dark face and hard black eyes, and a shock of hair, well-greased, and huge hairy hands. The other was shorter and more compact, with a bullethead, little piggish eyes, and a flat face, all of him as square and stocky as a blockhouse.

No need for Mr. Medary to whisper, after introducing them, that they were cousins—for the family favor was strong—and no need to add that they were sparking Miss Jinny—for both looked at her like she was something good to eat—and their enmity to Praxiteles, simply because he was in the room with her, was evident and immediate. He saw, also, the bright blush that rose from Jael's neck to the roots of her hair.

But when Mr. Medary added, behind his hand, that she would be making up her mind which one to choose, right soon, and that the reverend might have a wedding on his hands any day now, Praxiteles

21

was conscious of a wave of revulsion. He realized at once that he didn't want this to happen; he was later to search his soul in prayer over the violence that suddenly filled his heart, without receiving light on the matter.

The singing was resumed, Praxiteles standing manfully in his place by the organ, while Miss Jinny appeared to be nervous. She did not incline her body modestly away from him as he leaned to turn a leaf, and once or twice her hand went up and touched his on the music. When this happened, a pleasant excitement surged in him. The two boys were glooming like thunderclouds.

The atmosphere in the room was no longer friendly; you could, Uncle Jimmy says, fair smell the blood and guts on the floor.

The Reverend Grebs announced that it was his bedtime, and he reckoned his young brother had come a long way and was ready for the shucks—"only, it's not shucks, under this godly rooftree, brother; it's the finest goose feathers under elegant eiderdown quilts," he explained, so that Mrs. Medary colored with pleasure.

Let them, suggested Brother Grebs, have a lesson, and a sweet season of prayer before they sought their rest; ask a blessing on their labors in the morning.

Here the biggest Pike spoke his first word: "What labors, pahson?"

"Friend," Praxiteles answered him, "it is my intention to hold services at the settlement in the morning."

"Whar'bouts?" asked Mr. Pike.

"It is my intention to request your Mr.—Gadsen?—Gadsen to allow us the use of his place of business for two hours in the morning."

"Does Goat Gadsen know about it? Well, we was just ridin' on. We'll tell him what you want," said Mr. Pike ominously.

Praxiteles thanked him with the blandest air imaginable. "Do so, I beg, Mr. Pike. It is the Lord's work."

They departed without ceremony. Mr. Medary looked at Praxiteles thoughtfully, and the Reverend Grebs said he hoped his afflictions would let him out of bed tomorrow, but he was afraid they wouldn't. Nonetheless, he prayed at length and powerfully, and they all retired.

In the morning, they rode into town; the women and children in a wagon, Reverend Grebs, still feeble, riding with them, and the others on horseback.

Praxiteles hitched his mare to the rack and approached the front of the saloon steadily, his saddlebags, which contained his Bible and his hymnbooks, in his hand. A dozen unkempt individuals, not all of them sober, observed his approach. Within, the cheerful murmur of godless entertainment ceased. At once the door was crowded.

Two detached themselves from the knot of observers and stood out to meet the preacher—Bud Pike and Jim Pike, the gallants of the night before. Praxiteles was aware of a stiffening of the hair at the back of his neck, and a quiver along his bones, a sort of bugle call to action in his blood, for the aspect of the two was not peaceful. They were squarely in front of him, their arms hanging, but out a little from their bodies, and their faces dark and sneering—what a family resemblance they had, Praxiteles noted. He said, the skin around his mouth feeling stiff, "A good morrow to you, friends!"

"No friend of yours, pahson," snarled Jim Pike.

"That's right," agreed the other.

Praxiteles stopped because another step would have brought him into collision. "Young men—" he began.

"Listen, preacher. What would you do if we was to give you a damn good whippin'?"

"My friends," Praxiteles told them, keeping his voice under control, "if the Lord give me grace, I will bear it. But if He don't, woe to your hides!"

With that, Bud Pike slapped him—a slap at the end of a full-arm swing. Praxiteles might have taken a blow, but a slap, now— A second later, Jim Pike put his head down and charged, butting like a bull. Praxiteles side-stepped. Bud came in, his arms flailing, exactly in time to receive his cousin's bullethead in his stomach. The air went out of Bud with a great "whuff!" and the two fell, entangled, in a mud puddle. Before they could sit up, Praxiteles, his temper flaming like his hair, was upon them; he squatted on Jim Pike's shoulders, whipped a long thigh over his neck and ground his face into the mud. Bud Pike, dizzy from the impact, he seized by the stock as he came to his knees, hauled him close to, and began to buffet him with mighty short-arm punches that rocked his head loose on his shoulders. Jim, underneath him, threshed about like a chicken with a wrung neck, but never really got his head high enough to breathe.

The engagement was like San Jacinto fight in its brevity and violence and its astonishing and improbable outcome. The eagerness and fury of his enemies, together with the soft footing, delivered them into Praxiteles' hand. In time the action would assume legendary proportions, and take its place in the folklore of the region, but Uncle Jimmy Farrow, there present, swears it occurred exactly as he tells it.

It did not last long. The one was smothered and the other's face beat into a bloody pulp. But Praxiteles was conscious of a wild joy, and quite heedless of his cut knuckles. He heard, at first dimly, then with reluctant attention, the genial voice of Mr. Medary, and felt that gentleman's hand on his shoulder.

"Rev'rend! Rev'rend! They got enough, seh, sho'ly! Don't kill 'em, rev'rend; they's just boys!"

Giving the completely groggy Bud one last terrific back-hander in the mouth, Praxiteles flung him away and rose from Jim's back, turning that one over, not gently, with his foot. Jim's face was completely masked with mud, and he made distressed blowing noises through it as he tried to sit up. Bud Pike came to his elbow, spat out a tooth and opened one eye. When Praxiteles looked at him, he lay down again, hastily. And from the saloon fifty men whooped in Homeric laughter.

"Boys, did you see his arms going? Like Old Man Weyser's windmill with the governor off in a blue norther!"

"Ol' Jim, with the reverend sittin' on his head!"

"Make way for the reverend, boys! He's a bobcat with bristles on his belly. He's a cross between a catamount and a alligator!"—this from an enthusiast well drunken, who was immediately suppressed; for the ladies were getting down from the wagons. The men stood silent as Praxiteles Swan came toward them, having retrieved his saddlebags. They made way for him respectfully; some of them touched their hats.

One called, "Oh, Dutch, get the reverend a towel an' a basin, in case he wants to spruce up!"

Behind him walked Mr. Medary, his chest out a foot, saying to this acquaintance and that: "Reverend Swan, boys, from old Virginyeh. Particular friend of mine—stayin' at my house. They say he's a powerful preacher too."

The ladies followed. Miss Jael Medary, her skirts lifted daintily from the mud, disclosing the neatest ankles in the world, passed her fallen suitors with the effect of shying away from leprosy, but she was not thinking of them; she never thought of them again. Her cheeks flamed deliciously, and her eyes were at once speculative and tender, following the tall figure of Praxiteles Swan.

In Mr. Gadsen's Saloon and Billiard Parlors, saints and willing sinners hustled together with chairs and benches. The Negro bottle washer snatched the goboons out of sight behind the bar.

In his little room at one side, Mr. Goat Gadsen himself brought water and helped in the removal of the worst of the blood and mud with which the Church Militant was spattered; his expert judgment was, the eye where one of Bud's wild swings had landed wouldn't close altogether; he recommended a chunk of raw liver as soon as services was over. And the ladies would be glad to mend his coat, where it was split up the back. Uncle Jimmy passed out the hymnbooks.

The Rev. Elkanah Grebs, assisting, said he was miraculously restored in health, and he'd be pleased to deliver the opening prayer.

"You sho'ly smote the Amalekites hip and thigh, brother," he exulted. " 'The sword of the Lord and of Gideon'! And what, if I might make so bold, will be yore text this morning?"

"I'll give 'em a lesson from First Samuel, the ninth chapter—how Saul went looking for his father's asses," Praxiteles told him.

Brother Grebs knew his Bible; Uncle Jimmy says he rubbed his hands and allowed that he couldn't do better. It was the passage describing young Saul as being "from his shoulders and upward . . . higher than any of the people."

"And I don't know what you're looking for, exactly, but I do know what you've found, brother," he added, as Praxiteles pulled his coat on and went into the bar, where the congregation was settled down.

Uncle Jimmy laughed. "Reverend Grebs, he was right about it. He married the new preacher to Miss Jinny the next Sunday morning, and Brother Swan was the first man in Washington County that got married and was not shivareed by the neighbors."

O. HENRY

WILLIAM SYDNEY PORTER was born in Greensboro, North Carolina, September 11, 1862. His mother having died early, he was indebted both for his rearing and for most of his scant formal schooling to his Aunt Lina. At fifteen he stopped school to work in his Uncle Clark's drugstore, Greensboro's social center.

In 1882, threatened with consumption, Will came to Texas and, as O. Henry later put it, "ran wild on the prairies." He lived first on a ranch operated by the famous Captain Red Hall of the Texas Rangers, who became the heroic model for a number of O. Henry's lifelike portraits of Ranger officers. To a pale, skinny drugstore cowboy from Carolina, ranch life must have had its fears as well as its pleasures, but Will Porter enjoyed it. Red Hall opened for him the door to the romance of the Southwest. Since he was not a hand, but a guest, Will perhaps became less of a cowboy than O. Henry later claimed to be; but he was well liked by the men and did receive the "puncher's accolade" which O. Henry gives Curly in "The Higher Abdication."

Texas was to be Porter's home for the next sixteen years—one-third of his life. In Austin he worked as clerk in a tobacco store and in a drugstore, as bookkeeper for a real estate firm, as draftsman in the General Land Office, as teller in the old First National Bank, and as editor and publisher of the short-lived *Rolling Stone*. By day he was a genial but rather serious young man trying to get on. Outside office hours, however, he was a man-about-town, the witty baritone of the Hill City Quartet and the gallant lieutenant of the Austin Grays. His romance with delicate Athol Estes, a heroine straight out of Poe, was replete with a moonlight elopement and some idyllic though substantial satisfactions. Indeed, these years were probably the happiest of his life.

The story of Porter's embezzlement, flight, trial, and imprisonment has often been told. It is true that the First National Bank was rather irregularly run. It is not true that the authorities took advantage of the fact that Athol was ill with consumption. She died July 25, 1897, and Will was not brought to trial until the following February. It is not true that his lawyers did not do everything possible legally to free him.

There is little reason for believing that he was framed to protect others. Yet today most accounts of his life imply and Austin oldsters by the score would swear that the irresponsible, open-hearted Will Porter was innocent, at least of criminal intent.

Porter emerged from the federal penitentiary at Columbus, Ohio, July 21, 1901, with a better knowledge of the human heart and a number of salable manuscripts. The years from 1902 until his death, June 5, 1910, Porter spent giving away his money to the down-and-out, putting off editors who had paid him advances for stories not yet written, but yet becoming the chronicler par excellence of the little man and woman in New York City and making O. Henry the most important name in the short story of his day.

O. Henry's New York stories may, as he insisted, not depend for their truth or interest on their metropolitan settings, but most of his forty Texas stories provide a true though sometimes sentimental taste of Texas. Among the best known of them are "The Caballero's Way" and "The Reformation of Calliope," from the collection *Heart of the West,* which yields also a story less well known than it should be, "The Pimienta Pancakes." For this book, however, I have chosen a story not ordinarily reprinted, "Art and the Bronco." It does not depend upon a surprise ending, on which critics feel O. Henry placed too much reliance; and it does not possess the artistic finish the author sometimes attained. But for its picture of the legislature, of early Austin, and of the Boy Artist of the San Saba, it will, I think, prove highly enjoyable to most present-day lovers of things Texan.

Art and the Bronco

Out of the wilderness had come a painter. Genius, whose coronations alone are democratic, had woven a chaplet of chaparral for the brow of Lonny Briscoe. Art, whose divine expression flows impartially from the fingertips of a cowboy or a dilettante emperor, had chosen for a medium the Boy Artist of the San Saba. The outcome, seven feet by twelve of besmeared canvas, stood, gilt-framed, in the lobby of the Capitol.

The legislature was in session; the capital city of that great Western state was enjoying the season of activity and profit that the congregation of the solons bestowed. The boarding-houses were corralling the easy dollars of the gamesome lawmakers. The greatest state in the West, an empire in area and resources, had arisen and repudiated the old libel of barbarism, lawbreaking, and bloodshed. Order reigned within her borders. Life and property were as safe there, sir, as anywhere among the corrupt cities of the effete East. Pillow-shams, churches, strawberry feasts, and *habeas corpus* flourished. With impunity might the tenderfoot ventilate his "stovepipe" or his theories of culture. The arts and sciences received nurture and subsidy. And, therefore, it behooved the legislature of this great state to make appropriation for the purchase of Lonny Briscoe's immortal painting.

Rarely has the San Saba country contributed to the spread of the fine arts. Its sons have excelled in the solider graces, in the throw of the lariat, the manipulation of the esteemed .45, the intrepidity of the one-card draw, and the nocturnal stimulation of towns from undue lethargy; but, hitherto, it had not been famed as a stronghold of aesthetics. Lonny Briscoe's brush had removed that disability. Here, among

From *Roads of Destiny*, by O. Henry; copyright 1903 by Doubleday and Company, Inc.

the limestone rocks, the succulent cactus, and the drought-parched grass of that arid valley, had been born the Boy Artist. Why he came to woo art is beyond postulation. Beyond doubt, some spore of the afflatus must have sprung up within him in spite of the desert soil of San Saba. The tricksy spirit of creation must have incited him to attempted expression and then have sat hilarious among the white-hot sands of the valley, watching its mischievous work. For Lonny's picture, viewed as a thing of art, was something to have driven away dull care from the bosoms of the critics.

The painting—one might almost say panorama—was designed to portray a typical Western scene, interest culminating in a central animal figure, that of a stampeding steer, life-size, wild-eyed, fiery, breaking away in a mad rush from the herd that, close-ridden by a typical cowpuncher, occupied a position somewhat in the right background of the picture. The landscape presented fitting and faithful accessories. Chaparral, mesquite, and pear were distributed in just proportions. A Spanish dagger-plant, with its waxen blossoms in a creamy aggregation as large as a water-bucket, contributed floral beauty and variety. The distance was undulating prairie, bisected by stretches of the intermittent streams peculiar to the region lined with the rich green of live-oak and water-elm. A richly mottled rattlesnake lay coiled beneath a pale green clump of prickly pear in the foreground. A third of the canvas was ultramarine and lake white—the typical Western sky and the flying clouds, rainless and feathery.

Between two plastered pillars in the commodious hallway near the door of the chamber of representatives stood the painting. Citizens and lawmakers passed there by twos and groups and sometimes crowds to gaze upon it. Many—perhaps a majority of them—had lived the prairie life and recalled easily the familiar scene. Old cattlemen stood, reminiscent and candidly pleased, chatting with brothers of former camps and trails of the days it brought back to mind. Art critics were few in the town, and there was heard none of that jargon of color, perspective, and feeling such as the East loves to use as a curb and a rod to the pretensions of the artist. 'Twas a great picture, most of them agreed, admiring the gilt frame—larger than any they had ever seen.

Senator Kinney was the picture's champion and sponsor. It was he who so often stepped forward and asserted, with the voice of a bronco-buster, that it would be a lasting blot, sir, upon the name of this great state if it should decline to recognize in a proper manner the genius that had so brilliantly transferred to imperishable canvas a scene so typical of the great sources of our state's wealth and prosperity, land —and—er—live-stock.

Senator Kinney represented a section of the state in the extreme West—400 miles from the San Saba country—but the true lover of art is not limited by metes and bounds. Nor was Senator Mullens, representing the San Saba country, lukewarm in his belief that the state should purchase the painting of his constituent. He was advised that the San Saba country was unanimous in its admiration of the great painting by one of its own denizens. Hundreds of connoisseurs had straddled their broncos and ridden miles to view it before its removal to the capital. Senator Mullens desired re-election, and he knew the importance of the San Saba vote. He also knew that with the help of Senator Kinney —who was a power in the legislature—the thing could be put through. Now, Senator Kinney had an irrigation bill that he wanted passed for the benefit of his own section, and he knew Senator Mullens could render him valuable aid and information, the San Saba country already enjoying the benefits of similar legislation. With these interests happily dovetailed, wonder at the sudden interest in art at the state capital must, necessarily, be small. Few artists have uncovered their first picture to the world under happier auspices than did Lonny Briscoe.

Senators Kinney and Mullens came to an understanding in the matter of irrigation and art while partaking of long drinks in the café of the Empire Hotel.

"H'm!" said Senator Kinney, "I don't know. I'm no art critic, but it seems to me the thing won't work. It looks like the worst kind of a chromo to me. I don't want to cast any reflections upon the artistic talent of your constituent, Senator, but I, myself, wouldn't give six bits for the picture—without the frame. How are you going to cram a thing like that down the throat of a legislature that kicks about a little item in the expense bill of six hundred and eighty-one dollars for rubber erasers for only one term? It's wasting time. I'd like to help you, Mullens, but they'd laugh us out of the Senate chamber if we were to try it."

"But you don't get the point," said Senator Mullens, in his deliberate tones, tapping Kinney's glass with his long forefinger. "I have my own doubts as to what the picture is intended to represent, a bullfight or a Japanese allegory, but I want this legislature to make an appropriation to purchase. Of course, the subject of the picture should have been in the state historical line, but it's too late to have the paint scraped off and changed. The state won't miss the money and the picture can be stowed away in a lumber-room where it won't annoy any one. Now, here's the point to work on, leaving art to look after itself—the chap that painted the picture is the grandson of Lucien Briscoe."

"Say it again," said Kinney, leaning his head thoughtfully. "Of the old, original Lucien Briscoe?"

"Of him. 'The man who,' you know. The man who carved the state out of the wilderness. The man who settled the Indians. The man who cleaned out the horse thieves. The man who refused the crown. The state's favorite son. Do you see the point now?"

"Wrap up the picture," said Kinney. "It's as good as sold. Why didn't you say that at first, instead of philandering along about art? I'll resign my seat in the Senate and go back to chain-carrying for the county surveyor the day I can't make this state buy a picture calcimined by a grandson of Lucien Briscoe. Did you ever hear of a special appropriation for the purchase of a home for the daughter of One-Eyed Smothers? Well, that went through like a motion to adjourn, and old One-Eyed never killed half as many Indians as Briscoe did. About what figure had you and the calciminer agreed upon to sandbag the treasury for?"

"I thought," said Mullens, "that maybe five hundred—"

"Five hundred!" interrupted Kinney, as he hammered on his glass with a lead pencil and looked around for a waiter. "Only five hundred for a red steer on the hoof delivered by a grandson of Lucien Briscoe! Where's your state pride, man? Two thousand is what it'll be. You'll introduce the bill and I'll get up on the floor of the Senate and wave the scalp of every Indian old Lucien ever murdered. Let's see, there was something else proud and foolish he did, wasn't there? Oh, yes; he declined all emoluments and benefits he was entitled to. Refused his head-right and veteran donation certificates. Could have been governor, but wouldn't. Declined a pension. Now's the state's chance to pay up. It'll have to take the picture, but then it deserves some punishment for keeping the Briscoe family waiting so long. We'll bring this thing up about the middle of the month, after the tax bill is settled. Now, Mullens, you send over, as soon as you can, and get me the figures on the cost of those irrigation ditches and the statistics about the increased production per acre. I'm going to need you when that bill of mine comes

31

up. I reckon we'll be able to pull along pretty well together this session and maybe others to come, eh, Senator?"

Thus did fortune elect to smile upon the Boy Artist of the San Saba. Fate had already done her share when she arranged his atoms in the cosmogony of creation as the grandson of Lucien Briscoe.

The original Briscoe had been a pioneer both as to territorial occupation and in certain acts prompted by a great and simple heart. He had been one of the first settlers and crusaders against the wild forces of nature, the savage and the shallow politician. His name and memory were revered equally with any upon the list comprising Houston, Boone, Crockett, Clark, and Green. He had lived simply, independently, and unvexed by ambition. Even a less shrewd man than Senator Kinney could have prophesied that his state would hasten to honor and reward his grandson, come out of the chaparral at even so late a day.

And so, before the great picture by the door of the chamber of representatives at frequent times for many days could be found the breezy, robust form of Senator Kinney and be heard his clarion voice reciting the past deeds of Lucien Briscoe in connection with the handiwork of his grandson. Senator Mullens's work was more subdued in sight and sound, but directed along identical lines.

Then, as the day for the introduction of the bill for appropriation draws nigh, up from the San Saba country rides Lonny Briscoe and a loyal lobby of cowpunchers, bronco-back, to boost the cause of art and glorify the name of friendship, for Lonny is one of them, a knight of stirrup and chaparreras, as handy with the lariat and .45 as he is with brush and palette.

On a March afternoon the lobby dashed, with a whoop, into town. The cowpunchers had adjusted their garb suitably from that prescribed for the range to the more conventional requirements of town. They had conceded their leather chaparreras and transferred their six-shooters and belts from their persons to the horns of their saddles. Among them rode Lonny, a youth of twenty-three, brown, solemn-faced, ingenuous, bowlegged, reticent, bestriding Hot Tamales, the most sagacious cow pony west of the Mississippi. Senator Mullens had informed him of the bright prospects of the situation; had even mentioned—so great was his confidence in the capable Kinney—the price that the state would, in all likelihood, pay. It seemed to Lonny that fame and fortune were in his hands. Certainly, a spark of the divine fire was in the little brown centaur's breast, for he was counting the two thousand dollars as but a means to future development of his talent. Some day he would paint a picture even greater than this—one, say, twelve feet by twenty, full of scope and atmosphere and action.

During the three days that yet intervened before the coming of the date fixed for the introduction of the bill, the centaur lobby did valiant service. Coatless, spurred, weather-tanned, full of enthusiasm expressed in bizarre terms, they loafed in front of the painting with tireless zeal. Reasoning not unshrewdly, they estimated that their comments upon its fidelity to nature would be received as expert evidence. Loudly they praised the skill of the painter whenever there were ears near to which such evidence might be profitably addressed. Lem Perry, the leader of the claque, had a somewhat set speech, being uninventive in the construction of new phrases.

"Look at that two-year-old, now," he would say, waving a cinnamon-brown hand toward the salient point of the picture. "Why, dang my hide, the critter's alive. I can jest hear him, 'lumpety-lump,' a-cuttin' away from the herd, pretendin' he's skeered. He's a mean scamp, that there steer. Look at his eyes a-wallin' and his tail a-wavin'. He's true and nat'ral to life. He's jest hankerin' fur a cow pony to round him up and send him scootin' back to the bunch. Dang my hide! jest look at that tail of his'n a-wavin'. Never knowed a steer to wave his tail any other way, dang my hide ef I did."

Jud Shelby, while admitting the excellence of the steer, resolutely confined himself to open admiration of the landscape, to the end that the entire picture receive its meed of praise.

"That piece of range," he declared, "is a dead ringer for Dead Hoss Valley. Same grass, same lay of the land, same old Whipperwill Creek skallyhootin' in and out of them motts of timber. Them buzzards on the left is circlin' 'round over Sam Kildrake's old paint hoss that killed hisself over-drinkin' on a hot day. You can't see the hoss for that mott of ellums on the creek, but he's thar. Anybody that was goin' to look for Dead Hoss Valley and come across this picture, why, he'd jest light off'n his bronco and hunt a place to camp."

Skinny Rogers, wedded to comedy, conceived a complimentary little piece of acting that never failed to make an impression. Edging quite near to the picture, he would suddenly at favorable moments emit a piercing and awful "Yi-yi!" leap high and away, coming down with a great stamp of heels and whirring of rowels upon the stone-flagged floor.

"Jeeming Christopher!"—so ran his lines—"thought that rattler was a gin-u-ine one. Ding baste my skin if I didn't. Seemed to me I heard him rattle. Look at the blamed, unconverted insect a-layin' under that pear. Little more, and somebody would a-been snake-bit."

With these artful dodges, contributed by Lonny's faithful coterie, with the sonorous Kinney perpetually sounding the picture's merits, and with the solvent prestige of the pioneer Briscoe covering it like a precious varnish, it seemed that the San Saba country could not fail to add a reputation as an art centre to its well-known superiority in steer-roping contests and achievements with the precarious busted flush. Thus was created for the picture an atmosphere, due rather to externals than to the artist's brush, but through it the people seemed to gaze with more of admiration. There was a magic in the name of Briscoe that counted high against faulty technique and crude coloring. The old Indian fighter and wolf slayer would have smiled grimly in his happy hunting grounds had he known that his dilettante ghost was thus figuring as an art patron two generations after his uninspired existence.

Came the day when the Senate was expected to pass the bill of Senator Mullens appropriating two thousand dollars for the purchase of the picture. The gallery of the Senate chamber was early pre-empted by Lonny and the San Saba lobby. In the front row of chairs they sat, wild-haired, self-conscious, jingling, creaking, and rattling, subdued by the majesty of the council hall.

The bill was introduced, went to the second reading, and then Senator Mullens spoke for it dryly, tediously, and at length. Senator Kinney then arose, and the welkin seized the bellrope preparatory to ringing. Oratory was at that time a living thing; the world had not quite come to measure its questions by geometry and the multiplication table. It was the day of the silver tongue, the sweeping gesture, the decorative apostrophe, the moving peroration.

The Senator spoke. The San Saba contingent sat, breathing hard, in the gallery, its disordered hair hanging down to its eyes, its sixteen-ounce hats shifted restlessly from knee to knee. Below, the distinguished Senators either lounged at their desks with the abandon of proven statesmanship or maintained correct attitudes indicative of a first term.

Senator Kinney spoke for an hour. History was his theme—history mitigated by patriotism and sentiment. He referred casually to the picture in the outer hall—it was unnecessary, he said, to dilate upon its merits—the Senators had seen for themselves. The painter of the picture was the grandson of Lucien Briscoe. Then came the word-pictures of Briscoe's life set forth in thrilling colors. His rude and venturesome life, his simple-minded love for the commonwealth he helped to upbuild, his contempt for rewards and praise, his extreme and sturdy independence, and the great services he had rendered the state. The subject of the oration was Lucien Briscoe; the painting stood in the background serving simply as a means, now happily brought forward, through which the state might bestow a tardy recompense upon the descendant of its favorite son. Frequent enthusiastic applause from the Senators testified to the well reception of the sentiment.

The bill passed without an opposing vote. To-morrow it would be taken up by the House. Already was it fixed to glide through that body on rubber tires. Blandford, Grayson, and Plummer, all wheel-horses and orators, and provided with plentiful memoranda concerning the deeds of pioneer Briscoe, had agreed to furnish the motive power.

The San Saba lobby and its *protégé* stumbled awkwardly down the stairs and out into the Capitol yard. Then they herded closely and gave one yell of triumph. But one of them—Buck-Kneed Summers it was—hit the key with the thoughtful remark:

"She cut the mustard," he said, "all right. I reckon they're goin' to buy Lon's steer. I ain't right much on the parlyment'ry, but I gather that's what the signs added up. But she seems to me, Lonny, the argyment ran principal to grandfather, instead of paint. It's reasonable calculatin' that you want to be glad you got the Briscoe brand on you, my son."

That remark clinched in Lonny's mind an unpleasant, vague suspicion to the same effect. His reticence increased, and he gathered grass from the ground, chewing it pensively. The picture as a picture had been humiliatingly absent from the Senator's arguments. The painter had been held up as a grandson, pure and simple. While this was gratifying on certain lines, it made art look little and slab-sided. The Boy Artist was thinking.

The hotel Lonny stopped at was near the Capitol. It was near to the one o'clock dinner hour when the appropriation had been passed by the Senate. The hotel clerk told Lonny that a famous artist from

New York had arrived in town that day and was in the hotel. He was on his way westward to New Mexico to study the effect of sunlight upon the ancient walls of the Zuñis. Modern stone reflects light. Those ancient building materials absorb it. The artist wanted this effect in a picture he was painting and was traveling two thousand miles to get it.

Lonny sought this man out after dinner and told his story. The artist was an unhealthy man, kept alive by genius and indifference to life. He went with Lonny to the Capitol and stood there before the picture. The artist pulled his beard and looked unhappy.

"Should like to have your sentiments," said Lonny, "just as they run out of the pen."

"It's the way they'll come," said the painter man. "I took three different kinds of medicine before dinner—by the tablespoonful. The taste still lingers. I am primed for telling the truth. You want to know if the picture is, or if it isn't?"

"Right," said Lonny. "Is it wool or cotton? Should I paint some more or cut it out and ride herd a-plenty?"

"I heard a rumor during pie," said the artist, "that the state is about to pay you two thousand dollars for this picture."

"It's passed the Senate," said Lonny, "and the House rounds it up to-morrow."

"That's lucky," said the pale man. "Do you carry a rabbit's foot?"

"No," said Lonny, "but it seems I had a grandfather. He's considerable mixed up in the color scheme. It took me a year to paint that picture. Is she entirely awful or not? Some says, now, that that steer's tail ain't badly drawed. They think it's proportioned nice. Tell me."

The artist glanced at Lonny's wiry figure and nut-brown skin. Something stirred him to a passing irritation.

"For Art's sake, son," he said, fractiously, "don't spend any more money for paint. It isn't a picture at all. It's a gun. You hold up the state with it, if you like, and get your two thousand, but don't get in front of any more canvas. Live under it. Buy a couple of hundred ponies with the money—I'm told they're that cheap—and ride, ride, ride. Fill your lungs and eat and sleep and be happy. No more pictures. You look healthy. That's genius. Cultivate it." He looked at his watch. "Twenty minutes to three. Four capsules and one tablet at three. That's all you wanted to know, isn't it?"

At three o'clock the cowpunchers rode up for Lonny, bringing Hot

Tamales, saddled. Traditions must be observed. To celebrate the passage of the bill by the Senate the gang must ride wildly through the town, creating uproar and excitement. Liquor must be partaken of, the suburbs shot up, and the glory of the San Saba country vociferously proclaimed. A part of the programme had been carried out in the saloons on the way up. Lonny mounted Hot Tamales, the accomplished little beast prancing with fire and intelligence. He was glad to feel Lonny's bowlegged grip against his ribs again. Lonny was his friend, and he was willing to do things for him.

"Come on, boys," said Lonny, urging Hot Tamales into a gallop with his knees. With a whoop, the inspired lobby tore after him through the dust. Lonny led his cohorts straight for the Capitol. With a wild yell, the gang indorsed his now evident intention of riding into it. Hooray for San Saba!

Up the six broad, limestone steps clattered the broncos of the cowpunchers. Into the resounding hallway they pattered, scattering in dismay those passing on foot. Lonny, in the lead, shoved Hot Tamales direct for the great picture. At that hour a downpouring, soft light from the second-story windows bathed the big canvas. Against the darker background of the hall the painting stood out with valuable effect. In spite of the defects of the art you could almost fancy that you gazed out upon a landscape. You might well flinch a step from the convincing figure of the life-sized steer stampeding across the grass. Perhaps it thus seemed to Hot Tamales. The scene was in his line. Perhaps he only obeyed the will of his rider. His ears pricked up; he snorted. Lonny leaned forward in the saddle and elevated his elbows, wing-like. Thus signals the cowpuncher to his steed to launch himself full speed ahead. Did Hot Tamales fancy he saw a steer, red and cavorting, that should be headed off and driven back to herd? There was a fierce clatter of hoofs, a rush, a gathering of steely flank muscles, a leap to the jerk of the bridle rein, and Hot Tamales, with Lonny bending low in the saddle to dodge the top of the frame, ripped through the great canvas like a shell from a mortar, leaving the cloth hanging in ragged shreds about a monstrous hole.

Quickly Lonny pulled up his pony, and rounded the pillars. Spectators came running, too astounded to add speech to the commotion. The sergeant-at-arms of the House came forth, frowned, looked ominous, and then grinned. Many of the legislators crowded out to observe

37

the tumult. Lonny's cowpunchers were stricken to silent horror by his mad deed.

Senator Kinney happened to be among the earliest to emerge. Before he could speak Lonny leaned in his saddle as Hot Tamales pranced, pointed his quirt at the Senator, and said, calmly:

"That was a fine speech you made to-day, mister, but you might as well let up on that 'propriation business. I ain't askin' the state to give me nothin'. I thought I had a picture to sell to it, but it wasn't one. You said a heap of things about Grandfather Briscoe that makes me kind of proud I'm his grandson. Well, the Briscoes ain't takin' presents from the state yet. Anybody can have the frame that wants it. Hit her up, boys."

Away scuttled the San Saba delegation out of the hall, down the steps, along the dusty street.

Halfway to the San Saba country they camped that night. At bedtime Lonny stole away from the campfire and sought Hot Tamales, placidly eating grass at the end of his stake rope. Lonny hung upon his neck, and his art aspirations went forth forever in one long, regretful sigh. But as he thus made renunciation his breath formed a word or two.

"You was the only one, Tamales, what seen anything in it. It *did* look like a steer, didn't it, old hoss?"

EUGENE CUNNINGHAM

ON ONE OF HIS BOOK JACKETS his publishers state that Eugene Cunningham was "born bow-legged in Texas." Actually, the rider-writer missed being a native Texan, if we may believe *Who's Who in America*, by about a year. He was born at Helena, Arkansas, November 29, 1896, and moved to Texas in 1897. He was educated in the Dallas and Fort Worth public schools, by private instruction, and by a variety of work experiences: as he says, "chousing" cows and horses, repairing typewriters, and cub-reporting. From early 1914 to late 1919 he served in the Navy—with the Asiatic Fleet, Mexican Patrol Squadron, and the Atlantic Cruiser Patrol Squadron, after 1917 on escort duty in the submarine zone. His career as a writer, he says, began in 1915 on shipboard.

After World War I, Cunningham traveled widely in Central America, observing filibusters and revolutions, such as the Unionista overthrow of Estrada Cabrera in Guatemala, and writing fact and fiction for British and American newspapers and magazines. This travel resulted in the book *Gypsying through Central America*, published in London in 1922, the historical novel *Redshirts of Destiny* (1935), and other novels. After 1921 Cunningham did free-lance writing for three years from a San Francisco studio, specializing in sea and historical romances. Back in El Paso, he added to writing and research newspaper work, advertising, editing, and reviewing. He was literary editor of the *El Paso Times* from 1929 to 1936 and conducted the "Southwestern Bookshelf" of *New Mexico Magazine* from 1936 to 1941. A naval reservist, he returned to active duty in 1941. He now lives in San Francisco.

Despite collateral activities, Cunningham has devoted his life to writing, mostly fiction, short and long, predominantly western but including mystery, war, buccaneer, prize-fight, and other types of story. A few of his books—there are nearly thirty of them under his own and pen names—are *The Regulation Guy* (1922), *Trail to Apacaz* (1924), *Riders of the Night* (1932), *Triggernometry: A Gallery of Gunfighters* (1933), *Texas Sheriff* (1934), *Trail of the Macaw* (1935), *Red Range* (1939), *Spiderweb Trail* (1940), and *Gunfighters All* (1941). His published output has been estimated at nearly seven million words.

Like other western fiction, Cunningham's is strenuous, swift, and thrilling in its action. Cunningham is distinguished among writers of westerns, however, for his good craftsmanship, for the authenticity of his detail, and for his fidelity to the spirit of his region. He therefore has won a high place among the fictional chroniclers of our mounted frontier.

"Bar-Nothing's Happy Birthday," the only shoot-'em-up story in this collection, is based on a Ranger incident told to the author by "Jim" Gillett and Captain John Hughes. It reflects the resourcefulness and daring of a Texas Ranger in some of his lighter moments, which prove heavy enough to turn what seemed to be the worst birthday of his life into "a gen-u-ine P-cutter of a birthday."

Bar-Nothing's Happy Birthday

Six DINGY WALL TENTS among the giant cottonwoods at Bloody made the camp of Captain Hewey's ranger company. Down the sandy slope a quarter-mile to the south, the rangers could see the wide ribbon of silver that was the shallow Rio Grande. They could watch—and cover with their Winchesters—Bloody Ford. It was by this crossing that Garcia, El Bufalo, might be expected to come into Texas.

"Bar-Nothing Red" Ames, sprawling comfortably in the shade of a tent with three companions, was staring down at the river from beneath the wide rim of his Boss Stetson.

"Reckon the Buffalo really aims to come see us?" he drawled, without looking at the other rangers. "Here we are, imitating a bunch of old Dominecker setting hens, all because the Buffalo sent word to the folks in Pease City that he's coming and he's coming a-smoking. Seems to me if the hairpin's coming at all, he oughtn't to put it off like this. He ought to fog up like a decent scound'l so's we could bury him and high-tail it for a damper climate."

"You don't mean damper; you mean wetter, you hollow-laigged sponge," Step-and-a-Half Carstairs corrected him, grinning. "But we have been hunkered here longer'n X Company gen'ally decorates one spot. We come in on the fourth and here it is the twenty-sixth, today."

Bar-Nothing came with a snaky wriggle to stand staring.

"Twenty-sixth!" he yelled. "Step-and-a-Half, you wouldn't fool a man, now? But, now I come to think of it, you don't own brains enough to make up a lie . . ."

"Of course it's the twenty-sixth," Step-and-a-Half told him with dig-

Reprinted with permission of the author from *The American West,* ed. William Targ, by arrangement with The World Publishing Company.

41

nity. "I just pass over kind of contemptuous your remarks about my brains. Everybody knows it ain't that I can't lie with the best of 'em. It's just I got high religious principles against lying to jugheads that wouldn't know enough to cut out a lie from a whole herd of truth."

But Bar-Nothing was gone, moving as rapidly as the rocking of high heels permitted in the sand toward that tent where Captain Hewey, big, dark, quiet, headquartered.

"By Gemini!" Bar-Nothing said amazedly to himself. "If I didn't come inside a short inch of missing her. First time I ever forgot since I can remember; since I was just a button cowboy. I— Ah, hell! Cap'n's got company."

For out of Captain Hewey's tent voices carried to him. He moved up to hunker beside the canvas wall and wait the commander's leisure. Through the open flap he saw a big, tousled youngster in stained and shabby overalls and ancient boots, twisting a battered black Stetson in his two hands as he faced Captain Hewey.

"And so," the boy was saying, "now I come to be twenty year old, I guess it's time to make my throw at getting into the Rangers like I always wanted to all my life."

"Ah!" said Hewey in his deep, smooth voice. "Ah!"

Bar-Nothing shifted position until he could also see his commander, a big, immaculate figure in blue silk shirt, gray wool trousers and polished tan boots of alligator hide.

"I—don't know," Hewey drawled. "I'm just afraid— What have you been doing lately? Is that—can that be—calf dip that I smell on you? Surely not!"

"Why—yes, sir," the boy admitted nervously. "I been working with the calves all week. Dipping 'em, you know."

"Working!" Hewey cried. His tone held amazement, alarm—disgust. "Did I hear you say working? Just how long has that been going on? When did you begin this—what was that word?—working?"

"Ever since I was big enough to spin a loop in my twine and haze a calf, I reckon. I—I really am a hard worker, too!"

"My son," Hewey told him sadly, "I am very much afraid that all your dreams of becoming a Texas Ranger have been destroyed by one word—work. Automatically, you're disqualified. Rangers, my boy, never work! No ranger would even think of it. You—why, probably you've so hardened yourself in the awful habit that you couldn't break it. So—"

"But I sling the Mex' lingo like I was a chili-picker myself," the cowboy protested plaintively. "And I heard 'em say, over at Pease City, you needed to enlist a man could spiel it."

"Too, there are other qualifications to be considered. Let's see. . . . Suppose you had to lay out a man with your Colt. Would you strike him with the butt or the barrel?"

"With the barrel! Pa taught me that. You know he was in the Rangers with you thirty year back. He always says: Hold onto the cutter-handle and slam 'em with the barrel. Because you might have to shoot the *batardo* after all!"

"Right!" Hewey nodded solemnly. "If you were lone-wolfing it on the trail of five desperate outlaws, wanted dead or alive, how would you bring them into camp?"

"Well, if orders said 'dead or alive' I'd just bushwack 'em and load 'em onto their horses," the boy said simply. "Pa always says: They pack better, dead!"

"Right! Now, where do you live these days?"

"Up the road a whoop and a holloa; on the Box A between this and Pease City. Ten mile up, I reckon."

"Well, I think we can enlist you, if you'll promise faithfully not to work any more. Sit down over there while I talk to the gentlemen here."

Bar-Nothing's sandy brows lifted. Could Captain Hewey be referring to him? He half-rose, but an irritable voice in the tent, coming from someone invisible to him, checked the motion.

"Well, if you got done monkeying with Sim Cook, Cap'n, I would appreciate you taking my complaint about my blaze-faced sorrel being stole."

"Certainly," Hewey agreed. "When did you miss it?"

"Two days ago. I got word that it was tied to the hitch-rack in Pease City the day after it was stole. Some of that sticky loop gang of old Jay Bird Pease, they done the stealing. That damn' rustling old sidewinder! There he sets, saying he's the town and the town's him; he ain't only the justice of the peace, he's everything else in Pease. If I take my foot in my hand and fog it into town, trying to get back my horse, Jay Bird'll just wink at somebody and a gun'll go off accidental. Then Jay Bird'll prop my carcass up and try me for disturbing the peace and contempt of court and fine me whatever I got in my pockets and my horse and saddle."

"As bad as that?" Hewey drawled, black eyes twinkling.

"Likely, worse!" the robbed one cried. "So, I can't go and the sheriff, he won't go. I talked to him yesterday and he's sorry as hell he's got anyhow six months' work ahead before he can take on any new complaints. That sorrel's worth three hundred of any man's money. I want him back!"

"We'll certainly have to look into this," Hewey said thoughtfully. "Bar-Nothing! Something you want?"

"Oh, nothing much," Bar-Nothing answered. He got up and loafed into the tent. "It's just my birthday, Cap'n. I thought I'd like to drift over to Pease—it's just a short twenty mile—and buy myself a birthday present. Life-time habit of mine."

"Oh!" Hewey grunted. "You know, Red, we're supposed to be here because of Buffalo? That's why I've kept you wild buckaroos out of Pease."

"Yeh, of course. But, Cap'n! Birthdays make a lot of difference. Take me, now: If I hadn't started out with a birthday—right in the very beginning!—I couldn't be here with you watching for the Buffalo!"

"All right, then," Hewey surrendered. "You can go to Pease. But you're due back not later than nine tomorrow morning. You heard what Mr. Hawley said about his sorrel horse? Well, bring it back with you. Bring the thief, too, if you run into him. Take Sim Cook, here, with you. It will be experience for him. But, remember! Don't you get organized and start a riot. From what I've heard, Pease is quite—a—salty —community. You go in like a lamb, Red."

"I don't mind a bit going in like a lamb," Bar-Nothing said gravely, "if I don't go out like a light. From what I heard Mr. Hawley say, if I recover that horse of his, some kind of riot is mightily apt to start itself. You want me just to lie down under it?"

"That would be a lot to ask of a red-headed man," Hewey said with the flicker of a smile. "Particularly when that red-head is known from the Panhandle to the Big Bend as 'Bar-Nothing' Ames. What I mean is, don't you look for any trouble."

"Now I think of it, I never had to!" Bar-Nothing drawled.

44

It was a clean, extremely neat, Sim Cook who rode out from the Box A with Bar-Nothing. He had scrubbed himself in the horse trough and put on new black Stetson, new blue flannel shirt, new waist overalls. His half-boots, his Colt and holster belt, the .44 Winchester carbine beneath his leg in saddle scabbard, even the stamped swellfork hull and one-ear bridle, were also brand-new.

"You see, I been saving up and getting things ready for my coming into the Rangers," he explained shyly to Bar-Nothing. "I certainly am glad Cap' Hewey took me! But he had me boogering for a spell, hurrahing me from behind that solemnous face."

He rode with admiring eyes upon Bar-Nothing's easy, efficient figure. For the name of this tall, swaggering, happy-go-lucky red-head was known from border to border of Texas—and fairly well in adjoining states—as one of the deadliest two-gun rangers in the Frontier Battalion and as a puzzle-buster, a criminal-catcher, towering in the very front rank.

"So this Jay Bird Pease, he's the li'l' tin curly wolf with red stripedy legs," Bar-Nothing grunted, as they saw before them the "wide place in the road" which was Pease "City," with its lean rows of gray adobe and grayer frame buildings making "Main Street's" twin borders.

"He is that!" Sim Cook assured him earnestly. "He's been here since there wasn't nothing a-tall on this flat. He claims when he got here there wasn't ary mountain yonder—he planted 'em! Railroad coming by made the place and made him. Yes—sir! He rods Pease City from A to Big Casino. He's Big Auger."

"Railroad helped? How-come? I wouldn't guess Pease'd have a canary bird pack of stuff to ship out. Most of the ranches front on the West Spur and load out over there."

"It's the passengers," Sim explained, grinning. "Train stops ten minutes. Passengers look out and see Jay Bird's sign: *Cold Beer and Justice of the Peace*. They come a-racking it. Jay Bird, he reaches down and pulls out some bottled beer out of the wet sand under the bar. He slams it and his six-shooter on the bar. Beer ain't cold, but it's damp. Colt's staring right at the customers. Nobody's kicked yet about warm beer. Passenger gives Jay Bird maybe a ten dollar bill."

"Well, Jay Bird's Mex' kid runs out with the bill, hunting change. Passenger waits. Mex' boy don't show up. Train whistles—*toot-toot!* Still no Mex' boy; no change. (Jay Bird, he just can't figure how-come!) Conductor yells—*all aboard!* No Mex' boy showing. (Jay Bird's awful sorry.) Engine bell's a-ringing—*whangety-clang!* No Mex' boy yet. (Jay Bird do' no' what to do.) But that passenger, he has got to run so's not to miss his train. So he hightails, talking non–Sunday School lingo. Minute the train's down the track, out comes the Mex' boy from under the porch where he's been smoking cigareets. He hands over the five—or ten, or even twenty, to Jay Bird."

"Dear me, Suz!" Bar-Nothing cried, as they fox-trotted up Main Street toward Jay Bird Pease's thirst-and-justice headquarters. "That's not altogether downright honest, Sim. Maybe we can look into it. Well—no sorrel at this hitch-rack."

"One across the road, yonder," Sim contributed, shifting in the saddle. "But he ain't got a white hair on him and Hawley, he said his horse was blaze-faced and had four stockings."

Bar-Nothing's first glance at Jay Bird Pease gave him instant and complete dislike for the squat, wizened old man. Jay Bird had whitish hair, the few straggling locks of it looking as if they had been stuck sparingly at random on his shiny, egg-shaped skull. His eyebrows were of a mustard-tinted gray and so shaggy that they almost hid the tiny, shifting reddish-black eyes. His nose was like a buzzard's beak overhanging a huge, loose-lipped mouth in which showed a scattering half-dozen of yellow fangs.

"*Buenas dias!*" he cried as Bar-Nothing *cling-clumped* in with Sim Cook at his elbow. "*Como 'sta?*"

"*Muy bien*—very well," Bar-Nothing grunted. "*Muy bien.*"

Then he turned with artistic expression of bewilderment:

"Thought you said it was a white man, Sim—kind of . . ."

Malevolent rage twisted Jay Bird's face. One hand disappeared from the bar. The tiny black eyes glittered like a sidewinder's. But Bar-Nothing, standing with air of blandest innocence, had both thumbs hooked in crossed shell-belts . . .

"Smart Aleck, huh?" Jay Bird snarled. "Well, you better *sabe* this, right now: I'm Pease! I'm the town and the town's me! Folks that look for grief around here—they locate it!"

Bar-Nothing leaned over the bar until his face was hardly more than a foot from Jay Bird's.

"I have got just two questions to ask," he drawled. "First, what the hell are you talking about? Second, what the hell do I care? My name's Ames. I'm a ranger sergeant. Out of Hewey's X Company that's camped at Bloody Ford. I sing palpitating tenor when I sing, but I howl a lot better than I sing. I go where I'm a mind to go and I stay until I'm plumb ready to rattle my hocks. I ask for what I want, then see that I get it. And right now I want a drink!"

Jay Bird jumped at that sudden, unprefaced bellow. For there was a blaze in Bar-Nothing's blue eyes that failed to match the grin stretching his wide mouth.

"A' right! A' right!" he growled. "No call to be a bellowing around here like that. You can have your drink. Nobody aims to keep you drouthed up. But I don't like folks making remarks."

"Oh, me neither!" Bar-Nothing assured him. "Makes me fit to tie— and I never found the man, or men, could tie me."

He put a silver dollar on the bar, but stared at Jay Bird.

"Li'l' words have come floating to me, about the way you make your prices skip up and down, all-same the giddy gazellaroo. Now, me, I just don't like such. But I never massacreed a barkeep yet for charging me two-bits a throw."

"Two-bits is all right," Jay Bird told him sullenly—but with a furtive stare at the door behind the rangers. As if he expected—or hoped for— some relief from that direction, Bar-Nothing thought.

"Here's looking at you, Simmy," he said, when two tin cups of whisky were before them. "Look at her while she's red—"

"Can't," the boy disagreed, rolling a narrowed eye at Jay Bird. "Can't look at the liquor, account I got to keep looking at that door. Couple of good friends of Jay Bird's—couldn't you smell 'em; li'l' bit stronger'n a skunk?—they've been peeking in, trying to make out what Jay Bird means by all his funny motionings and eyebrow wigglings."

"I've been eyeing 'em, too, in that old mirror back there. Wouldn't it just be too sad, if something they tried to pull got poor old Jay Bird killed dead? Down her and take another."

They drank formally and Bar-Nothing refilled the cups, grinning cheerfully at the furious Jay Bird.

"Gullup that'n' and we'll ramble out where the air's fresh. I like to celebrate my new birthdays where things smell clean. Oh, Jay Bird! What'd you and the rest of your petty larceny thieves do with Mr. Hawley's sorrel horse, huh?"

"Never knowed Hawley owned a sorrel," Jay Bird snarled, choosing to ignore the bulk of the question. "Did he?"

"Says he did. Kind of sorrelish animal with a mane and—oh, yes, a tail!—and a leg sticking down towards the ground from each corner. Critter lived off grass and corn and hay and stuff like that. What'd you say you did with him?"

"I said I never knowed Hawley owned a sorrel!" the baited Jay Bird yelled. "And you looky here, young fellow! I told you before, I'm Justice of the Peace. Ranger or no ranger, you run no sandy around here, onto me!"

"You-all put him—where?" Bar-Nothing inquired, scowling. "I didn't just make out what place you said. Well, ne' mind! Ne' mind! I'll stumble onto him—always do. Then you'll be sorry, Mister Jay Bird, your tail in a crack and all!"

"Better watch you don't stub your toe trying," Jay Bird mumbled, as they turned toward the door. Bar-Nothing laughed.

"Any more juice-joints?" he asked Sim Cook. "I don't love to throw all my tremendous-tremens trade to one place, specially not a dump like Pease's. What-for a community is this, anyhow, that'll suck up its red-eye over a bar like that? Why, you'd think it'd sour on their stomachs! Me, I like to be happy and don't-give-a-hoot, all-same li'l' bitsy blue bird. You never catch me off in a mourning corner sucking a bottle of nothing. *Nunca! Jamás!* Never! I'm a sweet soul natural."

Approached, now, a citizen of the place who seemed to have suffered that souring of the stomach he had mentioned. It was a very tall man, six and a third feet in height. And he could not have weighed thirty pounds over the hundred. His dark hatchet face was marked by V-lines from hooked nose to savage gash-thin mouth. He stalked down the dirt sidewalk squarely in their path, gaunt arms swinging, one huge hand slap-slapping his pistol holster, glowering ferociously.

> "Her pay-rents don't like me,
> They say I'm too pore,
> They say I'm unworthy
> To enter her door.
> They say I drink whisky—
> Well, my money's my own
> And them that don't like me
> Can leave me alone!"

Bar-Nothing's tanned face was boyishly happy as he moved forward, his chin a trifle lifted, his head swaying gently in time with *Jack of Diamonds*. So he and the tall man met toe-to-toe and stopped short.

"Where the hell you think you might be going?" the townsman demanded. "Think you can hog the road in Pease, huh? Well—"

"Well?" Bar-Nothing repeated softly. "Flea bite you, or something? Family troubles, maybe? Old lady won't let you sleep in the house account of your Peasey smell? Or—could it be just growing pains, you not having your weight yet?"

The tall man made a wordless, rasping sound and flicked his hand to low-swung Colt. Sim Cook jerked out his new Colt with all the speed he could manage. But Bar-Nothing's hands twitched like nothing in the world so much as striking snake-heads. He slapped the tall man on one cheek with the right-hand gun-barrel, on the other with the left-hand Colt. His victim seemed to forget that he had begun to draw. He staggered backward with an agonized grunt, both hands up with palms out. A deft blow across the temple dropped him.

"Hey! You red-head!" a squat man yelled from across the street. "Cut that out! Don't you hit Casselberry no more!"

He came panting over to them. Bar-Nothing spun his Colts on the trigger guards. The butts slapped into his palms; twirled again so that they stared at the star-wearer—as he stared.

"I'm city marshal," the stocky man blustered. "You can't—"

"You can't . . ." Bar-Nothing repeated softly. "Seems to me that's the pet saying around this gawdforsaken village. And—know what's funny? I have been doing it, whatever it is, all the time! Now, my good advice to you is, ram that cutter back into the scabbard and quit trying to howl like a wolf! Good idea to file off the front sight of the hogleg, too: Because if a gunfighter comes along and takes it away from you and rams it down your neck, you won't get scarred up so much!

"I'm a sergeant in the rangers. This folding contraption on the ground come interfering with me in the execution of my doings. According to the statutes made and provided, I discussed that interfering with him in the way and the fashion I figured his intellects would understand best. Perfectly simple!"

"Casselberry interfered? How-come? Execution of what?"

"Celebrating my twenty-seventh birthday! And don't you think for one minute that's not a serious doing! Come on, Sim. We are turning over the prisoner to the city authorities. Now that he understands what's what, he's going to save—a—heap—of—trouble."

They went on, leaving behind them a silent marshal—pistol reholstered—bending over the unconscious Casselberry.

At the far end of the town was an ancient and bullet-pocked 'dobe house with the customary "gallery" along its street-front. A dingy tin sign bearing a faint likeness of a billygoat hinted of beer inside. They entered, to face a brown, still-faced man with sun-squinted gray eyes. He looked flashingly at Sim, then watched Bar-Nothing steadily.

"Hi, Pegleg!" Sim greeted the saloonkeeper. "Touch paws with Bar-Nothing Red Ames of the rangers. I'm a ranger, too, since today. Red, this-here's Pegleg Scott. He'll do!"

"Howdy," Pegleg drawled, relaxing. "I been watching out for some of that coyote-crew of Jay Bird's. They went racking past last night and shot some more nicks into my wall. But when they scallyhooted back to try it over, me and Bill Jameson the blacksmith, and Squeaky Conner the freighter, we happened to be all out at the end of the c'ral a-cleaning our Winchesters—except me, being I al'ays favor a Sharps .50 buffalo gun. It made us so skittery when they got to howling that our long guns went off accidental-like and we come close to rubbing some of 'em out. Happened some of us did kind of buttonhole Hognose Judd, that trifling swamper at Jay Bird's wagon yard. Plumb killed the horse he was forking. Kind of sad, how it happened."

"They—bother you any, after?" Bar-Nothing asked owlishly.

"Not as I recollect, no. Of course, that nitwit marshal did come this way a li'l' piece yelling some kind of foolishness about me surrendering to the law up at Jay Bird's. He was yelling in English, too. He speaks tol'able Mex', too. Most of Jay Bird's thieves do. Handy for 'em. Lets 'em lie in two languages. But I couldn't just make out what he wanted. So I went around the Widow Jenk's c'ral to hear better and I motioned him to come closer. He must've mistooken my intendings because he singlefooted right away from there. Maybe I was waving at him with the hand I had my Sharps rifle in. What'll it be?"

"Beer and—who plays that fiddle? It's my birthday, Mr. Scott. So I just pine for happiness."

"I'll call Old Black Joe. He's asleep out back. Got a pickaninny, too, can double-shuffle and buck-and-wing."

At his yell an ancient negro appeared, grinning, to get the battered fiddle from the wall. He sawed the bow across the strings and swept into *Sugar in the Gourd*. A tiny black boy stole in, teeth splitting his face with a white crescent. His twinkling pink heels slapped a tattoo on the rough floor. Bar-Nothing fished a harmonica from his pocket and joined in.

Then, suddenly, a rapid rattle of shots carried to them, followed by raucous, high-pitched howl. Bar-Nothing jerked the harmonica from his mouth and swore irritably as he moved to the door and looked out.

In front of Jay Bird Pease's saloon a man was reloading his pistol, howling wolfishly the while. His hand jerked and again the Colt was emptied in air.

"I wish he wouldn't do that," Bar-Nothing said plaintively. "It plumb sends the shivers down my spine—that howl."

He went quickly along Main Street. Sim Cook trailed him, tight-faced, hand on Colt. The howling one was pulling more shells from his belt when Bar-Nothing stopped before him.

"What's the idea of these vulgar noises?" Bar-Nothing demanded coldly. "You just trying to bother people?"

"When I feel like howling—" the celebrant thrust stubbled, liquor-swollen face out belligerently "—howling's what I do!"

To Sim Cook was presented a sort of dust-wreathed Punch and Judy show accompanied by sounds as of applauding hands. It continued for only a minute or so, then Bar-Nothing stepped back with a sigh and the ex-howler began slowly to get to his feet. There were faces at every opening of Jay Bird's place. Bar-Nothing, seeing everything, stepped quickly in and twisted the man's right hand behind him. Holding that wrist and the left arm, he hustled him into Jay Bird's door.

"Pease!" he called grimly. "You have been bragging about being a justice. A' right! I'm not only a ranger, I'm a man with an ear for music. On both counts I give this two-legged tomcat into your custody for disturbing the peace. I certainly expect you to take charge of his case!"

"'Sta bueno," Jay Bird mumbled, without meeting Bar-Nothing's glare. "I—I'll take him in charge."

"Better see that you do," Bar-Nothing advised him.

Back in Pegleg Scott's place, he waved at the fiddler.

"Now, let her rip!" he cried. "I'm not in right good practice, Joe.

51

You get so far ahead of me that I need spec's to make out what you're playing. Let's try *Going Up Cripple Creek!*"

Again the bow sawed frantically and Bar-Nothing, setting down his beer glass, wiped his mouth and lifted the harmonica.

"*Oooeeee! Yip! Yip! Yip!*" came to them from down street.

"Coyote's out again," Pegleg said gravely. "Believe I'd tie a knot in his tail this time, Red—a hard knot. But—that gang's likely ribbed up something, this trip. You could easy slide up behind this row of buildings and—whisper in his ear . . ."

"Can happen!" Bar-Nothing agreed, grinning one-sidedly.

A quick, barehead glance from the front door showed heads in Jay Bird's windows, figures in his doorway. Then, trailed again by the faithful Sim, he ran awkwardly down the room and through Pegleg's back entrance. They trotted up the rear walls of this row until at the corner of a store neighboring Jay Bird's 'dobe—but separated by a space of two yards—they could look at the howling figure in the street.

"Ah, he ain't coming, Harrigan!" someone in Jay Bird's yelled. "Yellow's up in his neck. Heave some lead in the air!"

Bar-Nothing turned to look at the half-dozen horses standing "hitched to the ground" behind the saloon. He crossed to them, looking at the ropes on the saddles. With quick, tight grin he took down a coil of slim rawhide *riata* and shook out a loop. Sim grinned, also, as Bar-Nothing came back to him.

"Now, I'll show you I used to be a right tol'able buckaroo before my health gave out and I had to quit work and go to rangering," Bar-Nothing grunted. "This is a California string; sixty-footer. Just what Doc' Ames would've ordered. A Texas thirty-two foot manila wouldn't reach our Howling Harrigan, but—"

He went quietly along Jay Bird's side wall to stop at the corner. The loop went up and out snakily, settled around Harrigan's neck and tightened. With a ferocious Comanche yell Bar-Nothing hauled in the slack hand-over-hand. Harrigan was dragged to him and he stooped to loosen the choking noose. He jerked the strangling man up, half-pushed, half-carried him out and to Jay Bird's door.

"Back you go, you mangy fices!" he snarled at the audience. "I wouldn't trust one of your cur-faces behind me!"

He had one Colt out and sullenly they surged into the saloon before its muzzle—and Sim Cook's.

"Now, you Jay Bird!" Bar-Nothing snapped at Pease. "You listen to me prophesy and you listen good and hard: I'm tired of this pet sack of wind of yours and if I hear anything louder'n a Number Two whisper out of him, there's going to be more trouble around this skunk-den than your clothes'll stand. You *heah* me? I'm telling you in the solemnest tone I've got to lock him up until he's sober or plumb out of howls. You *heah* me?"

"I—I'll take care of him," Jay Bird promised, with downward glance, longing glance, at something behind the bar, but without moving either dirty hand out of Bar-Nothing's sight.

Once more they returned to Pegleg Scott's. But this time they had hardly passed through the door when Harrigan popped into the street. He had a pistol in each hand, Sim reported—Bar-Nothing had gone quietly on to the bar and motioned twice, once at the beer, again at the sawed-off shotgun hanging conveniently in Pegleg's rear. Six shots sounded, then a howl.

"He's keeping one loaded," Sim called. "Rammed her in his belly-band; loading the other one. You certainly got to get out from under your hat to his stubborn gall!"

Bar-Nothing drank his beer deliberately and bought one for Black Joe. Then he accepted the shotgun from the still-faced Pegleg and made a second departure through the back door. This time he and Sim ran through the litter of tin cans and bottles behind the buildings until they could cross Main Street at that end of town farthest from Jay Bird's. They came back in the rear of the buildings on that side, crossed again while the men in and around Pease's looked toward Pegleg's place, or watched that corner from which Bar-Nothing had roped Harrigan.

They slipped soundlessly into Pease's rear door and the crowd at the front had no warning of their presence until Bar-Nothing clicked back both shotgun hammers and yelled savagely:

"Yup! Yup! Grab your ears or grab a harp! Over to the wall, all of you polecats; my patience has come unraveled. If 't wasn't I promised Cap'n Hewey I'd be tender as a barbecued calf, today, I swear I'd take you nine at a time and I'd sweep this county clean with you. Sim! Dab a loop on that laughing jackass, huh?"

"Looky here!" Jay Bird yelled shakily. "I'm justice and—"

Bar-Nothing let the shotgun slide to the crook of his left arm. His right hand flashed down; came up with a Colt. The slug jangled a pyramid of tin cups on the bar at Jay Bird's very elbow. The old man made a squeaking noise and jumped two yards to the side, hands uplifted.

"Was a man, once," Bar-Nothing remarked casually, "got himself a lot in Boot Hill, talking when he ought've been listening. What's it, Sim?"

Sim, at the front door, steadied his new Colt against the frame. He let the hammer drop and, blending with the bellow of it, a yell half-startled, half-pained, came from Harrigan. Sim moved outside, pistol easily at hip-level.

"Just wondered could I shoot it out of his fist," he called back. "Come on, Harrigan. Singing school's done shut up. We have got language to pour into your long, dirty ears."

"Which is your goat?" Bar-Nothing demanded, when Harrigan came meekly inside, shaking his bleeding gunhand.

"Big black out behind," mumbled Harrigan. "I—I never meant no harm, Sergeant. I—It was just the whisky. I'll hightail!"

"You bet you'll hightail—right out to camp with us. Come along. Jay Bird—and all the rest of you—if there's anything happening as we rack out of this, Pease City's going to look like a Kansas twister hit her. Only way you can stop us is to down us, both. If that was to happen, Cap'n Hewey and the boys'd certainly enjoy piling up the carcasses of everybody that Sim and me left for 'em. Cap'll likely have a word or two to say to you, anyhow, time he hears what kind of justice you are."

While Sim prodded Harrigan ahead of him through the back door, Bar-Nothing watched with ready shotgun. Then he backed out and saw Harrigan climb into the saddle of the tall black.

"Why, that's the hull I took the California twine off of," he told Sim. "Bring our horses around, will you? I'll wait."

When Sim reappeared with their mounts, they swung up and jogged quietly toward the road. Pease City was sullenly quiet behind them. But within a mile they met the city marshal, riding out of a pasture. He gaped at them.

"What's all this?" he blustered. "You rangers needn't to think you can take a man out of town without seeing me first—"

"Take that gun out—slow!" Bar-Nothing commanded, gesturing with Pegleg's shotgun. "Get it, Sim. Now, my homely friend, just turn around and side us. I sort of want to hear what Cap'n Hewey will have to say to you. It'll be as good as reading a big, thick book, for you. It'll be a talk on how to live a lot longer'n you figure to last, way you've been heading. Come on!"

So, with the silent prisoners leading, they went toward Bloody Ford at the long, mile-eating hard trot. The sun was sliding toward the western horizon; the air grew noticeably cooler. It was nearly sunset when they came to the tents of X Company.

"What's this, Red?" Captain Hewey inquired from his door. "Prisoners? Did you recover Mr. Hawley's horse?"

With the question and sight of Hawley behind the captain, Bar-Nothing made a vague, self-reproachful sound.

"Blamed if I never forgot all about that bronc' in the arguring! We looked the place over and he wasn't in sight and then that skunk Jay Bird set this coyote to howling and—"

"That's my horse!" Hawley bellowed, surging out. "They colored up his nose and his stockings and hair-branded him, but I raised him from a colt and I'd know him in a million in the dark. And—And you, Ed Welch! You was riding him!"

With which he hauled the city marshal from the saddle and fell to committing assault, battery and minor mayhem upon him. Bar-Nothing swung down and separated them—after a time.

"This Harrigan," he told Captain Hewey, "he was disturbing the peace and every time I'd arrest him Jay Bird'd turn him loose and give him another drink and start him out again. So I packed him out here. I do think you'd enjoy talking to Jay Bird and Welch about the way they handle the law in Pease."

"I'll talk to Jay Bird, all right," Hewey said ominously. "As for Welch, we'll hold him on a charge of horse-theft. As for Harrigan—" he looked long and thoughtfully at the silent, glaring prisoner "—we'll keep him, too. Oh! Have a good time?"

"Worst birthday in my life! Them Peasers are half-skunk and half-coyote. Run a white man crazy."

From a hip pocket the captain drew a leather case. Out of it came a sheaf of folded papers. He riffled them, selected one and held it out to Bar-Nothing, whistling softly. Bar-Nothing unfolded the printed notice—and Harrigan's ugly likeness was there, under twin lines of heavy Gothic capitals—$1500 REWARD—MURDER—HIGHWAY ROBBERY—

"Happy birthday, Red," Captain Hewey drawled.

"Fif-teen hun-dred dollars!" Bar-Nothing breathed reverently. "Thanks, Cap'n! Thanks! She certainly is. She—She's a gen-u-ine P-cutter of a birthday!"

GEORGE PATTULLO

Of Scottish ancestry, George Pattullo was born in Woodstock, Ontario, Canada, October 9, 1879. He was educated at the Woodstock Collegiate Institute and, briefly, at the University of Toronto. Like many other writers, he began his career in newspaper work, in Montreal, London, and Boston.

In 1907 the *Boston Herald* published his full-page illustrated feature article on the work of the Texas student sculptor Erwin E. Smith, who was then studying in Boston. His doctor having recommended outdoor activity, that summer Pattullo came with Smith to Texas, to the JA Ranch, near Clarendon. In the fall they returned to Boston, where they shared a studio, Pattullo writing stories and Smith modeling and sketching. Smith, indeed, illustrated Pattullo's first *Saturday Evening Post* story, with photographs; and Pattullo years later repaid the debt, by cataloguing the collection of Smith's films and plates of range life presented to the Library of Congress after Smith's death (see Smith and J. Evetts Haley, *Life on the Texas Range*).

In 1909 and succeeding years, Pattullo and Smith returned to the range, where they visited with such men as Charles Goodnight, "Uncle Hank" Smith, and Frank Hastings, and stored all they saw and heard until they could give it the permanence of record. Pattullo often made an amateur hand on roundups throughout the Southwest, in Texas with the Matador, SMS, and Spur outfits. He soon became one of the *Post's* leading writers of articles and fiction.

During World War I, Pattullo was attached to the First Division, A.E.F., as special correspondent for the *Post,* and accompanied the division into Germany with the Army of Occupation. For the *Post* he wrote the first story of the exploits of Sergeant York, under the title "The Second Elder Gives Battle," a story which by what the author admits was sheer good luck scooped all American newspapers on the famous hero. Another product of Pattullo's war years was a book, *One Man's War* (1928), in collaboration with J. E. Rendinell, a Marine corporal who had kept a diary.

Pattullo's other books include two collections of Southwestern short stories, *The Untamed* (1911) and *A Good Rooster Crows Everywhere*

57

George Pattullo

(1939), and *Horrors of Moonlight* (1939), *All Our Yesterdays* (1948), *Always New Frontiers* (1951), and *Era of Infamy* (1952).

C. M. Russell, who illustrated the present story on its first appearance, in *McClure's Magazine,* called it "the best horse story ever written." Pattullo replied that Russell's illustration was "the finest ever done of a pitching horse." Both men may very well be right.

Corazón

A man is as good as his nerves.
—Cowboy maxim

WITH MANES STREAMING in the wind, a band of bronchos fled across the grama flats, splashed through the San Pedro, and whirled sharply to the right, heading for sanctuary in the Dragoons. In the lead raced a big sorrel, his coat shimmering like polished gold where the sun touched it.

"That's Corazón," exclaimed Reb. "Head him or we'll lose the bunch."

The pursuers spread out and swept round in a wide semicircle. Corazón held to his course, a dozen yards in advance of the others, his head high. The chase slackened, died away. With a blaring neigh, the sorrel eased his furious pace and the entire band came to a trot. Before them were the mountains, and Corazón knew their fastnesses as the street urchin knows the alleys that give him refuge; in the cañons the bronchos would be safe from man. Behind was no sign of the enemy. His nose in the wind, he sniffed long, but it bore him no taint. Instead, he nickered with delight, for he smelled water. They swung to the south, and in less than five minutes their hot muzzles were washed by the bubbling waters of Eternity Spring.

Corazón drew in a long breath, expanding his well-ribbed sides, and looked up from drinking. There in front of him, fifty paces away, was a horseman. He snorted the alarm and they plunged into a tangle of sagebrush. Another rider bore down and turned them back. To right and left they darted, then wheeled and sought desperately to break through the cordon at a weak spot, and failed. Wherever they turned,

Reprinted from *The Untamed*, by George Pattullo; copyright 1911 by the author and used by his permission.

a cowboy appeared as by magic. At last Corazón detected an unguarded area and flew through it with the speed of light.

"Now we've got 'em," howled Reb. "Don't drive too close, but keep 'em headed for the corral."

Within a hundred yards of the gate, the sorrel halted, his ears cocked in doubt. The cowboys closed in to force the band through. Three times the bronchos broke and scattered, for to their wild instincts the fences and that narrow aperture cried treachery and danger. They were gathered, with whoops and many imprecations, and once more approached the entrance.

"Drive the saddle bunch out," commanded the range boss.

Forth came the remuda of a hundred horses. The bronchos shrilled greeting and mingled with them, and when the cow-ponies trotted meekly into the corral, Corazón and his band went too, though they shook and were afraid.

For five years Corazón had roamed the range—ever since he had discovered that grass was good to eat, and so had left the care of his tender-eyed mother. Because he dreaded the master of created things and fled him afar, only once during that time had he seen man at close quarters. That was when, as a youngster, he was caught and branded on the left hip. He had quickly forgotten that; until now it had ceased to be even a memory.

But now he and his companion rovers were prisoners, cooped in a corral by a contemptible trick. They crowded around and around the stout enclosure, sometimes dropping to their knees in efforts to discover an exit beneath the boards. And not twenty feet away, the dreaded axis of their circlings, sat a man on a horse, and he studied them calmly. Other men, astride the fence, were uncoiling ropes, and their manner was placid and businesslike. One opined dispassionately that "the sorrel is shore some horse."

"You're damn whistlin'," cried the buster over his shoulder, in hearty affirmation.

Corazón was the most distracted of all the band. He was in a frenzy of nervous fear, his glossy coat wet and foam-flecked. He would not stand still for a second, but prowled about the wooden barrier like a jungle creature newly prisoned in a cage. Twice he nosed the ground and crooked his forelegs in an endeavor to slide through the six inches of clear space beneath the gate, and the outfit laughed derisively. "Here goes," announced the buster in his expressionless tones. "You-all watch out, now. Hell'll be poppin'."

At that moment Corazón took it into his head to dash at top speed through his friends, huddled in a bunch in a corner. A rope whined and coiled, and, when he burst out of the jam, the noose was around his neck, tightening so as to strangle him. Madly he ran against it, superb in the sureness of his might. Then he squalled with rage and pain and an awful terror. His legs flew from under him, and poor Corazón was jerked three feet into the air, coming down on his side with smashing force. The fall shook a grunt out of him, and he was stunned and breathless, but unhurt. He staggered to his feet, his breath straining like a bellows, for the noose cut into his neck and he would not yield to its pressure.

Facing him was the man on the bay. His mount stood with feet braced, sitting back on the rope, and he and his rider were quite collected and cool and prepared. The sorrel's eyes were starting from his head; his nostrils flared wide, gaping for the air that was denied him, and the breath sucked in his throat. It seemed as if he must drop. Suddenly the buster touched his horse lightly with the spur and slackened the rope. With a long sob, Corazón drew in a life-giving draught, his gaze fixed in frightened appeal on his captor.

"Open the gate," said Mullins, without raising his voice.

He flicked the rope over Corazón's hind quarters, and essayed to drive him into the next corral, to cut him off from his fellows. The sorrel gave a gasp of dismay and lunged forward. Again he was lifted from the ground, and came down with a thud that left him shivering.

"His laig's done bust!" exclaimed the boss.

"No; he's shook up, that's all. Wait awhile."

A moment later Corazón raised his head painfully; then, life and courage coming back with a rush, he lurched to his feet. Mullins waited with unabated patience. The sorrel was beginning to respect that which encircled his neck and made naught of his strength, and when the buster flipped the rope again, he ran through the small gate, and brought up before he had reached the end of his tether.

Two of the cowboys stepped down languidly from the fence, and took position in the center of the corral.

"Hi, Corazón! Go it, boy!" they yelled, and spurred by their cries, the horse started off at a trot. Reb tossed his loop,—flung it carelessly, with a sinuous movement of the wrist,—and when Corazón had gone a few yards, he found his forefeet ensnared. Enraged at being thus cramped, he bucked and bawled; but, before Reb could settle on the rope, he came to a standstill and sank his teeth into the strands. Once, twice, thrice he tugged, but could make no impression. Then he pitched high in air, and—

"NOW!" shrieked Reb.

They heaved with might and main, and Corazón flopped in the dust. Quick as a cat, he sprang upright and bolted; but again they downed him, and, while Reb held the head by straddling the neck, his confederate twined dexterously with a stake-rope. There lay Corazón, helpless and almost spent, trussed up like a sheep for market: they had hog-tied him.

It was the buster who put the hackamore on his head. Very deliberately he moved. Corazón sensed confidence in the touch of his fingers; they spoke a language to him, and he was soothed by the sureness of superiority they conveyed. He lay quiet. Then Reb incautiously shifted his position, and the horse heaved and raised his head, banging Mullins across the ear. The buster's senses swam, but instead of flying into a rage, he became quieter, more deliberate; in his cold eyes was a vengeful gleam, and dangerous stealth lurked in his delicate manipulation of the strands. An excruciating pain shot through the sorrel's eye: Mullins had gouged him.

"Let him up." It was the buster again, atop the bay, making the rope fast with a double half-hitch over the horn of the saddle.

Corazón arose, dazed and very sick. But his spirit was unbreakable. Again and again he strove to tear loose, rearing, falling back, plunging to the end of the rope until he was hurled off his legs to the ground. When he began to weary, Mullins encouraged him to fight, that he might toss him.

"I'll learn you what this rope means," he remarked, as the broncho scattered the dust for the ninth time, and remained there, completely done up.

In deadly fear of his slender tether, yet alert to match his strength against it once more, should opportunity offer, Corazón followed the buster quietly enough when he rode out into the open. Beside a sturdy mesquite bush that grew apart from its brethren, Mullins dismounted and tied the sorrel. As a farewell he waved his arms and whooped. Of course Corazón gathered himself and leaped—leaped to the utmost that was in him, so that the bush vibrated to its farthest root; and of course he hit the earth with a jarring thump that temporarily paralyzed him. Mullins departed to put the thrall of human will on others.

Throughout the afternoon, and time after time during the interminable night, the sorrel tried to break away, but with each sickening failure he grew more cautious. When he ran against the rope now, he did not run blindly to its limit, but half wheeled, so that when it jerked him back he invariably landed on his feet. Corazón was learning hard, but he was learning. And what agonies of pain and suspense he went through!—for years a free rover, and now to be bound thus, by what looked to be a mere thread, for he knew not what further tortures! He sweated and shivered, seeing peril in every shadow. When a coyote slunk by with tongue lapping hungrily over his teeth, the prisoner almost broke his neck in a despairing struggle to win freedom.

In the chill of the dawn they led him into a circular corral. His sleekness had departed; the barrel-like body did not look so well nourished, and there was red in the blazing eyes.

"I reckon he'll be mean," observed the buster, as though it concerned him but little.

"No-o-o. Go easy with him, Carl, and I think he'll make a good hoss," the boss cautioned.

While two men held the rope, Mullins advanced along it foot by foot, inch by inch, one hand outstretched, and talked to Corazón in a low, careless tone of affectionate banter. "So you'd like for to kill me, would you?" he inquired, grinning. All the while he held the sorrel's gaze.

Corazón stood still, legs planted wide apart, and permitted him to approach. He trembled when the fingers touched his nose; but they were firm, confident digits, the voice was reassuring, and the gentle rubbing up, up between the eyes and ears lulled his forebodings.

"Hand me the blanket," said Mullins.

He drew it softly over Corazón's back, and the broncho swerved, pawed, and kicked with beautiful precision. Whereupon they placed a rope around his neck, dropped it behind his right hind leg, then pulled that member up close to his belly; there it was held fast. On three legs

63

now, the sorrel was impotent for harm. Mullins once more took up the blanket, but this time the gentleness had flown. He slapped it over Corazón's backbone from side to side a dozen times. At each impact the horse humped awkwardly, but, finding that he came to no hurt, he suffered it in resignation.

That much of the second lesson learned, they saddled him. Strangely enough, Corazón submitted to the operation without fuss, the only untoward symptoms being a decided upward slant to the bank of the saddle and the tucking of his tail. Reb waggled his head over this exhibition.

"I don't like his standing quiet that a-way; it ain't natural," he vouchsafed. "Look at the crick in his back. Jim-in-ee! he'll shore pitch."

Which he did. The cinches were tightened until Corazón's eyes almost popped from his head; then they released the bound leg and turned him loose. What was that galling his spine? Corazón took a startled peep at it, lowered his head between his knees, and began to bawl. Into the air he rocketed, his head and forelegs swinging to the left, his hind quarters weaving to the right. The jar of his contact with the ground was appalling. Into the air again, his head and forelegs to the right, his rump twisted to the left. Round and round the corral he went, blatting like an angry calf; but the thing on his back stayed where it was, gripping his body cruelly. At last he was fain to stop for breath.

"Now," said Mullins, "I reckon I'll take it out of him."

There has always been for me an overwhelming fascination in watching busters at work. They have underlying traits in common when it comes to handling the horses—the garrulous one becomes coldly watchful, the Stoic moves with stern patience, the boaster soothes with soft-crooned words and confident caress. Mullins left Corazón standing in the middle of the corral, the hackamore rope strung loose on the ground, while he saw to it that his spurs were fast. We mounted the fence, not wishing to be mixed in the glorious turmoil to follow.

"I wouldn't top ol' Corazón for fifty," confessed the man on the adjoining post.

"Mullins has certainly got nerve," I conceded.

"A buster has got to have nerve." The range boss delivered himself laconically. "All nerve and no brains makes the best. But they get stove up and then—"

"And then? What then?"

"Why, don't you know?" he asked in surprise. "Every buster loses his nerve at last, and then they can't ride a pack-hoss. It must be because it's one fool man with one set of nerves up ag'in a new hoss with a new devil in him every time. They wear him down. Don't you reckon?"

The explanation sounded plausible. Mullins was listening with a faintly amused smile to Reb's account of what a lady mule had done to him; he rolled a cigarette and lighted it painstakingly. The hands that held the match were steady as eternal rock. It was maddening to see him stand there so coolly while the big sorrel, a dozen feet distant, was a-quake with dread, blowing harshly through his crimson nostrils whenever a cowboy stirred—and each of us knowing that the man was taking his life in his hands. An unlooked-for twist, a trifling disturbance of poise, and, with a horse like Corazón, it meant maiming or death. At last he threw the cigarette from him and walked slowly to the rope.

"So you're calling for me?" he inquired, gathering it up.

Corazón was snorting. By patient craft Reb acquired a grip on the sorrel's ears, and, while he hung there, bringing the head down so that the horse could not move, Mullins tested the stirrups and raised himself cautiously into the saddle.

"Let him go."

While one could count ten, Corazón stood expectant, his back bowed, his tail between his legs. The ears were laid flat on the head and the forefeet well advanced. The buster waited, the quirt hanging from two fingers of his right hand. Suddenly the sorrel ducked his head and emitted a harsh scream, leaping, with legs stiff, straight off the ground. He came down with the massive hips at an angle to the shoulders, thereby imparting a double shock; bounded high again, turned back with bewildering speed as he touched the earth; and then, in a circle perhaps twenty feet in diameter, sprang time after time, his heels lashing the air. Never had such pitching been seen on the Anvil Range.

"I swan, he just misses his tail a' inch when he turns back!" roared a puncher.

Mullins sat composedly in the saddle, but he was riding as never before. He whipped the sorrel at every jump and raked him down the body from shoulder to loins with the ripping spurs. The brute gave no signs of letting up. Through Mullins' tan of copper hue showed a slight pallor. He was exhausted. If Corazón did not give in soon, the man would be beaten. Just then the horse stopped, feet a-sprawl.

"Mullins,"—the range boss got down from the fence,—"you'll kill that hoss. Between the cinches belongs to you; the head and hind quarters is the company's."

For a long minute Mullins stared at the beast's ears without replying.

"I reckon that's the rule," he acquiesced heavily. "Do you want that somebody else should ride him?"

"No-o-o. Go ahead. But, remember, between the cinches you go at him as you like—nowhere else."

The buster slapped the quirt down on Corazón's shoulder, but the broncho did not budge; then harder. With the first oath he had used, he jabbed in the spurs and lay back on the hackamore rope. Instead of bucking, Corazón reared straight up, his feet pawing like the hands of a drowning man. Before Mullins could move to step off, the sorrel flung his head round and toppled backward.

"No, he's not dead." The range boss leaned over the buster and his hands fumbled inside the shirt. "The horn got him here, but he ain't dead. Claude, saddle Streak and hit for Agua Prieta for the doctor."

When we had carried the injured man to the bunk-house, Reb spoke from troubled meditation:

"Pete, I don't believe Corazón is as bad as he acts with Mullins. I've been watching him. Mullins, he didn't—"

"You take him, then; he's yours," snapped the boss, his conscience pricking because of the reproof he had administered. If the buster had ridden him his own way, this might not have happened.

That is how the sorrel came into Reb's possession. Only one man of the outfit witnessed the taming, and he would not talk; but when Reb came to dinner from the first saddle on Corazón, his hands were torn and the nail of one finger hung loose.

"I had to take to the horn and hang on some," he admitted.

Ay, he had clung there desperately while the broncho pitched about the river-bed, whither Reb had retired for safety and to escape spectators. But at the next saddle Corazón was less violent; at the third, recovering from the stunning shocks and bruisings of the first day, he was a fiend; and then, on the following morning, he did not pitch at all. Reb rode him every day to sap the superfluous vigor in Corazón's iron frame and he taught him as well as he could the first duties of a cow-horse. Finding that his new master never punished him unless he undertook to dispute his authority, the sorrel grew tractable and began to take an interest in his tasks.

"He's done broke," announced Reb; "I'll have him bridle-wise in a week. He'll make some roping horse. Did you see him this evening? I swan—"

They scoffed good-naturedly; but Reb proceeded on the assumption that Corazón was meant to be a roping horse, and schooled him accordingly. As for the sorrel, he took to the new pastime with delight. Within a month nothing gave him keener joy than to swerve and crouch at the climax of a sprint and see a cow thrown heels over head at the end of the rope that was wrapped about his saddle-horn.

The necessity of contriving to get three meals a day took me elsewhere, and I did not see Corazón again for three years. Then, one Sunday afternoon, Big John drew me from El Paso to Juárez on the pretense of seeing a grand, an extraordinary, a most noble bullfight, in which the dauntless Favorita would slay three fierce bulls from the renowned El Carmen ranch, in "competency" with the fearless Morenito Chico de San Bernardo; and a youth with a megaphone drew us both to a steer-roping contest instead. We agreed that bull-fighting was brutal on the Sabbath.

"I'll bet it's rotten," remarked Big John pessimistically, as we took our seats. "I could beat 'em myself."

As he scanned the list, his face brightened. Among the seventeen ropers thereon were two champions and a possible new one in Raphael Fraustro, the redoubtable vaquero from the domain of Terranzas.

"And here's Reb!" roared John—he is accustomed to converse in the tumult of the branding-pen—"I swan, he's entered from Monument."

Shortly afterwards the contestants paraded, wonderfully arrayed in silk shirts and new handkerchiefs.

"Some of them ain't been clean before in a year," was John's caustic comment. "There's Slim; I KNOW he hasn't."

They were a fine-looking body of men, and two of my neighbors complained that I trampled on their feet. The horses caught the infection of excitement from the packed stands and champed on their bits and caracoled and waltzed sideways in a manner highly unbecoming a staid cow-pony.

There was one that did not. So sluggish was his gait and general bearing, in contrast to the others, that the crowd burst into laughter. He plodded at the tail-end of the procession, his hoofs kicking up the dust in listless spurts, his nose on a level with his knees. I rubbed my eyes and John said, "No, it ain't—it can't be—"; but it was. Into that arena slouched Corazón, entered against the pick of the horses of the Southwest; and Reb was astride him.

We watched the ropers catch and tie the steers in rapid succession, but the much-heralded ones missed altogether, and to John and me the performance lagged. We were waiting for Reb and Corazón.

They came at last, at the end of the list. When Corazón ambled up the arena to enter behind the barrier, the grandstand roared a facetious welcome; the spectacle of this sad-gaited nag preparing to capture a steer touched its risibilities.

"Listen to me," bawled a fat gentleman in a wide-brimmed hat, close to my ear. "You listen to me! They're all fools. That's a cow-horse. No blasted nonsense. Knows his business, huh? You're damn whistlin'!"

Assuredly, Corazón knew his business. The instant he stepped behind the line he was a changed horse. The flopping ears pricked forward, his neck arched, and the great muscles of his shoulders and thighs rippled to his dainty prancing. He pulled and fretted on the bit, his eyes roving about in search of the quarry; he whinnied an appeal to be gone. Reb made ready his coil, curbing him with light pressure.

Out from the chute sprang a steer, heading straight down the arena. Corazón was frantic. With the flash of the gun he breasted the barrier-rope and swept down on him in twenty strides. Reb stood high in the stirrups; the loop whirled and sped; and, without waiting to see how it fell, but accepting a catch in blind faith, the sorrel started off at a tangent.

Big John was standing up in his place, clawing insanely at the hats of his neighbors and banging them on the head with his programme.

"Look at him—just look at him!" he shrieked.

The steer was tossed clear of the ground and came down on his left side. Almost before he landed, Reb was out of the saddle and speeding toward him.

"He's getting up. HE'S GETTING UP. Go to him, Reb!" howled John and I.

The steer managed to lift his head; he was struggling to his knees.

68

I looked away, for Reb must lose. Then a hoarse shout from the multitude turned back my gaze. Corazón had felt the slack on the rope and knew what it meant. He dug his feet into the dirt and began to walk slowly forward—very slowly and carefully, for Reb's task must not be spoiled. The steer collapsed, falling prone again, but the sorrel did not stop. Once he cocked his eye, and seeing that the animal still squirmed, pulled with all his strength. The stands were rocking; they were a sea of tossing hats and gesticulating arms and flushed faces; the roar of their plaudits echoed back from the hills. And it was all for Corazón, gallant Corazón.

"Dam' his eyes—dam' his ol' eyes!" Big John babbled over and over, absolutely oblivious.

Reb stooped beside the steer, his hands looping and tying with deft darting twists even as he kept pace with his dragged victim.

"I guess it's—about—a—hour," he panted.

Then he sprang clear and tossed his hands upward, facing the judges' stand. After that he walked aimlessly about, mopping his face with a handkerchief; for to him the shoutings and the shifting colors were all a foolish dream, and he was rather sick.

Right on the cry with which his master announced his task done, Corazón eased up on the rope and waited.

"Mr. Pee-ler's time," bellowed the man with the megaphone presently, "is twenty-one seconds, ty-ing the world's re-cord."

So weak that his knees trembled, Reb walked over to his horse. "Corazón," he said huskily, and slapped him once on the flank.

Nothing would do the joyous crowd then but that Reb should ride forth to be acclaimed the victor. We sat back and yelled ourselves weak with laughter, for Corazón, having done his work, refused resolutely to squander time in vain parade. The steer captured and tied, he had no further interest in the proceedings. The rascal dog-trotted reluctantly to the center of the arena in obedience to Reb, then faced the audience; but, all the time Reb was bowing his acknowledgments, Corazón sulked and slouched, and he was sulking and shuffling the dust when they went through the gate.

"Now," said John, who is very human, "we'll go help Reb spend that money."

As we jostled amid the outgoing crowd, several cowboys came along-

69

side the grandstand rail, and Big John drew me aside to have speech with them. One rider led a spare horse and when he passed a man on foot, the latter hailed him:

"Say, Ed, give me a lift to the hotel?"

"Sure," answered Ed, proffering the reins.

The man gathered them up, his hands fluttering as if with palsy, and paused with his foot raised toward the stirrup.

"He won't pitch nor nothing, Ed?" came the quavered inquiry. "You're shore he's gentle?"

"Gentler'n a dog," returned Ed, greatly surprised.

"You ain't fooling me, now, are you, Ed?" continued the man on the ground. "He looks kind of mean."

"Give him to me!" Ed exploded. "You kin walk."

From where we stood, only the man's back was visible. "Who is that fellow?" I asked.

"Who? Him?" answered my neighbor. "Oh, his name's Mullins. They say he used to be able to ride anything with hair on it, and throw off the bridle at that. I expect that's just talk. Don't you reckon?"

BARRY BENEFIELD

JOHN BARRY BENEFIELD was born and bred in Jefferson, Marion County, in the northeast corner of Texas. As a boy he worked after school in his father's feed store and wagon yard. His attendance at the University of Texas was interrupted for a term of schoolteaching but led to his B.Litt. degree in 1902. For a year Benefield was a reporter on the *Dallas Morning News;* for nearly seven years more, on the *New York Times.*

Like Eugene O'Neill, Benefield was led to creative writing by a failure in health. Retiring to rural New Jersey to rest, Benefield began to write fiction in order to pass the time constructively. The result was publication in some of the country's leading magazines: *Century, Collier's, Scribner's, Smart Set, Woman's Home Companion,* and others. A volume of short stories, *Short Turns* (1926), may be said to have established Benefield as a short-story writer; it was highly praised by Edward J. O'Brien. *The Best Short Stories of 1926* reprinted "Carrie Snyder" and gave three-star ratings to three other Benefield stories. Thereafter, his work was frequently singled out for such commendation.

Not wishing to devote his full time to writing, Benefield has usually had a part-time editorial position with a New York publisher. For many years he was associate editor of the Century Company; from 1935 to 1947 he served on the editorial staff of Reynal and Hitchcock. A six weeks' stint in Hollywood seems to have left him less disillusioned than most writers, but he did not go to the coast to stay. Now retired, he lives in Peekskill, New York.

Besides *Short Turns,* Benefield's principal works include *The Chicken-Wagon Family* (1925), *Bugles in the Night* (1927), *A Little Clown Lost* (1928), *Valiant Is the Word for Carrie* (1935), *April Was When It Began* (1939), and *Eddie and the Archangel Mike* (1943).

Since his fiction has often treated victims of injustice, it has been hard for so warmly human and sympathetic a writer as Benefield always to avoid lapsing into sentimentality. His novels suffer in this respect perhaps more often than his short stories. Even among the latter, however, sentimentality mars such an otherwise excellent story as "Ole Mistis," usually cited as one of the few good examples of Southwestern

Barry Benefield

fictional treatment of the Negro. The present story, "Incident at Boiling Springs," shows Benefield's characteristic sympathy for the underdog but restrains it through the limited point of view of the manly boy-narrator. This story was rated "distinctive" in Martha Foley's *The Best American Short Stories of 1949.*

72

Incident at Boiling Springs

I WAS THIRTEEN, thin and weedy, shock-headed, fish-mouthed, unbelievably homely. And because my left leg was shorter than my right I could never be a real rider, could never do any fancy riding while a prospective buyer settled the price with Bass Howie. Bass hated me and called me Crip, making it sound like a curse. I hated him and called him Mr. Howie. Thirteen is not a heroic age. So I was glad of what happened at Boiling Springs.

Bass didn't fit the usual pattern of a Texas horse trader. No high-heeled boots with stuffed-in pants, no bandanna, no ten-gallon hat, no big-roweled spurs to jingle noisily whether he was riding or walking. And no big talk or bluster or bawling overheartiness. He was as quiet as a snake and dressed like a small-town storekeeper. Medium-sized, round-shouldered, clean-shaved and medium even in age—thirty-seven —Bass was entirely unspectacular. He wore a .45 Colt in his right hip pocket under his coat.

For a dozen years Bass had been coming up from southwestern Texas with a herd of trading horses. We had started in August and, following his customary route diagonally across Texas, we were now only three stops from the Louisiana border and the scheduled end of the trip. Through swapping and selling the herd was low in numbers and quality.

As the herd had dwindled, Bass had paid off and brushed off the half-dozen drifting riders and horse busters he had hired at the beginning of the trip. The only help he still had was old Gus Wills, an ex-cowboy that he kept all the year round as a handy man. Bass didn't rate me as help—he rated me as a useless unprofitable pestiferous infliction

Copyright 1948 by Barry Benefield and reprinted by his permission. First published in *Woman's Home Companion*, September, 1948, under the title "Beautiful Calico."

that had been put on him by a dead wife and the inescapable compulsion of social custom. I was his stepson.

On a sharp bright morning in mid-December the three of us drove into Boiling Springs with thirty-one horses and corralled them in the annex yard opening off McAtee's main wagon yard.

Even as late in the trip as Boiling Springs, though, there was still one spectacular item in our outfit. Calico was young and lovely and had the spirit and bearing of a sweet queen. She was a bay with great splatterings of white that made her look like something camouflaged, as indeed she was in a way. Since she was obviously Bass' personal mount, people thought nothing of it that they always saw her under the saddle.

It was five blocks to his hotel, the Pawnee House; Gus and I of course cooked and slept in the wagon yard bunkhouse. But Bass never walked where he could ride. One block or ten, he swung himself into the saddle, barely touched his small spurs to Calico's sides and set out for his destination, showing at least three of her gaits within each block.

This was advertising. People would say, "That's Trader Howie—he's at McAtee's for the week. And isn't that calico mare something?"

Until his last day in a town Bass would turn aside (but not finally reject) all offers for her. At nearly every stop so far she had done her selling so effectively that several admiring victims had absorbed Bass' calculated evasions and stimulating short answers and kept on coming back to the yard until the last day and the showdown.

There was one die-hard victim in Boiling Springs, which, after all, had only two thousand souls. That first Monday when Bass opened for business, Jules Guines heard about it and hurried down to McAtee's yard. Here was a chance, as he saw it, to square himself for his latest and most serious social sin. And he saw Calico.

Is there sometimes a quick bond that ties together those who have been hurt? Do they say in their secret hearts, "He is my brother and I'll help him all I can"? Anyway, Jules and I, thirty-three and thirteen, became brothers during Bass' business week in this little town. And before the week was over I was trying to save Jules from the Calico trick.

Jules worked in the primitive little foundry on the east side of town. He was the one who battered to pieces, with a fourteen-pound sledge, old stoves and other scrap. He was the foundry's strong-arm man.

Almost every week the half-dozen foundry workers were laid off a couple of days. It was partly to make use of these off days that Jules had bought a five-acre farm three miles west of town. He had been driven to seek the companionship of plants and animals rather than that of people—people other than his wife and three little black-eyed boys.

The plants and animals never made fun of him, never made him ashamed and then furious at himself for being ashamed. Jules was a Belgian immigrant—a late immigrant—and his way of talking and acting, his way of life generally, was foreign and different and therefore comical to Boiling Springs. It knew him as Frenchy or The Frog.

His mates at the foundry were all native Americans and of the few foreign-born people in the town and county he and his family were the only Belgians. His seeming preference for plants and animals was only a gesture on Jules' part. Actually he wanted desperately to be well-liked, to be taken seriously, to be accepted, to be a regular American. And he wanted it more, even, for his wife and boys than for himself. She was shy and still scared of the strange country and the boys had to run the gauntlet at school five days a week.

They were already a family of lonely wistful outcasts when Jules made his worst blunder. Since he needed a work animal on his five acres and something also to ride to and from his job in town, he had bought a mule from a neighboring farmer. The mule, Renée, was young and sound and willing and he had thought he was doing the right thing in buying her. But no, it appeared that he had done the wrong thing again. His mates at the foundry—and other people too—seized on Renée as another hilarious way of getting at The Frog. What could be more comical than a frog on a mule!

After buying Renée and suffering the gibes of Boiling Springs, Jules studied his situation. He noticed that men riding around town used horses and that mules were used only for hard work. Since it would be a waste to have a horse to ride on the foundry days and also a mule to work only a couple of days on the farm, he decided that it was bound to be right to part with Renée and get a double-duty horse—especially if the horse could be a handsome one and do the fancy steps without his trying to make him do them. Jules wouldn't know how.

So the first day we came Jules led Renée into the yard where Bass' animals were. They were nibbling at some scattered hay in the middle of the yard and Gus Wills, a dozen or so hesitant farmers and a few horsy loafers were standing near them in a loose group, laughing and

75

talking. Bass stood a little apart, listening and giving short answers to occasional idle questions.

Jules kept to the outer edge of the group, an uneasy set smile on his big dark face. Behind the mask of his smile he was puzzled and worried. He was all set to do business but nobody paid any serious attention to him.

Turning from the baffling men to the herd of horses he didn't see a single animal that he thought was anywhere near as good as Renée. And then he saw Calico. She was saddled and bridled, but since the boss trader was holding her reins in the crook of his left arm, she must belong to him. Jules had heard that traders would sell or swap anything they had. She was lovely, she was unmistakably young and strong and not too little or too big.

Just then he heard Bass say, impatiently answering a loafer's idle question, that she was as good in harness as under the saddle; and that under the saddle she pranced, paced, did all the fancy gaits. If he had her, Jules thought, she would give him all the help he needed on his five acres and surely nobody could ever make jokes about this so-beautiful animal that could do all the fancy steps as he rode through the town to and from his job.

So he changed his mind again; he was determined to stay around and listen as long as there was anything to hear and to watch lest someone get ahead of him and carry off the enchanting speckled horse.

Even before today Jules had been eagerly absorbing information about horse traders and his understanding was that you could pick out any of their animals that pleased you and turn in as part payment for it another horse—or even a mule. You almost always paid some money which was, strangely, called boot. If this boot thing had to be paid it had to be paid—the thought no longer gave Jules pain.

As the afternoon wore on a farmer would from time to time ask Bass a question that seemed to touch on the matter of his selling or swapping Calico, but the answers confused Jules to the point of desperation. At one moment Bass sounded as if he were saying, "No," at the next, "Maybe so."

Jules wanted to march up close to this insolent unclear man and pin him down with two perfectly clear questions. But he hesitated. He might not only lay himself open to the belittling laughter of all these men but also lose the beautiful horse as well.

76

He got no clearer light on Bass' intentions as to Calico, however, nor did he see any real trading done that afternoon. Since it was our first day in town, the farmers and other possible buyers were just scouting the herd and would be back later in the week.

The western sky flamed red, turned purple, quietened to gray and Bass swung himself up on Calico. When Gus Wills had run ahead, opening the gates, Bass pulled Calico back on her heels, curvetted gracefully about the yard and streaked out through the gates to the street—a tantalizing spectacle which poor Jules shouldn't have seen. Later Gus would go up to the Pawnee House and bring Calico back.

After Bass had gone, the loafers, some of whom knew Bass from other years and had already learned about me, teased me about carrying on the business when Bass was old and worn out; and Jules gathered that I was his son. Following me into the main yard he asked where he could water his mule, please. While there were no others around to hear his questions, he planned to get from the boss' son some light on the question of Calico.

While Renée was drinking at the trough by the yard well he said, "Your papa, he is angry about something, is it not?"

"No," I said, "that's just his way. Do you want to talk to him about one of his horses? Did you see one that you liked? I'll tell him to look for you tomorrow."

And then I got something of what was in Jules' mind; and on Wednesday and Saturday when he came back, I got more. As he could see, I was a hurt one and I could feel that he was too somehow.

I suppose I am now trying to put into the tight mold of words things that then were but vague cloudy notions floating around in Jules' head and mine. And yet I know that I understood how serious it would be for him if he made the mistake that he seemed headed for.

Back in the annex yard I'd heard some half-whispered snickering about The Frog and his mule. I knew from experience the extra price in pain and shame that the odd, the different child must pay for his mistakes and I took it for granted that the odd man must pay it too. He and all that are his—his wife, his children, all who stand close to him, as my mother had been to me.

Buying Calico would expose him to the eager mockery of the whole town, not just his small circle of foundry acquaintances. But I couldn't say outright that to him Renée was worth a hundred Calicos and then tell him why. After all, one doesn't squeal on his outfit and besides, I was afraid of Bass. And yet some boyish huggermuggery in thinking made it all right to help Jules if I could do it by the back door, indirectly.

So that afternoon, after Renée had finished drinking, I celebrated the whole tribe of mules and sang Renée's manifold excellences.

Using all the airs I had picked up from traders, I stood off and looked at her admiringly. I held open her mouth and spoke of the youth that her teeth proved beyond the shadow of a doubt. Pressure on a leg at the right place made her lift it and I gravely studied her small hoofs and found them all good.

Putting my ear to her side I listened intently. I pounded her ribs. And then I stood close to him and pronounced my verdict. I said Renée was as sound as a nut, as gentle as a lamb and worth a hundred silver dollars of any man's money. That was a handsome price in those days.

Jules' black eyes were full of admiration for my parade of mule knowledge, full of gratitude for my praise of his animal.

"Yes, yes," he said, "of a certainty my Renée is a mule among mules."

I did not, as a matter of fact, need to pretend a bias in favor of mules. They, I felt, also belonged to the brotherhood of the hurt. People mocked them and penalized them for looking odd and homely and told supposedly funny lies about them.

Back in Carthage, one of the towns we had made, there had been a competing trader who handled mules only. The yard he used was near ours and afternoons and nights I'd sat at his feet, listening and approving. Bass was sparing and dry in his talk but under the spell of the mule trader's fiery torrent I had a kind of contempt for horses—the soft gaudy things!

In one way and another, on Jules' three trips to McAtee's yard, I gave him everything I had so eagerly absorbed from the mule trader, repeating his words and phrases.

Only fools, I said, laughed at mules and sold them short. The whole world knew where to turn when there was tough work to be done. Had he, I asked sternly, ever taken note of how a mule goes around the curves in a cotton field? Had he not noticed that a mule has eyes in all four of her little feet as well as in her head? See how she'll not trample down a single one of the young plants, not even with her hind feet.

"True, true, all true!" Jules said, his eyes shining and his voice excited.

But I was soon to discover that all my ingenuity and eloquence had been worse than wasted on Jules. While he listened he was deliberately storing up ammunition to use on Bass to make him take Renée as a large part payment on Calico. Maybe—who knew when a miracle might happen?—he might not have to pay any boot at all. That is, if he could ever get to Bass.

I kept telling him that Calico was Bass' personal mount and that therefore he wouldn't consider letting her go until his very last hour in town and possibly not then. I hoped Jules couldn't come on Saturday. Maybe there'd be a rush job at the foundry or on his farm. I had lost hope that he'd keep Renée and save himself from humiliation.

But no last-minute stroke of fortune kept him away on Saturday. He came early in the afternoon. I had a dismal—dismal to me—talk with him in the main yard and then saw him march into the annex yard, holding Renée's reins over his crooked left arm as he'd seen Bass holding Calico's. At a considerable distance behind I followed unhappily.

Renée was neat and trim. Jules had been working on her to increase her trading value. Her glossy white coat shone in the sun. Her tail was clipped clean of hair except for a decorative little brush at the end. Her mane was clipped and scalloped and twined around the headband of her bridle was a red ribbon.

Jules, too, was furbished for the occasion. A country gentleman in town to attend to a certain large matter. No foundry smut about him this day. The coat of his pressed black suit seemed a dangerously tight fit across his bulging shoulder muscles. There had been a morning shave but already the vigorous black beard was a dark stain on cheeks and chin. And when he took off his black derby to fan himself it was a gesture to relieve nervous tension, not to cool the December air. And it showed his stiff black hair closely clipped and all but scalloped.

There was no hesitant ingratiating set smile on Jules' face today. He did not award so much as a half-smile to the loud jokes and silly antics of the loafers. And he stood around only a moment, waiting for an opening to broach his business—then he battered an opening for himself through the crowd.

79

The first few men he knocked aside growled, "What in blazes!" and glared at him but they cleared a lane for his approach to Bass. This rough elbowing was only nervous tension on Jules' part. He was no bully, he was a passionate gentle man with an obsession.

Leading Renée, he màrched up to Bass and stood at his side. Bass knew what this was. Habitually he went around with stooped shoulders and bent head as if preoccupied with thinking. But not now—he had covertly studied Jules on both of his previous visits and he was set for the usual profitable triumph.

The crowd drew in and tightened itself, watching and listening. Obviously The Frog was all keyed up and this looked as if it might be different from the ordinary horse trade.

"What can I do for you?" Bass said quietly, turning his head an inch toward Jules.

Jules' mind, now that his climactic time had come, was a log jam of horse-trading arguments and he couldn't break the jam at once. Bass prompted him with deadly quiet words. "You like any of my animals?"

Jules, desperately throwing aside his prepared words, exploded into spontaneous speech. "My mind, she makes herself up. I take Calico— you take Renée—I pay the boot thing."

"You call the mule Renée?"

I stood on the inner edge of the crowd—I wanted to see and hear everything. Bass' voice hadn't been loud—it seldom was—but I had heard his question and caught the sneer in it. So had several of the town loafers near me. One of them, taking his cue from Bass, slapped his thigh and hooted, "Renée! Whoa there, Renée! Whoa, I tell you!" The other loafers whooped and bellowed, "Renée, Renée! Whoa, Renée!"

Looking steadily at Bass Jules said simply, "It is her name." Then, recalling a few of his prepared trading words, he rushed into business and tense eloquence: "Mister 'Owie, she is sound as the nut—she is worth a hundred silver dollars of any man's money."

My words were coming back to me and my neck and ears burned. Jules' log jam was broken up now and his arguments came stampeding out in wild incoherence.

Smiling and watching his audience, Bass held up his hand. "Hold it, hold it, my friend! And get this—I don't like mules. I handle them if I have to but I do *not* like them."

"I pay the boot thing, Mister 'Owie. How many if you shall be so kind to say?"

"You know me? I don't know you. Your name?"

"Me! Jules Guines, Mister 'Owie."

"I seem to remember seeing you around here several times already, Mister Guines. I take it you've looked at my mare all you want by this time but have another look to make sure, doubly sure. Then, since you insist, we'll talk business. I'll look at your mule."

Bass handed Calico's reins to Jules and took Renée's into his own hands. Quickly he went through the trader's short routine of examination, his own eyes more on Jules than on Renée.

If Jules had made any move to take off Calico's saddle, Bass would have said he didn't want the mule in his herd at any price and abruptly called the deal off.

But Jules merely rubbed his hand along Calico's neck two or three times and she stamped her left forefoot, worked the bit around in her mouth and finally took a playful nip at him. Smiling fatuously, he faced around, stood erect; he was saying without words that he knew all he needed to know about this lovely Calico.

"Mister Guines," Bass said, "as they stand, I'll swap my mare Calico for your mule Renée and you'll pay me fifty dollars boot. Cash. Now." He held out his hand.

"Jules Guines accepts, Mister 'Owie."

Even as he said it Jules was reaching for his left hip pocket. Pulling out his billfold, he counted into Bass' hand three tens and four fives. Bass, having rolled the bills around his forefinger, making of them a tight round wad, pushed it with affected indifference into the left front pocket of his trousers.

Throwing Renée's reins to one of the obsequious loafers, Bass turned to Calico. With swift practiced movements he unbuckled her rear girth and then her front girth, swept off the saddle and blanket, stood back so that everybody could see clearly what he wanted them to see.

Poor Calico. The broad strong rear girth had concealed and held in the swelling low in her left flank.

One of the loafers, always ready to attract attention by speaking first the public mind, gave a long shocked whistle, then said to those near him, "Lord in heaven! She has to stay saddled all the time, night and day I reckon."

And then for a moment, while the shock was wearing off, the crowd was silent, staring at the lump on Calico's side. It was a serious rupture and already, as her insides began pushing through the inner break and enlarging the lump, she was feeling pain.

She shook her head nervously and pawed the ground and I could see too much white in her eyes. Jules went on patting her neck, his lips making the soft half-whispered words of a lover. She was his now, at last, and he was paying no attention to any of the talk.

As the surprise and shock wore off the crowd, it got back its voices. Most of the voices anyhow, though I did notice several grim silent faces. There was snickering now and presently loud jeers and hoots. It was as if Jules had entered a contest with Bass in which the rules were perfectly clear to both and Jules had lost the fair contest of wits by a stupid mistake.

Imagine a frog who couldn't even talk straight English playing a game with a horse trader—why you just had to laugh at the fool.

In other towns when Bass pulled the Calico trick, the victims had forced a sickly smile at this point and asked Bass, "How much?"

If the transaction had been a plain sale, his standard charge to call off the deal was fifty dollars and no hard feelings. To have made Calico whole would have required an operation by an expert veterinarian and long and expensive aftertreatment. Horses were too cheap for that as Bass well knew and he was aware that the victims and the witnesses knew too.

If the transaction had been a trade, Bass had said, "My friend, it'll cost you exactly the boot you've already paid. But you can keep your own animal and I'll keep Calico. She has her little weakness but I like her."

In the other towns, amidst laughter and loud banter, victor and victim and most of the witnesses had then gone off and had drinks. Whatever hard feelings there were had not been allowed to show. It was the code. Let the buyers beware.

Most of the crowd on this Saturday afternoon in McAtee's yard, while the hooting and jeering were going on, kept their eyes delightedly on

Bass. This was his moment and a faint smile of triumph played about his lips.

I was watching Jules. At long last he had come out of his infatuated trance, had listened to the talk around him and had bent down and scrutinized the swelling lump on Calico's side and now he knew what the others knew about the so-beautiful horse.

I saw his great chest rising and straining at the buttons of his vest. His wide-open black eyes, shining with tears of rage, went back and forth from Calico's side to Bass' face.

Somebody else was watching Jules. Out behind me I heard: "Look at The Frog!" The excited babble of jeers and laughter quieted down, died into tight stillness. I heard Calico nervously rattling the metal on her bridle and pawing the ground; I heard sparrows chittering faintly in the feedboxes of the stalls set around the outer edge of the yard; I heard a shrill panicky screech: "Look out, Bass! He's going to blow up!"

My eyes still on Jules, I listened for a single heavy shot. As I knew from horrid experience, Bass needed but one for an unprofitable crippled horse and surely he would need no more for a man only a couple of yards away.

But Jules was too quick and mad beyond all fear. With two steps he was on Bass. With one motion he lifted him high, with another he slammed him down to the ground. Lucky for Bass—and lucky for Jules too—that the strong man of the foundry didn't have handy his fourteen-pound sledge.

Bass lay still, face up. The witnesses had scuttled back when they saw Bass' hand go to his hip pocket. He and Jules were now in the clear. Renée and Calico had been pulled back with the crowd.

I saw Jules, now hatless, bend over Bass, the white of his shirt showing through the wreckage of his black coat and vest. He put his hand on Bass' chest, held it there a moment; then he rose and began cleaning up.

Picking up the gun and the wad of bills that had fallen out of Bass' pocket, he lifted both hands high above his head for the witnesses to see. Then he dropped the gun at Bass' feet and shoved the bills into his own pocket.

Moving out to the edge of the crowd, he hooked Renée's reins over his left arm, patted Calico's neck again, made a gesture in my direction that I couldn't make head or tail of and glared inquiringly around at the faces of the crowd. Then he marched toward the wagon-yard gate, Renée stepping along daintily behind him.

It was Jules who now held all eyes. A path opened for him. A loafer, quick to speak the public's changed mind, picked up the fallen derby, carefully brushed the dirt off with his sleeve and ran after Jules, calling out eagerly, "Mister Guines, Mister Guines! Here's your hat, sir."

For two weeks Bass' trading business stopped still while he lay in bed at the Pawnee House, suffering a local bonesetter to snatch out by degrees the kink in his back. Meanwhile the herd ran up a distressful bill for feed and yard charges at McAtee's.

Meanwhile too, Boiling Springs, all two thousand of it, was opening its eyes and taking to its repentant wayward heart an amazed hero, one of its very own.

MARGARET COUSINS

SUE MARGARET COUSINS was born, of Texas pioneer people, at Munday, Knox County, January 26, 1905. At the age of sixteen she made her first appearance in print with a poem. In 1926 she received her B.A. degree from the University of Texas, where she was winner of the D. A. Frank Poetry Prize.

Miss Cousins was virtually born with a writer's or editor's pencil in her hand. For three years she was a staff writer on her father's important trade publication, the *Southern Pharmaceutical Journal,* and from 1929 to 1937, its editor. In 1936 she sold her first magazine story. Hers are, alas, among the many good brains which are one of Texas' principal exports. From Dallas she went to New York, where she worked on the staff of *Pictorial Review.* In 1939 she moved to Hearst Magazines. In 1943 she became associate editor, then in 1946 managing editor, of *Good Housekeeping,* where she has remained. But the Texan, no matter how long in exile or how well acclimated there, cannot forget his origin. In her Dobbs Ferry, New York, home Margaret Cousins proudly displays the Lone Star flag and state seal.

However busy editing the writings of others, Miss Cousins has continued on occasions to produce poems, articles, and stories of her own for the leading popular magazines. Several of her stories have been judged "distinctive" by the editors of the annual *Best American Short Stories.* "A Letter to Mr. Priest" made Martha Foley's Roll of Honor for 1947 and was reprinted in *The Best American Short Stories of 1948.* Though it makes use of a Texas setting, it is much less specifically set and less characteristically Texan than the story offered here, "Uncle Edgar and the Reluctant Saint." This fine tale of a girl's remembered Christmas contains topographical and historical references which will keep lovers of Texana long guessing.

Uncle Edgar and the Reluctant Saint

ALMOST EVERY GROWN PERSON remembers with a kind of tender sadness the year he found out who Santa Claus was. Because, after that Christmas, no Christmas ever was quite the same again, nor was anything else. The world, held at bay by the gentle legend and unshaken trust of childhood, thereafter encroached upon the virgin country, and all the things that hitherto had been taken on faith became suspect. Something went out of the heart, and, for the time being, there was nothing to put in its place.

I was luckier than most. When Santa Claus departed my life, Uncle Edgar came into it in a new and significant way.

When I was a little girl, I had a whole passel of uncles, some satisfactory and some only fair; but Uncle Edgar was the one we never mentioned outside the home. Uncle Edgar did not turn up at family gatherings, except in conversation, when aunts, knitting fast and speaking with compressed lips, referred to him as a scapegrace and a black sheep; uncles, tamping down their pipe tobacco and scratching matches on the seats of their pants, opined that it did look as if Ed had played the fool long enough, and even my grandmother, with a hint of tears behind her mild blue eyes, admitted wistfully that she wished Eddie would marry some good girl and settle down.

Naturally Uncle Edgar was the uncle who interested me most. I tried to fit him to the various descriptions I heard in family conclaves, but he did not seem to be much like anything they said. Occasionally he turned up at our house unannounced in the middle of the night, wanting lodging, and my mother would have to get up and fly around, putting fresh linen on the spare-room bed and dragging out my father's best

Reprinted from *Good Housekeeping Magazine* by permission of the author; copyright 1944 by Margaret Cousins.

pajamas, while my father muttered condemnation. These occasions always filled me with such excitement I could hardly sleep, because I knew that in the morning there would be hot popovers and Uncle Edgar would be sitting across the table, with the sun flaming in his shock of red curly hair and burnishing the sunburned column of his throat, while my mother plied him with her most ambitious cooking.

He was a lean man—lean and hungry. His hips were narrow and his legs, slightly bowed, were thin and muscled; his shoulders were wide but without surplus flesh, as if they were the base of an inverted triangle of bone. There was nothing soft about him except his face, which had a way of looking startled, like a small boy's. His eyes were very blue and a little bewildered. His red hair fell down on his freckled forehead, and his nose quivered when he got mad, which was often. His mouth would have looked gentle, but he seemed determined to make it surly, and he kept his jaw jutting forward by some conscious effort. My mother said the root of Edgar's trouble was stubbornness, but my father said he was just plain wild.

I had a kindred feeling for Uncle Edgar. I, too, was said to have a trouble rooted in stubbornness, and I used to stare at him while he ate breakfast, trying to ferret out the nature of his wildness. He was interesting to look at, anyway, for he did not wear a stiff collar or a fawn-colored coat or a derby hat, like my father. He wore an old flannel shirt, open at the neck, a tooled russet leather belt, mounted with Mexican dollars, faded blue breeches, and a pair of high-heeled black boots with a small, neat pair of roweled spurs. Uncle Edgar was a cowboy.

Nobody in the family wanted Uncle Edgar to be a cowboy, for that was the time when the ploughshares were beginning to turn over the great ranches and make cotton fields out of them, and the cowboys who had a wink of sense were climbing off their horses and going into professions and businesses that had a future. Uncle Edgar, however, never had been one to listen to counsel or take orders, and no sooner did the family decide to make him a lawyer than he left home and got a job punching cattle for thirty dollars a month. He had no cheer for civilization, Uncle Edgar said. They could mind their own business. My mother was the only member of the family who stood by him. He was her youngest brother, and, as she said, you can drive a horse to water but you can't make him drink. That was Uncle Edgar all over. Whatever he did, he had to do it himself.

I do not know what species of trouble Uncle Edgar had got into, but I suppose he must have shot up something one Saturday night in an excess of youthful spirits. He never talked about himself or his exploits, even to my mother, for he was a silent man, absurdly bashful, sometimes stumbling over his own feet or the furniture when he got caught in a house. But I used to hear my mother begging him to control his temper and not get in any more fights, because the sheriff was already down on him.

Such was Uncle Edgar. He always called me Sis, and just before he would disappear for another long period of time he would press a silver dollar into my grimy palm, adjuring me to buy candy with it.

I loved him.

I did not know what Uncle Edgar really thought of me until the Christmas I was six years old. I had been sent on a visit to my grandmother just before the holidays, while my father and mother made a flying business trip to St. Louis. My grandmother had expected to accompany me home, but the day before Christmas Eve she had come down with sciatica and could scarcely move. As it was unthinkable that I should spend Christmas away from home (how would Santa Claus know where I was?), there was a great stir, and at length it was decided by Grandma and two uncles and three aunts that I would have to make the four-hour day trip on the train alone, entrusted to the care of Mr. Smith, the conductor of the Brazos Valley & Central passenger train. If I had started out to cross the Great Plains solo and afoot, there could not have been more confusion, brow-wrinkling, and concern.

As a matter of fact, the Brazos Valley & Central passenger train (once per day) ran over a spur of some hundred miles, so slowly that any horse could outrun it. Mr. Smith, who had been on the train since the spur was built, had lifted me on it and off it since I had been a babe in arms (the whole family lived in various small towns up and down this spur), and his celluloid collar and walrus mustache were as familiar to me as the characteristics of any uncle. I was also personally acquainted with Mr. Bolander, the engineer, who sometimes waved his bandanna to me when we drove down to the station on Sunday evenings to watch the train pass through; and Chester, the brakeman, once had let me hold his lantern. It seemed unlikely that I could be safer in my mother's arms than on the Brazos Valley & Central. I myself had no qualms about the matter, and, indeed, I looked forward to the journey with somewhat ungrateful pleasure. I was almost glad sciatica had come along.

Nobody else shared my aplomb. Aunt Josephine buttoned me into my moleskin coat with the braided frogs and tied on my velvet bonnet and gave me lengthy instructions about how to divest myself of these outer garments once I got in that overheated coach. I had been taking off my coat for years and was very bored. Aunt Eliza handed me a shoebox filled with enough lunch to feed several men, though I would be home well before supper. Uncle Garland gave me a dollar bill, which Aunt Mae pinned with a safety pin to the lining of my silk purse. Grandmother, lying stiffly in bed, begged me to be a good girl and not to speak to strangers. Then Uncle Whit came, whirled me off to the station in a hired hack, bought my ticket, and held a whispered conference with Mr. Smith as soon as the train, heaving and sighing, paused at the weather-beaten station. Mr. Smith nodded his head again and again, and I was handed up into the coach, and Uncle Whit followed me with my suitcase. He put the bag in the rack overhead, settled me firmly on a red plush seat, and delicately pushed the white granite spittoon out of sight under the next seat.

"Now, you stay right here," Uncle Whit said, as if I were a baby, "and before you know it, your papa will be taking you off the train. And if you want anything, ask Mr. Smith. Don't move unless you ask Mr. Smith!"

It occurred to me that there were some things I could not possibly ask Mr. Smith, but I didn't want to unnerve Uncle Whit any more, so I said, "All right."

Uncle Whit bade me good-bye, and after one more conference with Mr. Smith he swung off the train and came back beside the window where I was sitting and continued his worried gesticulations to the effect that I was to stay in that seat until my journey was over. I kept nodding my head to reassure him, until with many a creak and groan, which justly had earned the Brazos Valley & Central the title "Wooden Axle," the train pulled away from the station and picked its lackadaisical way across the prairie among the clumps of prickly pear and mesquite trees.

I originally had had no intention of obeying my elders' orders once I got out of sight, but as the train hove away and I looked around the car, I began to feel small and serious. Not only were there no other children in the car, there were no ladies. I had had some hazy and high-colored notion that the Brazos Valley & Central would be full of merry progeny about my age and that I could run amok, having no grownup around with the authority to quell me. But it was the day of Christmas Eve, and everybody who was going to spend Christmas with his grand-mother already had gone. There was not even a stray mother around in case something terrible happened.

I craned my neck toward the door, for I was glued to my seat by this startling realization, and looked toward the other car. It was a smoker, and naturally no lady would be caught dead in there. The car ahead was the mail car, and I could see the government man, in a green eyeshade and a black apron, handling the mailbags. The car ahead of that, I knew, was the baggage car. The Brazos Valley & Central boasted only four cars. I was adrift in a world of men.

At once I began to remember what everybody had told me to do, so I got up and took off my coat, folded it neatly, divested myself of my bonnet, and sat down again, clutching my purse and my lunchbox. Nobody said anything to me, so I was saved the necessity of not speaking to strangers. I gazed around the coach at its occupants. There was a rough-looking man in the front seat; he had long hair and a beard, and was wearing an old flat hat, very greasy and dirty. I took him to be a sheepherder. He had a tremendous sack of wool. Across the aisle and one seat closer there was a small, swarthy man with heavy eye-brows, piercing black eyes, and a mustache. He had a large pack on the seat beside him, and I recognized him as a peddler—one of those itinerant vendors who used to travel the West with a stock of indispensa-ble merchandise and shoddy pretties, which brought cheer to many a hard-bitten rancher's wife. The seat directly in front of me was filled with the bulk of a fat man wearing a black alpaca suit, a white shirt, a black string tie, and a large, fawn-colored Stetson hat. On the lapel of his shiny black suit, I discovered later, was pinned a glistening silver star. His coat was unbuttoned, and stretched across the vest encasing his pendulous stomach was a heavy gold watch chain with an unusually fierce-looking elk's tooth depending from it. In spite of his heavy jowls and beetling black eyebrows, he was a dapper man, and his black, high-topped boots were fastidiously shined. He was dressed up for Christmas.

As the train ground along with a seasick motion, there was no sound but the creaking of the worn wheels on the track and occasional shouts from the smoker, where the men were smoking black cigars and playing faro and, for all I know, nipping Christmas cheer out of a bottle.

I was very lonely and stiff from sitting so still, and I began to wonder what had become of Mr. Smith. I felt that soon I must look on a familiar face. Just as I began to get really restless, the fat man in the seat ahead folded his newspaper and stood up, probably bent on going into the smoker. He paused beside me and said: "Hello, kid."

Grandma had told me not to speak to strangers, so I dropped my eyes and toyed with my purse.

"Aren't you Charlie Grant's kid?" the man asked in his deep, bass voice.

I cut my eyes toward him and nodded; but as I did so, I read the legend on the silver star. "S-h-e-r-i-f-f," it said. Here, here in the flesh, was the archenemy of Uncle Edgar. A shiver ran over me. Any enemy of Uncle Edgar's was bound to be an enemy of mine. I looked busily out the window.

"Looky here," the sheriff said. He obviously thought he had a great way with children. "What's the matter? Has the cat got your tongue?"

I was moved to stick it out at him for proof that he was mistaken, but controlled the impulse and simply shook my head. He put a heavy hand on my shoulder and turned me around so that the elk's tooth just grazed my nose, and I jumped.

"Scaredy cat, ain't you?" he said.

"I am not," I blazed. "I'm not supposed to speak to strangers."

"I'm no stranger," he said. "I've known your daddy since he was so high—no bigger than you. You look exactly like him. The spit and image."

"Well, Grandma told me—"

"Know her, too," the sheriff remarked. "Fine old lady."

Mr. Smith came by at this point. "How you doing, Sis?" he asked kindly.

"Just fine," I said in a thin voice.

"Well, well, Charlie Grant's kid," the sheriff said to Mr. Smith. "I remember mighty well the day he was no bigger than this urchin."

I didn't know what "urchin" was, but I didn't like the sound of it.

I glowered, now that Mr. Smith's kindly presence was there to protect me.

"Yep," Mr. Smith said. "This is Little Sissy Grant. She's been down to her grandma. Her folks are going to take her off the train in Porterfield."

"Well, I declare," the sheriff said with heavy jocularity. "A Christmas package. Why isn't she riding up in the mail car with the parcel post?"

Mr. Smith smiled benignly, somewhat pleased to be engaged in conversation by the man of the law.

"Tell you what we could do," the sheriff pursued. "Write out a tag and tie it around her neck and let Jack toss her in the mailbag for Porterfield."

I was not unaccustomed to the teasing ways of adults, but this notion sounded pretty plausible to me, and I began to feel qualms. I had no doubt that this horrible sheriff could arrange it. I inched away from them and pressed my face to the windowpane.

Sheriff Bonner—that was his name—yawned, stretched, and dropped into the seat opposite mine. Mr. Smith went on into the smoker to announce the name of the next town, which everybody on the Brazos Valley & Central knew anyway. The train was imperceptibly slowing to a stop at the dull-red station, where a little knot of people waited to get on.

"Never saw such a young'un," the sheriff said, winking at the peddler. "The only lady on the train, and I am getting no place fast."

The swarthy man stretched his mouth into a tired smile.

The sheriff continued to harass me. "You know what's liable to happen," he said. "When you get to Porterfield, I bet old Charlie Grant won't be at the station to meet you."

"He will, too!" I sputtered.

"Been gone, hasn't he? Been up to St. Louis on a trip, Mr. Smith said. How do you know he's home yet?"

"He is, he is!" I cried. "My daddy *will* meet me."

"Bet you a jawbreaker he won't," Mr. Bonner said.

"You wait and see!" I threatened.

"Like as not he and your mama are having such a good time in St. Louis they won't remember anything about you," the sheriff went on, having discovered a hole in my armor.

My distress suffused me. I had been homesick at Grandma's. That week had seemed like a year. Maybe St. Louis *was* a wonderful place. Maybe they *had* forgotten me. But at Christmas— They couldn't. They couldn't! I defended them hotly against my aroused suspicion. I wanted to cry, but I felt too old for that. My chest seemed tight and funny. I did not know which way to turn, and then I looked up and there was Uncle Edgar, standing at the door of the coach, his red hair tousled, his face flushed, a crooked smile on his lips. He must have got on at that station. I didn't know where he was going on Christmas Eve. I doubt if he himself knew.

"Uncle Edgar!" I cried and left the seat and ran to him.

"Why, Sissy," he said. "What are you doing here? Is Mama with you?"

"I'm by myself," I said importantly. "Grandma got sciatica."

We got back to my seat, and Uncle Edgar looked down from his six-foot eminence on the sheriff.

"Who's your friend?" Uncle Edgar snarled.

"Hello, Ed," Sheriff Bonner said. "Keeping yourself straight, I hope."

"No credit to you," Uncle Edgar said. "How do you happen to be hanging around Sissy?"

"She's in my custody," Sheriff Bonner said jovially.

"I am not," I put in. "Uncle Whit gave me to Mr. Smith, the conductor."

"You better not let me catch you picking on this kid," Uncle Edgar said thickly. "Keep your teasing to yourself!"

"Are you threatening me?" Sheriff Bonner inquired humorously. "Sounds like liquor talking."

"You can take it any way you want to," Uncle Edgar said. "You old sorehead!"

"Keep a civil tongue in your head, my boy. Remember there's a lady present."

"You remember it," Uncle Edgar said, and stalked toward the smoker.

"Uncle Edgar!" I cried. "Don't go. Please don't go."

"Sit down, Sis," Uncle Edgar said. "I'll be back."

"Doesn't seem to care for you much, does he?" nagged Sheriff Bonner.

"He does, too," I said vehemently. "He's my uncle." This seemed to me to be enough to prove it.

"I never saw an honest-to-goodness uncle act like that."

"I like the way he acts," I shouted. And I did. But I wished he would come back.

The slow hours passed, and the early winter dark began to come down. Sheriff Bonner had gone to sleep and was snoring loudly. Every now and then Uncle Edgar stuck his head into the coach and looked at me to see that I was all right. He didn't come in, and I didn't know whether this was because he had been overcome by shyness, after having talked more than I had ever heard him talk in my life, or simply because he was afraid the sheriff would wake up. I had the impression that he was lurking in the vestibule against any emergency that might come up, and that made me feel safe and comfortable and sure about everything again—sure I wouldn't be tossed in the mailbag and sure my father would be at the station in Porterfield.

As the afternoon had worn away, the weather had changed and it had begun to snow. The sharp wind drove the flakes against the window and the whole world outside was a swirl of white. It had been a rainy winter, full of storms and floods, but this was the first snow, and I felt gratified that heaven had come through with the right weather for Christmas. I began to feel drowsy and to think about home, and hanging my stocking at the mantel and the Christmas tree, and my father and mother, and Santa Claus coming down the chimney with the sleepy-doll I had ordered. We must be almost to Porterfield by now. We had just to go over the Brazos River Bridge and a little way beyond that was home.

Sheriff Bonner came up out of slumber with a loud snort and roused me from my reverie. He pulled out his ponderous watch and looked at it. "Five o'clock," he said. "Must be about two hours late."

"Two hours late!" I cried. No such exigency had ever occurred to me.

"Yep," he said. "Looks as if you might not get to hang up your stocking after all!"

The full horror of such a possibility smote me amidships and I was speechless.

"Well," he said, "I reckon it won't make much difference. You're too old not to know who Santa Claus is."

"Santa Claus is Santa Claus!" I quavered. "I know that."

"Now, Sissy, you can't fool Old Man Bonner. You're too smart not to know that Santa Claus is just your papa and mama! A big girl like you."

I was six years old. I was an only child and never had known many children. The myth was fresh and pure in my mind. Nobody had ever

94

cast a doubt on the authenticity of Santa Claus. But the horrid truth fell on my ears with the ring of authority. I began to wail.

"He is not! He is not!" I shrieked. The peddler and the sheepherder both started up out of dozes.

"Sure thing. Santa Claus is just your mama and papa," Sheriff Bonner reiterated loudly.

These words were no sooner out of his mouth than a long, lithe shape leaped like a panther through the doorway leading from the vestibule and Uncle Edgar had Sheriff Bonner by the collar.

"What did you say that for?" Uncle Edgar rasped, shaking the sheriff the way a dog shakes a rat. "Trying to make a little kid miserable. You old devil!"

"Take your hands off me," Sheriff Bonner shouted, trying to reach his gun. "You outlaw!"

Uncle Edgar pinioned his arm, took the gun, and threw it into a seat. They began to scuffle up and down the aisle, and the men poured out of the smoker into our coach. Uncle Edgar was pummeling the sheriff.

"What's going on?" shouted a drummer.

"He told the little girl there wasn't any Santa Claus," the sheepherder said.

"The old reprobate!" another man yelled. "Let me help you, Edgar."

"I can manage," Uncle Edgar panted, "if I can just keep him in reach."

The peddler put out his foot and tripped Sheriff Bonner as he was backing away, and Uncle Edgar landed a blow that caught the sheriff full on the nose. His nose began to bleed, and Uncle Edgar let up.

"I reckon that'll hold him," Uncle Edgar said and stood up and hitched up his belt.

"You're under arrest," Sheriff Bonner exploded, holding his handkerchief to his nose, which was rapidly beginning to swell.

"Wait'll I tell the judge how this happened," Uncle Edgar said.

Sheriff Bonner didn't say anything more, but departed for the washroom to attend to his nose.

The train suddenly ground to a stop.

Mr. Smith came rushing out of the mail car, staring myopically at the remains of the scene of carnage. "What's going on, boys?" he asked worriedly.

"Just a little private discussion," Uncle Edgar said.

"Ed just decided to whip the sheriff for a Christmas present to himself," one of the other men put in.

"This is no time to be fighting," Mr. Smith said, his walrus mustache trembling. "It's Christmas Eve. Besides, I've got bad news for you—for all of us." Mr. Smith had a family at the other end of the line waiting to hang up stockings, too.

"What is it?" everybody said at once.

I had been crouched in the corner of the seat, my little world a tumbled heap of ruins about me and the sobs strangling my throat, but I sat up and dug my fists into my eyes, because Mr. Smith's voice was so sad and worried.

"I just got word—" Mr. Smith gulped. "The bridge is blocked over the Brazos. It's a blinding blizzard. No chance to get the track cleared before tomorrow. Looks like we'll be here all night."

A groan went up, and Sheriff Bonner burst out of the washroom to hear the latest disaster. A hubbub of questions, talk, and complaining followed. Not knowing what to do, I began to weep again. They all stopped talking and looked at me, and the enormity of the thing broke over them. Here they were, caught for the night in the middle of a prairie in a blinding snow with a girl-child whose illusions had just been shattered. And it was Christmas Eve. Distress filled their faces; they turned to me in despair. Not one of them knew what to say or do.

"Now don't cry, Sissy," Mr. Smith said bravely. "There's not a thing to be afraid of. You'll be home all right tomorrow."

I howled afresh.

They looked at one another, mutely asking, "What'll we do?"

I continued to bawl.

"You fellows go on into the smoker," Uncle Edgar said finally with superhuman courage. "I'll try to get her quiet."

They filed out, and Uncle Edgar sat down gingerly beside me.

"I want my mo-ther!" I shrieked, adding, "And there isn't any Santa Claus!" I was unable to separate the two cataclysms. One was as bad as the other.

Uncle Edgar fastened on the latter as the more likely topic of discussion. "Now, you listen here, Sissy," he said. "There is too a Santa Claus." Uncle Edgar then gathered me in his arms and proceeded to embroider this theme with what he remembered inexpertly from Clement Moore's Christmas poem. I think he even recited a few stanzas.

He talked and he talked, until he was hoarse, and at last I began to get sleepy and to believe him.

"But if there is a Santa Claus," I said, "how'll he know where I am—on this old train?" I sniffled again.

"He'll know!" Uncle Edgar said hastily.

"I want to see him," I insisted, like the archfiend a six-year-old girl is.

"All right," Uncle Edgar weakly promised. "You'll see him."

Thus reassured, I gave up and sagged against Uncle Edgar's shoulder in the peaceful surrender of sleep.

I don't know how long Uncle Edgar held me there, but it must have been only a few minutes. I have some strange and lingering recollection of his curly hair's touching my face and his laying me gently down and covering me with something. I found out later it was his saddle blanket. That was about all he had. All night I had vivid dreams of scurry and bustle, and I knew somehow that I wasn't at home and that people were moving about on tiptoe; but I was so worn out by the violences of the day that I was never able to get my eyes open.

Nor did I open them until the sunlight, falling through the window of the stalled train and reflected from the dazzling whiteness of the landscape outside, shone square in my eyes. And what a sight awaited me! They must have put in a night of superhuman endeavor—that ill-assorted group of passengers on the Brazos Valley & Central. They were all standing in a huddle at one end of the coach, waiting ecstatically for me to become conscious. Young as I was, I saw how pleased they were with themselves, and I gave them a brilliant smile.

On the seat opposite me was a small sagebrush scrub, which had been uprooted and trimmed with wizened apples, elderly candy and chewing gum, and even a sack of chewing tobacco, tied on with white twine. On the arm of the seat hung a man's sock, probably from the drummer's valise. It contained one of the most unusual and enticing collections of presents any little girl ever was awarded. A rabbit foot, a string of rattlesnake rattlers, which were sometimes worn to cure rheumatism, a deck of cards, slightly used, a large jackknife, a good-luck dollar with a bullet hole through the middle, a small, sentimental-looking pair of lady's spurs, and an elk's tooth.

97

But we still had not reached the climax. When I had examined these tributes with an enthusiasm I do not have to assure you was not feigned, there was suddenly a great ringing of the train engine's bell, and through the mail-coach door burst an apparition that had all the earmarks of Santa Claus. It was fat and shook; it had a wealth of silvery whiskers and hair, strangely like sheep's wool. Its eyes were twinkling and it had a red nose. It had a pack on its back. It capered and cavorted in the approved manner, though somewhat ponderously. The fact that it wore a pair of blue denim overalls and a windbreaker of the same, and that its peaked cap was made of a red bandanna, completely escaped my notice. To my bedazzled eyes, it was certainly Santa Claus; and I thought with renewed wonder what a miracle it was he had known where to find me, way out here on a dead train in the middle of the prairie. I do not really know how this oddly caparisoned figure ever sold itself to my already suspicious mind, but I know it did. I suppose I had the same kind of blind spot most young children have who are able to take all sizes and shapes and costumes of Santa Claus in the stores at Christmas. I just desperately wanted to believe that it was true. And so I did.

When the assembled company noted this, a sigh of relief went up and such jollity broke out as I never have seen before or since. All those sad, homeless men, who never would have been on the Brazos Valley & Central passenger train on Christmas Eve if they really had any place to go (they were probably all going up to Wichita to get drunk), embraced the Christmas spirit and we were children together. Santa Claus did not open his mouth, but he led a snake dance up the aisle and back, and then, with a great flourish, he put his hand into the pack and from among the shoelaces, saddle soap, needle books, and boxes of arnica, he withdrew a splendid hair ribbon and a china doll without legs, obviously salvaged from the peddler's one remaining pincushion, and presented them to me. I shrieked with joy, fondled the red ribbon, and folded the maimed baby to my chest.

All my friends were proud and happy at the success of their hard work. They laughed and slapped one another on the back, and the peddler took out a harmonica and played *Dixie* and *When the Work's All Done This Fall*. Uncle Edgar did a hat dance, stepping high and delicately around the brim of his sombrero in the intricate steps of the figures. The drummer recited *The Shooting of Dan McGrew* from beginning to end, to loud applause. Mr. Smith, still a little mournful from having missed the hanging of his children's stockings, made me a cat's cradle out of his slightly grimy handkerchief, and the sheepherder took the jackknife in my loot and carved me a whistle from a mesquite switch.

While celebration was still at its height, the whistle of the engine gave forth a loud toot and Mr. Smith ran forward and then came back with the news.

"The road's open," he shouted. "Got the track all cleared. Be to Porterfield in sight of an hour."

I didn't know whether to be glad or sorry, but I didn't have time to think, for the Brazos Valley & Central chugged, sighed, picked up steam, and lurched slowly forward toward the river. We were going home.

I do not have to tell you that pandemonium had reigned all night in Porterfield and that my distracted parents could not believe their eyes when I was handed down to them, rosy, smiling, and well pleased with life, my face smeared with the candy I had consumed for breakfast and my arms loaded with strange but compelling presents.

"Santa Claus found me!" I cried, and a sigh went up from the anxious knot of my fellow passengers, collected in the vestibule to bid me farewell. My Uncle Edgar had a funny grin on his face and his chest seemed to expand.

"Edgar!" my mother cried, noticing him at last. "For heaven's sake, what are you doing there? Get right off that train and come home to dinner with us."

"Lordy, Ed," my father said, dragging Uncle Edgar off the train just as it was beginning to move toward Wichita. "I'm glad you were on there to look after Sissy."

Uncle Edgar blushed. It was about the first time my father had addressed a kind word to him.

"Nothing to it," Uncle Edgar said casually, but he walked straighter. He had at last accepted responsibility, and what's more, he had made good.

Sated with a second Christmas that afternoon, I sat playing with my legless doll among stacks of store-bought presents, and my mind began to go over the events of the day. It seemed strange to me that Santa Claus had deigned to visit me in Porterfield and also in the day coach of the Brazos Valley & Central. I told myself that it must have been

Santa Claus on the train, because how in the world could somebody who looked so like him have got way out there? And then a sharp thought occurred to me, and I knew, once and for all, who Santa Claus was. Santa Claus could be anybody, even Sheriff Bonner. The thing that gave it away was not the fact that he was wearing Mr. Bolander's overalls and bandanna, or wore a beard made of sheep's wool right out of that herder's sack, or carried the pack that belonged to the peddler, but that he had a bulbous nose—red as a cherry and big only as the nose of Santa Claus, or of somebody who has just been hit on it, can be big!

Uncle Edgar had done the whole thing—even to the right kind of nose. I thought of my strange Uncle Edgar with such a surfeit of love that it almost squeezed the wind out of my small chest. I immediately transferred all the love I had ever borne Santa Claus to Uncle Edgar, who certainly needed it more. And I swore I never would let him know that I knew.

Years later I did tell him, of course, after he had a little girl of his own. He roared with laughter, remembering it all, especially Mr. Bolander standing in his long underwear ringing the bell while Sheriff Bonner wore his overalls.

"Never had any more trouble with Old Man Bonner from that day on," Uncle Edgar reminisced. "Though naturally he didn't have any yearning to be Santa Claus that day right at first. He was mighty mad, and his nose was sore. I reckon that was the last time I ever used a pistol." Uncle Edgar looked a little sheepish, remembering. "But I persuaded him, and finally he entered into the spirit of it. He was the only one for that part. He had the figure for it.

"Sheriff Bonner turned out to be one of my best friends," Uncle Edgar continued. "When I ran for office, he stumped for me. He seemed different to everybody from that time on. Kind of thought of himself as Santa Claus. And the kids used to follow him around. I reckon he was teasing you that day because he really wanted to make up to you. He loved children—never had any family of his own."

I didn't say it, but I thought Uncle Edgar was always different from that time on, too. The angry wildness seemed to go out of him. Shortly after that Christmas, even as Grandmother had hoped, he married a nice girl and settled down. He made a wonderful father. He made a wonderful lawyer, too. Maybe you know him, Judge Edgar West of the Circuit Court of Appeals?

100

CHESTER T. CROWELL

THOUGH BORN IN CLEVELAND, Ohio, October 14, 1888, Chester Theodore Crowell spent a large part of his life in Texas. He was educated in the public schools of San Antonio. For the first half of his adult life he was a newspaperman. Between 1905 and 1910 he was a reporter for the *San Antonio Express,* with two years out as managing editor of the *Mexican Herald,* in Mexico City. From 1911 to 1916 he was editorial writer and managing editor of the *Austin Statesman.* From 1917 to 1919 he was a staff correspondent for the *Dallas Morning News.*

Crowell believed, however, that all newspaper editorial men who amount to much get out of that business as soon as they can. After a short term on the *New York Evening Post* in 1923, he became a freelance writer. In the next fifteen years he contributed hundreds of stories and articles to the principal magazines. Throughout the twenties his was a name very familiar to readers of the *Saturday Evening Post.* In 1924 his story "Margaret Blake" was second winner of the O. Henry Memorial Award. In 1926 three of his stories were given three-star ratings in the O'Brien collection, and other stories by him have been similarly recognized. His "Ruth" was reprinted in the anthology *The Hundred Best Short Stories of the World. Liquor, Loot, and Ladies* (1930) was a novel about machine politics. *Recovery Unlimited: The Monetary Policy of the Roosevelt Administration* (1936) followed the author's appointment as a special assistant to the Secretary of the Treasury. "Mamma and Papa," a delightful chapter from an unfinished autobiography, was published in the *Post* after his death.

In his later years, Crowell made his home in Washington, D.C., and at "Millermore," near Dallas. He died in Washington, December 26, 1941. His widow is the writer Evelyn Miller Crowell. "The Stoic," here printed, is interesting not only as a story but also because it is an early treatment of oil workers and because it reflects, though in caricature, some folkways of the Texas of that day.

The Stoic

I<small>T WAS DURING</small> the never-to-be-forgotten September when my father promised me long trousers for Christmas that Wallace Hutchins came to our community, bringing with him his beautiful wife and their little girl, five years of age. They were the only total strangers who established a home there during my lifetime. Any others who came had kinsfolk in the community. It was not a town, but a cross-roads, marked by a general store, a cotton-gin, several churches, and a side-track for freight. People in the county referred to this place as "The Corners." Pine-forest and sandy, cut-over lands surrounded it. Here and there the forest or the stumps had been cleared away, and either corn, cotton, or sweet potatoes were planted. The farmers lived in unpainted, pine-board shacks, which looked as drab and discouraged as their corn crops during dry weather.

This part of eastern Texas was the first to be settled. Among the family names in that county were Washington, Lincoln, Hamilton, Jefferson, Franklin, Davis, and Henderson. They were represented on the battlefield of San Jacinto when independence was won from Mexico. Some of the oldest county records are beyond question the work of scholarly men, but poor soil and generations of isolation took their inevitable toll, until finally not a school in the county boasted more than a five-months' term, and most of them offered only three months out of the twelve. Our neighbors were almost illiterate.

Wallace Hutchins and his partner, Paul Davidson, came to drill for oil. A deep well had been sunk for artesian water and had struck natural gas. Paul Davidson, who was the business man of the partnership, had heard of this, and leased several thousand acres from a lumber com-

Reprinted from *Century Magazine*, May, 1924; copyright 1924 by the author and used by permission of Evelyn Miller Crowell.

pany. Wallace Hutchins came to superintend the drilling of four test wells. With him came a crew of workmen, and I trailed along with my dog, wondering where they were going to find shelter and food. The community was afraid of them, and, after consultation, not only decided against taking them in, but thought it might be necessary to guard against thievery.

My eyes opened wide with astonishment as these men set up large, comfortable tents, oil-cooking-stoves, neat beds, mirrors, and little stands on which their toilet articles were displayed. They came one morning, and early in the afternoon they were not only established, but provisioned from the general store. Moreover, they paid cash. I had never seen anyone do that before. Cash was available only once a year, when the cotton was sold.

On the table for their first meal were three vegetables, meat, sweet pickles, great platters of bread, dishes of preserves, and jellies, cake, and bananas. We should have considered that a wedding-feast. After eating, they turned their attention to the largest tent and soon had a floor built. Then they hauled up Mrs. Hutchins's three trunks, her brass-bound cedar boxes and furniture, placing the articles as she directed. By night her tent was beautiful. She went for a stroll with the little girl at sunset, wearing what I described at the supper table that night as a party dress.

Wallace Hutchins stood before his tent silhouetted against the vivid evening sky, and I felt such a thrill as I had never known before. He looked a general grown accustomed to victory, a very emperor. The incredible speed, efficiency, and cheerfulness of this camp were mere routine accomplishments to him. His profile was classic, his posture erect, confident, and his blue-gray eyes calm, imperious, a trifle scornful without being unkindly.

"Sonny, can you get a quart of fresh milk for the little girl?" he asked.

"Yes, sir," I replied, confident that I could hold out that much when I milked three cows. At any rate, I was determined to take a chance, for he was a demigod, and the little girl in her pretty, clean clothes an angel. He stepped into the tent and reappeared with a glass milk bottle, the first I had ever seen.

"Thank you, sonny," he said, and handed me twenty-five cents. At the local market price he was entitled to two and a half gallons of milk. That was how we became acquainted.

103

Never was milk delivered with greater enthusiasm. The glass bottle was my ticket of admission to a new world twice a day.

Our sandy roads were so rutted that the front axle of a truck would strike the middle of the road. Mr. Hutchins bought a steel scraper to smooth the roads he intended to use. He did this without complaining about the government or his taxes. Mrs. Hutchins used the tea leaves or coffee grounds only once, then threw them away. She wore a house dress while cooking, but changed to her party dress before serving the food. The little girl laughed a great deal and seldom cried. One day she asked her father to buy her a Shetland pony, and the very next morning he telegraphed for it. When she climbed on his knee, he didn't tell her to go away because he was tired. He changed clothes when he came home in the evening and wore a coat at the table. His khaki working-clothes were washed regularly and always looked clean. He didn't seem to have any old clothes to work in. When he came home from the derricks in the evening he took a bath and even washed his head. Every morning he shaved. Instead of wasting hours at these tasks, he consumed only a few minutes.

Observing all this made me think of my aged grandfather, who lived with us. He always put on an old smoking-jacket with a velvet collar when he came to supper. I had supposed this was the childish foible of an old man, but now I began to wonder; so I asked him why he did it. He was a very tall man and still as straight as an arrow. His eyes were bright, and although he was very old, his teeth were beautiful. He drew himself up proudly, pleased with my question.

"We are poor," he said, "but not white trash. When I was a young man in New Orleans, my boy, I dressed for dinner. I continued to dress for dinner while your father and I were clearing this land. The reason I do not dress for dinner now is that I have only one suit. The smoking-jacket is all I have, boy; so I wear that."

I walked away, choked with emotion, my eyes blinded with tears, and there was born in me a determination, which never thereafter cooled, to fight my way back to that mysterious, but desirable, station in life from which we had fallen.

But to return to the Hutchins household, another innovation I encountered was the kiss. Mrs. Hutchins would often kiss her husband without any excuse, and neither seemed embarrassed by my presence.

One day a truck thundered into camp carrying the Shetland pony. With it came a collie dog. I begged permission to feed the pony, and Mr. Hutchins not only granted the request, but insisted on paying me one dollar a week. It was like accepting wages to attend the circus. The dog adopted the little girl at first sight, and thereafter paraded wherever she romped, looking at her with such pride and affection that it seemed to me the very animals knew instinctively these were superior people.

One evening while I was leading the pony up and down in front of the tent, and the little girl, holding tight to the saddle, squealed with delight, Preacher Jackson called. I don't know why we used the title "Preacher," but we did. The word now sounds disrespectful, but we meant quite the opposite. He was an awe-inspiring person who struck terror in me whenever I saw him—a spiritual descendant of the old Hebrew prophets. His black, deep-set eyes burned with such intensity that one expected him to speak passionately. Instead, his voice was deep and calm. He was tall, gaunt, and determined. Saving sinners was only the least part of the task he had set for himself. He purposed also to prevent sin.

"Are you a member of any church?" he asked Mr. Hutchins.

"No," was the prompt reply. Mr. Hutchins was watching the little girl.

"I am the Reverend Mr. Jackson. We shall be pleased to receive you—"

"Yes, sir. Thank you." Mr. Hutchins replied too promptly.

Preacher Jackson glanced at the pony, and, beyond it, saw a group of the workmen sitting around a table playing cards. They were in front of a tent and had large lanterns hanging over the table.

"Are those men playing cards?" he demanded.

"They are."

"That will have to stop." Preacher Jackson started toward the table. Mr. Hutchins placed his hands to his mouth and called:

"Look out, boys! He may upset the table. If he bothers you, throw him into the creek."

Preacher Jackson returned and faced Mr. Hutchins.

"You tolerate that in the sight of your innocent child?" he asked, pointing at the card game.

Mr. Hutchins became very angry now.

"Move on, old malaria; you are blocking traffic," he said. His lips smiled, but his eyes blazed.

"We shall pray for you Wednesday evening," Preacher Jackson announced.

At that sentence things swam before my eyes, and my knees felt weak. In our church we prayed for people who were so wicked it was time to put the community on notice. If they yielded to Preacher Jackson's entreaties, their sins might not find them out; but if they refused, we were called upon to pray for them, and he left us in no doubt as to the reason. But Mr. Hutchins didn't know what a terrible thing it was to be prayed for in The Corners.

"All right," he said; "enjoy yourself."

I was so weak I had to go home. Why Mr. Hutchins would thus bring down the wrath of Providence was more than I could understand. It seemed to me that any one venturing upon such uncertain labor as drilling holes in the ground to find oil had need of all the influence he could array on his side. Such behavior was calculated to send his drills right into a protruding crevasse of hell and open a volcano.

Children were not required to attend Wednesday prayer meeting, but I heard about it Thursday morning. On my way to the camp to deliver the milk I met Mrs. Hobbs. She was talking to herself, as was her custom, and when I appeared she merely raised her voice.

"And you delivering them milk," she said. "Next we'll be praying for you."

I trembled and hurried on, feeling very guilty. Mrs. Hobbs talked a great deal about God; what He would like and wouldn't like; what He would punish people for, and sometimes she said He would reward someone, but not often. One of her eyes was dim from a cataract that had grown over it, so that it looked like the eye of a dead fish. Her complexion was sallow, as, indeed, nearly all complexions were thereabout, because of the prevalent malaria. My grandfather called Mrs. Hobbs the town-crier because she spread so much news, but at that time I didn't know what a town-crier was. I supposed he referred to her habit of attending all funerals for miles around and weeping noisily. Also, she had a peculiar voice, and when she talked about God it seemed to me there was a sort of sob barely controlled.

When I delivered the milk Mr. Hutchins was in high good humor as usual. Mr. Davidson, his partner, was with him, and had evidently just heard of the encounter with Preacher Jackson.

"Well, sonny, did they pray for me?" he asked. I had to smile, because he was so jolly and handsome and unafraid.

"Yes, sir," I said. "I'm awful sorry."

"Sorry?" He was astonished. I explained what it meant.

"So you think my social standing here is just about ruined?"

"I like you," I managed to say.

"Were none of your family ever prayed for?"

The question was asked as a joke, but it exposed the family skeleton.

"Grandfather was," I answered. "He made some wine."

They laughed. This was many years before national prohibition. Then Mr. Davidson told Mr. Hutchins not to "stir up a hornet's nest." He talked very calmly and affectionately. It was interesting to watch their eyes when they looked at each other. Anyone would see they were wonderful friends. I did not know then how soon I was to see that friendship tried and proved in tragic circumstances.

When I reached home I asked Grandfather if he thought it was all right for me to deliver milk to Mr. Hutchins.

"What do you think?" he demanded sternly.

"I don't see any harm in it," I said, trying to catch a glimpse of my father and mother at the same time.

"Then deliver it," he shouted. "The sorriest human on earth is a coward. You've got good blood in your veins, boy, if this sand hasn't clogged it. I'm not afraid of death, so you ought not to be afraid to deliver milk."

"Don't talk like that!" my mother pleaded.

I escaped before anything more could be said about the milk.

My Friday evening visit to the camp was rewarded with a view of the constable and his enormous leather pistol-holster, which he wore over his stomach instead of on his hip. The figure he presented was absurd, but if you will go through the motions of drawing your pistol, first from the hip and then from the belt-buckle, you will at once see that the constable's holster occupied a decidedly strategic position. Preacher Jackson had sent the constable to stop card-playing. Perhaps this requires the explanation that it was not necessary to prove the men were gambling. Playing cards in a public place was, and still is, a misdemeanor under Texas law, even though the game were solitaire.

Fortunately, however, the men were not playing this evening. They were laying pipe from the old gas-well to the tents, so they would have unlimited fuel for approaching cool weather. The constable seemed glad not to have caught them. He advised that future games be played in the tents, which had the status of private houses and could not be invaded unless the men were gambling.

During the succeeding three weeks before tragedy closed the Hutchins tent, I became much better acquainted with the head of this charming family and his partner. Mr. Davidson was not so busy now, and spent more time in the camp. I learned that they had been to Alaska and Mexico together. Mr. Hutchins had been to South America, and Mr. Davidson knew India. Both could speak Spanish and some French. This was very impressive to a boy who had never heard a word of any foreign language.

When Mr. Hutchins told me of the failure of their gold hunt in Alaska, and the long, dangerous return to the coast, I asked him if he had not felt very discouraged.

"No; it was great sport," he said. "Most of the things men try to do fail of success. We had a very interesting experience. Always take your failures standing up, boy. Then they don't amount to much."

On another occasion I remarked upon the beauty of his wife and their evident deep affection.

"She is the only woman you have ever loved, isn't she?" I asked. To my astonishment, he laughed.

"Not at all, sonny," he said. "But she's the best woman I ever loved. She's a human being."

"Aren't all women human beings?" I inquired.

"Decidedly not," he snapped.

That puzzled me for a long time. I wanted to ask his opinion of Mrs. Hobbs, but hesitated. Not long after, however, I got it.

Mr. Davidson was older than Mr. Hutchins and more demonstrative in the expression of his affections. He called Mrs. Hutchins "Wally's doll baby," and the little girl "papa's pet."

Hopeful of a tale of adventure, I asked him one day if he had ever saved Mr. Hutchins's life or what they had done for each other to establish so warm a friendship.

"Nothing," he replied. "That's why we can love each other. There aren't any obligations in the way."

Years passed before that remark ceased to be a conundrum.

Mr. Davidson was not very tall, but the strongest man I had ever seen. He wore a great mop of curly red hair and had the peculiar shade of brown eyes appropriate to it. There was long red hair on his arms and some on the backs of his hands. The muscles of his forearms swelled and receded even when he used a knife and fork. Sometimes he would put the little girl in her chair, then lift both with one hand across the room to the table, without apparent effort. The gentleness of such a giant impressed me deeply.

One night, late in November, during our first cold weather, when I went to feed the pony, Mr. Hutchins had not returned. Something had gone wrong with the machinery at one of the derricks, and he was delayed. Mrs. Hutchins was in bed, reading, and the little girl was playing about the room, dressed in her sleeping-suit and looking like a baby bear from a toy store. The new gas-stove was blazing, and the tent was quite warm.

When I delivered the milk next morning Mr. Davidson came to the back door and said:

"We won't need any more, sonny. The two little girls are dead." I dropped the bottle. "It was that gas-stove," he explained very calmly. "It went out. When Wally came home about eleven o'clock, they were dead."

I couldn't believe it. Without realizing what I was doing, I pushed past him and looked at them lying side by side in bed. Then I went into the little front room—there were three rooms in the tent—and saw Mr. Hutchins sitting in a rocking-chair, smoking a pipe and staring blankly. He was not aware of my presence, but he looked up when Mr. Davidson entered, and resumed their interrupted conversation.

"There is a finality about death, Paul, which is beyond grief," he said in a firm voice. "I know their lives have been as near untouched by trouble as is humanly possible. Who knows that it could always have been so? That child's five and a half years are as perfect as the whitest diamond. Would that they might have gone on so forever, but such is not in human destiny. I take this like the rest of life, Paul, standing up. The little one is dead, and that's an end without worry. My wife and I could,

I think, have grown old together gracefully; but if that is not to be, then I have nothing to regret in our relations. We painted a masterpiece, and now it is ours forever, beyond the danger of future marring. We could not have done better in a century than we have done in seven years."

"You are a good Stoic, Wally," Mr. Davidson said.

I slipped out of the room and ran home to tell my mother what had happened. On the way I met Mrs. Hobbs and very foolishly told her also. In fact, I may have told several persons. Mrs. Hobbs said:

"That's what comes of behaving like he did."

I hated myself for telling her. My mother sent me back to ask Mr. Hutchins if there was anything she could do. I picked up a bone for the collie dog and returned.

Four of the workmen were making a coffin near the tent. Inside, the two men were sitting silently side by side. I summoned Mr. Davidson to the door and delivered my message.

"That is very kind, my boy," he said. "If there is anything, I will let you know."

I stood and looked at Mr. Hutchins while tears came into my eyes.

"Can't you say anything to help him?" I asked.

"Nothing, my boy," Mr. Davidson replied. "There is nothing to say. I am just standing by. Maybe you don't know the term standing by?" I didn't. "Once when I was off the China coast there was a great storm, and the ship's rudder jammed," he explained. "The captain sent a wireless call and shot up rockets. Presently out of the rain and spray there loomed the great steel hull of a ship, and we could see her sailing lights looking very brave in such a sky. Then we heard a man on that ship shout through a megaphone, '*Green Castle* of Glasgow standing by.' Our ship didn't go down. They fixed the rudder. But it was very comforting to know the *Green Castle* of Glasgow was standing by. So to-day the old tug, Paul Davidson, is standing by."

Before I could say anything, he walked away to meet Preacher Jackson, who was coming toward the tent. I did not hear their first words, but Mr. Davidson was evidently trying to detain him and not succeeding. As they came nearer I heard Preacher Jackson say:

"It is in the hour of their affliction that men turn to—"

"I'll go in and tell him you are here," Mr. Davidson interrupted.

Inside the tent he said:

"Better let him come in, Wally. He wants to console you. Better have it over with. Let's don't have any trouble at a time like this."

"He doesn't want to console me," Mr. Hutchins replied. "He wants to tell me I brought this on myself. Into the creek with him, Paul!"

Mr. Davidson came out, shaking his head gravely.

"Broken down completely, parson," he said; "unconscious."

But I fear Preacher Jackson had heard their voices, because his eyes narrowed.

"Has an inquest been held?" he asked.

Mr. Davidson said it had not, and Preacher Jackson went away.

"Did you tell him I had broken down?" Mr. Hutchins asked.

"Yes, Wally."

"But, Paul, I want them to know there are men who don't break down. I want them to know there is a religion with no whine in it."

"Wally, they wouldn't understand. In their formula the bereaved breaks down and they console him. It's harmless enough if you let them go through with it, but you'll stir up a hornet's nest if you don't."

I was sitting at the door of the tent petting the collie and listening when skirts brushed my cheek, and Mrs. Hobbs was inside. Her voice, strident and hysterical, filled the tent a moment later.

"You poor, dear man!" she moaned. "But put your trust in the Lord, and He will comfort you. Find your strength in prayer and lean on the blessed—"

"Are you enjoying that?" Mr. Hutchins asked, rising from his chair. Mrs. Hobbs rushed over and took hold of his arm. "Take your hands off me and make less noise," he ordered.

She recoiled at the angry tone and stood staring with her one clear eye.

"We are commanded to comfort the afflicted," she resumed, "and Heaven knows I was good enough to come past all that iniquity,"— indicating the alfresco card-table,—"but if this is the way you receive a humble messenger of mercy—"

"He's very nervous," Mr. Davidson explained.

"I am not nervous," Mr. Hutchins interrupted. "I want that ugly old she out of here."

Mrs. Hobbs was out as though propelled from a gun.

111

"Now you've done it, Wally," Mr. Davidson muttered. "We're in for something, and I don't know what."

He saw me at the door, and asked if Mrs. Hobbs was not an old witch. I, poor innocent, never having seen her ride a broomstick, replied that she was not, but that she talked a lot. Both men smiled; then Mr. Davidson went out to see the coffins. They were nearly ready. I heard him order a large truck brought to the tent, along with Mr. Hutchins's automobile. Then he went into the kitchen and began preparing lunch.

I walked to the general store and heard talk. It alarmed me. They were waiting for the constable and a justice of the peace, who would conduct an inquest. They waited for three hours, but neither official had yet arrived; then Preacher Jackson suggested that they go back to the tent. Some ten or twelve persons were about to start, so I ran ahead to give notice.

"What do you think they'll do?" Mr. Davidson asked me.

"I think they want to console him, but if he won't let them, they may arrest him."

"For murder?"

"Yes, sir."

"Just what I thought."

He re-entered the tent and put his hand on Mr. Hutchins's shoulder.

"Wally," he said, "they are coming back. I know these people, old-timer, and you don't. They haven't very much entertainment and they don't propose to be beaten out of this. If you don't break down and let them console you, you'll go to jail. Now, be a good fellow and fall across the lounge over there. I'll get them out pretty soon. It won't last twenty minutes. They mean well. Humor them. They want to see what's in this tent. Remember you are a widower now, and maybe some of the girls want to look you over. Widowers always remarry right away in places like this. And don't forget that you are already in bad standing. Try to be diplomatic."

Mr. Hutchins laughed. Anyone would have understood he meant no. Mr. Davidson shook his head disconsolately and went to the medicine closet, where he took out a little bottle. He wet a corner of his handkerchief with its contents, then folded the handkerchief very tight and placed it in his pocket. After that he came to the door and told me to run along. I started to obey, but had not moved ten feet when I heard sounds of a violent scuffle and returned.

112

Mr. Davidson had pinned Mr. Hutchins's arms behind him and was struggling to throw him face down on the lounge, but Mr. Hutchins was as agile as a cat. Both men were breathing hard and both were smiling. In fact, it looked as though they could barely keep from laughing aloud. I stood speechless and unable to move until I saw the crowd coming. Just as Mr. Davidson pinned Mr. Hutchins down and sat on his legs, I ran around the tent and came up behind the crowd, entering with them.

The first sound we heard was a groan that began in deep bass and trailed off to a whine.

"The poor dear man!" Mrs. Hobbs said, and tears streamed into her eyes. Preacher Jackson kneeled beside the bed where the bodies were and began praying. Then Mr. Hutchins groaned again, and I went over to investigate. Mr. Davidson had pinned him down in such a way that the hand he was holding so tenderly was a lever for his arm, which was twisted back until the slightest movement caused excruciating pain. After each of these sobs or groans Mr. Hutchins tried to talk, but his mouth was pressed down on the pillow. Mr. Davidson did this very cleverly by resting his elbow on the back of Mr. Hutchins's head when he leaned over him to place a handkerchief to his nose. Once, however, I understood the muffled sounds clearly enough. He said, "Let me up, damn you, Paul!" Mr. Davidson was so strong he could handle Mr. Hutchins and appear to be sitting on the edge of the lounge. His own eyes were red, as though he had been crying. Without advance information their positions looked natural enough, but I saw clearly. Mr. Hutchins groaned five times, then he relaxed. As I knelt down beside him, Mr. Davidson placed his finger to my lips, warning me to say nothing. I could smell chloroform.

The people prayed, and sang "Rock of Ages," and looked at the pretty cedar chests, and carried in the coffins and placed the bodies in them very tenderly. Mrs. Hobbs wailed most dismally. Mr. Davidson picked up Mr. Hutchins as though he were a sleeping child and carried him to the automobile. He opened his eyes then and said:

"Where are we, Paul?"

Mr. Davidson made an ear-shattering noise starting the car, and I heard no more. Two workmen rode on the truck which carried the coffins and they set off toward the main line of the railroad.

Mr. Hutchins never came back, but Mr. Davidson did, and when he finally left The Corners, I went away with him, eager to see Mr. Hutchins again and to win back a place in that world from which my grandfather had so unfortunately banished himself.

The great love Mr. Hutchins bore his wife became a tradition in The Corners. If Mrs. Hobbs is alive, she is still telling about it. This tradition rests entirely upon those five groans. None like them had ever been heard before nor are they likely to be again, for Mr. Davidson nearly overdid the job. Mr. Hutchins couldn't use his left arm for a month.

GEORGE SESSIONS PERRY

ONE OF THE BEST-KNOWN of living Texas authors, George Sessions Perry was born at Rockdale, Milam County, May 5, 1910. He was educated, as the phrase has it, at Allen Academy, Bryan; Southwestern University, Georgetown; Purdue; and the University of Houston. But the statement omits the significant education of his part-time jobs. He hung around his father's small-town drugstore. At the age of ten, he reports in his autobiographical *Tale of a Foolish Farmer*, he once successfully waddied some cattle all alone to a dipping vat. At eleven he brought in an escaped convict on his horse behind him. Later he was a deck boy and sailor as far as Africa, a victim of shipwreck, and an oil-field roustabout at twenty-one dollars for a seven-day week. Somewhere along the way he wrote eight novels which no one saw fit to publish.

Perry's first work to appear in print, in 1937, was the short story "Edgar and the Dank Morass," in the *Saturday Evening Post*. In 1938 he did some movie-writing. In 1939 appeared his first novel, *Walls Rise Up*, a humorous story of the arrival in Texas of three hoboes from California. His romantically conceived, realistically told *Hold Autumn in Your Hand* (1941) recounts Sam Tucker's poor year on his sixty tenant acres of Texas bottom land, his all-summer battle with a catfish, and his unshaken confidence, shared by all who love and work the soil everywhere, that the next year will be better. This novel, which was filmed as *The Southerner*, won the National Booksellers Association award for 1941 and the Texas Institute of Letters award as the best Texas book of that year.

In 1942, Perry published a biography of his state, *Texas: A World in Itself*, and was a war correspondent, in the Mediterranean Basin, for the *Saturday Evening Post* and the *New Yorker*. In 1943 he edited a good anthology of Southwestern writing, *Roundup Time*. Other books by him are *Hackberry Cavalier* (1944), a collection of linked short stories; *Cities of America* (1947), profiles of great cities (including his own Rockdale as well as San Antonio and Dallas–Fort Worth); *My Granny Van* (1949), a most appealing biography of his most appealing grandmother; and *The Story of Texas A&M* (1951).

The Perry story here chosen, "The Fourflusher," offers a needed

George Sessions Perry

gentle corrective to the tendency to romanticize the past which in the typical western story and motion picture is still too often with us. Its hero has "involuntarily fallen into the mannerisms of an old-time, Indian-fighting sheriff west of the Pecos"—whence his nickname, Powderhorn, and his calling every gully an arroyo, every surrey horse a cayuse.

The Fourflusher

Powderhorn Flinders had just finished a satisfying breakfast of skillet bread and what he, at least, called coffee. He laid his plate and pan on the earthen floor of the tent for Penrose, the only pig he'd ever seen who could truly be said to have good manners, to polish clean. Then he walked outside to savor the morning. It was autumn in Hackberry, when the mustard has flowered and the field larks have come back for the winter. Over on Grass Bur Hill to the left, a jackass gave tongue to a jackass' limited repertoire. Powderhorn lit his pipe, gently plucked a seed tick off the underside of his right forearm, popped it, and was at peace.

Next, according to morning ritual, he feasted his eyes on his slowly, but over the years steadily, mounting pile of scrap lumber and roofing tin. Soon now, there'd be enough to start building the cozy two-room house of which he had so long dreamed. That stack of building material was to Powderhorn a visible token of his faith that someday Myrtle Bledsoe—Myrtle with the flaming red hair—would come back to him.

For Powderhorn Flinders—despite the fact that he was one of the people who, by life, "had been drove hard and put up wet"—was not the kind of man to hold a grudge. Just because Myrtle had run off with a book agent three days before she was to have married Powderhorn did not alter the fact that he loved her. Myrtle, he realized, was impulsive. Maybe, just as impulsively, she'd come back to him. But, now that the years of her absence had grown to seventeen, it was becoming harder all the time for Powderhorn to keep his faith alive. It was something of a strain even to maintain hope. In fact, the one thing that illuminated

Copyright 1950 by The Curtis Publishing Company; reprinted from the *Saturday Evening Post*, May 20, 1950, by permission of the author and the publisher.

his life these days was the demands of his public career in law enforcement.

For fifteen years—ever since, after a violent political campaign, Hackberry had voted to bar livestock from the public thoroughfares, lawns and flower gardens—his had been the responsibility of enforcing the stock law. He'd loved the job so much that he'd involuntarily fallen into the mannerisms of an old-time, Indian-fighting sheriff west of the Pecos. A tall, unkempt man, he was almost invariably garbed in tattered canvas brush clothes, an ancient hat with the widest possible brim, and a pair of high-heeled, narrow-toed rodeo boots with a rattlesnake design stitched on the sides. Moreover, he usually wore a pair of low-slung Spanish spurs which raked the sidewalk as he walked and did duly jingle, jangle, jingle. Not only did he carry a lariat and pigging string on his saddle but a carbine holster as well. Though he did not, as it happened, own a carbine, he made out with, and felt a certain emanation of authority from, the holster in which, when he could afford it, he carried an extra sack of tobacco and a penny box of matches. To Powderhorn, every gully was an "arroyo," every surrey horse a "cayuse." And it was this predilection for Western ways of a century ago that had caused his neighbors, behind his back, to dub him "Powderhorn," although his parents had named him "Kavanaugh."

However, this nickname was coined and used in a friendly spirit. Powderhorn was, and was proud to be, a necessary figure in the governmental structure of the town. He took his duties with extreme seriousness and arrested all cows, pigs, horses and mules that dared wander abroad within its limits. He impounded them in a pen on the back of his little lot, and levied a fine of a dollar per animal upon careless owners. Fifty cents went to the city treasury, the other fifty cents to Powderhorn as his stipulated fee.

At this very moment a winsome Jersey heifer and her baby calf were out in the pen. Powderhorn had picked them up the preceding afternoon after the calf, with a calf's curiosity, had wandered into the Three Brothers' Barbershop and started licking the lather off the face of a recumbent patron.

It was odd, Powderhorn thought, that he didn't recognize his two prisoners, since among the town's quadruped population his acquaintance was wide indeed. As he pondered this fact, he saw the town taxi

118

come roaring down the road, leaving behind it a plume of fine, pale, copper-colored dust. Skeet Clymore, the driver, drew to an abrupt stop in front of Powderhorn's tent, and a woman climbed out. She was sturdy and fortyish, but agile. Her hair was as red as a field of poppies.

Powderhorn's heart leaped with hope. Then, as the woman hurried up to him, he saw that it wasn't Myrtle.

In her eyes was the fire of anger. "You the pound-pen feller?" she asked. "The one they call Powderhorn?"

Powderhorn bristled. "Not to my face, ma'am. My name is Kavanaugh Flinders, law-enforcement officer of Hackberry, Texas, livestock division."

"Well, you must not be very much on the ball. I came to report a cattle theft."

Powderhorn was all keen interest now. "You don't say? How many?"

"All I had. What I got when we divided up the property after the divorce over at Lampasas. I came here to Hackberry yesterday to start a new life, slinging hash at the Bluebonnet Café. And now this had to go and happen."

"Jest exactly how many, Miss—er—"

"Dilsey Dunnington's the name. Been robbed of a Jersey cow and a Jersey calf, my seed stock. Planned to let 'em multiply till I had enough cattle to quit hashin' and open a dairy."

"Well, Miss Dilsey Dunnington—" Here Powderhorn turned to Skeet Clymore and remarked in an aside, "Cute name, ain't it? . . . Well, Miss Dilsey, I got a surprise for you. As an official of the Hackberry government, I know I speak for the whole town when I say, 'Welcome to our fair city.' Had we any keys to same to pass out, I'd present you with the shiniest one. 'Stead, Hackberry wishes to return to you safe and sound, with its best compliments and 'thout any pound fees whatsoever, the two charter members of its future leadin' enterprise, Dunnington's Dairy. Please to step out to the lot."

At the sight of her cow and calf, contentedly gnawing opposite ends out of an old burlap bag that had once contained salt, Miss Dunnington was so overjoyed that impulsively she threw her arms around Powderhorn's neck and kissed him. It was a freckled neck, sporting the most memorable Adam's apple she'd ever seen. But she hugged it just the same, and gave him a big, lipstick-leaving kiss on the cheek.

When Skeet was telling the boys uptown about it later on, he said he'd have gladly given a wheel off his car to have had a camera in his hand. He said first Powderhorn looked scared, next he blushed, and then he just stood there and sort of whinnied.

From that moment on, the citizens of Hackberry had a new and absorbing topic of conversation. During the next few days, they noted with surprise that Powderhorn had got a haircut, begun to shave regularly, and had even washed his clothes. He cleaned his hat and had his boots half-soled. They came quickly to know that when, during the day, Powderhorn made a good catch of law-breaking animals, he'd take Dilsey to the movies that evening. Thereafter, if the weather was fine on Sundays, he usually took Dilsey for a ride in his old buggy during her off hours from the café. When, eventually, Powderhorn spent seventeen-fifty, of the twenty-three dollars he had on earth, for a weanling Jersey calf, everybody knew that calf was destined to be the third charter member of what he dreamed of as the Flinders-Dunnington dairy herd.

But the keystone in this arch of circumstantial evidence was fitted into place when Powderhorn began to set the cedar blocks on which his house was to be built. Hackberry knew precisely what that meant, just as well as if he'd carved "K. F. loves D. D." on the city-hall door with his pocketknife.

Hackberry was titillated by the thought of Powderhorn Flinders, Hackberry's own buckskin de Bergerac, in the role of an ardent lover. But to one person other than Powderhorn and Dilsey, who found Powderhorn's doglike devotion flattering at least, there was nothing funny about the affair at all. That person was Ruby Frazier, who cooked at the Bluebonnet.

For years Ruby and Powderhorn had been friends. They'd grown up together in two of the neighboring communities which dotted Hackberry's outer reaches: Ruby at Gunsight, and Powderhorn, only two miles distant, at Bug Tussle.

Now that Ruby had reached maturity, she was, alas, almost as plain as a woman can be. Her face had the usual number of features, but none of them really added anything in the way of comeliness. Her hair was precisely the color of Johnson-grass hay which had been cut on time, but, due to showers, baled three days too late. She kept it out of sight and the French fries by wearing a ribbon-laced boudoir cap

120

whenever she was presiding over the Bluebonnet's cookstove. But even if Ruby did have to endure being homely, there was, nevertheless, nobody in Hackberry who didn't love her. From her, goodness and warmth emerged just as naturally as did bale-to-the-acre cotton from the black, waxy land of the San Pedro River bottoms where she was born.

Ever since the days when, as youngsters, she and Powderhorn had run trotlines together, gathered pecans and herded the turkeys to the spots where the grasshoppers were thickest, Ruby had always had a warm spot in her heart for him. It was from Ruby that the flame-haired Myrtle had taken Powderhorn, then in his twenties. But Ruby's love for Powderhorn had never wavered. To her, he really was the dashing figure he fancied himself to be. Since Powderhorn thought of himself as, roughly speaking, a Texas Ranger, so did Ruby. And to Ruby, a Texas Ranger meant sheer daring and romance.

Ever since Ruby had moved to Hackberry and begun cooking at the Bluebonnet, she had saved the restaurant scraps for Powderhorn. On them each year he had raised and fattened a pig. But she was never so thoughtless in packaging these scraps as not to lay carefully on top the choice morsels, bits of cold meat, stale cake or biscuits, on which Powderhorn himself subsisted. Of her love for Powderhorn no one knew but Ruby herself. On his part, Powderhorn thought of Ruby as an old and trusted friend in need—in much the way, say, as he felt about Mr. Sibert, with whom he played checkers at the harness shop, or his faithful buckskin mare.

Weeks passed before Ruby could bring herself to mention *l'affaire* Dunnington to Powderhorn. Then, one morning when he brought his empty ten-gallon lard can to be exchanged for a similar one filled with scraps, Ruby, peeling potatoes, said casually, "Mornin', Kav. Hear you been seeing right smart of our new hasher."

"Folks will talk, won't they?" Powderhorn said, sampling a left-over slice of bacon on the back of the stove. "But seein' we're such old friends, Ruby, I'll admit to you that something new has come into my life. Used to, I just went around sorta . . . I don't know, plum flopsy doodle, you might say, not takin' no real interest in nothing. But now, when I wake up in the morning, my first thought is that somewhere over in Scuffle Gut Valley my little Dilsey is having her morning bath, then slipping into her stiff-starched green uniform. In my mind, I walk with her all the way here to the café. I imagine what we talk about. Hit's always kind of cute talk, and frisky. I guess the answer is that little rascal, Cupid, has done fogged one o' his arrows in me smack up to the feather on the end."

Ruby swallowed and went on peeling potatoes. From up front Dilsey trumpeted, "Stack a pair . . . one with bacon, one with air!"

"Coming up!" Ruby replied, and to Powderhorn, as she began preparing the order, explained, "That's two orders of hot cakes, one with bacon."

"Oh, I get the meaning of the poetry all right," said Powderhorn, fastidiously whittling a matchstick into a toothpick. "It's a blessing for you to have Dilsey here, Ruby, with that good clear voice o' hern. Must be awful to have to cook for a mumbler."

"I ain't complaining, Kav."

He got up. "I'll pick up my pig vittles in a minute, Ruby. Right now, I b'lieve I'll step up front and, as you might say, tilt a chili with my lady love."

As he left the kitchen, Ruby went into the pantry, locked the door, leaned her head against a shelf and, heartbroken, hopeless, wept.

As if Powderhorn's confession to Ruby about the joys of new love was not enough to crush her, there were the even less welcome confidences of the self-assured Dilsey which had to be borne. Dilsey made it clear that to her Powderhorn was a kind of devoted clown, a mildly comical convenience who'd build a house for her and whose knowledge of livestock would be useful in the dairy of which she dreamed.

Worse yet, Ruby could not avoid seeing that Steve Baker, the short, dark, slightly oily man who owned the Bluebonnet Café, was at least physically attracted to Dilsey. It was just as obvious that Dilsey's response to him was far more direct and electric than it would ever be to Powderhorn. Ruby alone knew that it was only with great difficulty that Dilsey kept Steve from ordering Powderhorn permanently off the premises.

However, Ruby did not know of the joke Steve Baker had up his sleeve. Just before daylight one morning, Steve, with Skeet Clymore as helper, went over to Sam Creadick's barn, put a rope on his milk cow and led her downtown. Sam Creadick was the town tough and its preeminent fist fighter. They arranged to get word to Powderhorn that there was a stray cow downtown, just as Sam went out to milk, and also just as the café was opening.

Everything worked according to schedule. Sam caught Powderhorn with the cow. But when the officer levied the customary fine, Sam Creadick simply snatched the lead rope away from him, and then yanked Powderhorn's beloved vintage sombrero down over his face with such violence that Powderhorn's head shot through the top.

Looking out over the top of the hat he now wore for a collar, Powderhorn saw Steve Baker out in front of the Bluebonnet, laughing and holding his sides. Both Dilsey and Ruby were there. There were tears in Ruby's eyes. Dilsey turned and went inside.

Powderhorn, braving out this humiliation as best he could, went right on working on the house. It was the single-wall sort. Those walls consisted of upright planks twelve inches wide and one inch thick, with tasteful little strips nailed over the cracks. A dog trot ran through the middle between the two rooms. It was the kind of house in which most old-time Texans were born and grew up, and which three handy carpenters can build in two days.

When Dilsey came down to look the job over, she, being not very learned in the fundamentals of house construction, was so well pleased that she gave Powderhorn permission to announce their engagement and approaching marriage on the following Wednesday, her next night off from the café.

But there was one problem concerning the house which did not attract her attention. That was the fact that Powderhorn was short of two-by-fours. With his wedding day only five days off and his funds almost at the point of exhaustion, Powderhorn had to economize the only place he could, which is to say, on ceiling joists, the timbers that reached from the top of one wall to the other and held the house together. Certain of Powderhorn's visitors who paused to watch the progress of the work said the house was dangerously shy of bracing. But Powderhorn, whose heart was pure, expected the few two-by-four ceiling joists he'd nailed up to hold with the Galahad-like strength of ten-by-tens.

All this, of course, was town talk too. And it was as the house neared completion that Steve Baker thought of his second joke.

Two nights before the wedding, after the café had closed, he fixed it up with Skeet Clymore as they sat in the kitchen, drinking.

"What we might do," Steve said, stopping to laugh now and then, "is just wait till the wedding gets going at the justice of the peace's office, then slip down and pry the nails loose in the ceiling joists. We could hold the house up with a lariat rope tied to the big oak tree just behind it. Then on the wedding night, as soon as the lamp's turned out, let 'er go. Everybody in town'll think it was because Powderhorn built it wrong. And we'd have something to laugh over for many a day."

The wedding was scheduled for six o'clock in the afternoon when the justice of the peace would have finished his day's official labors.

By a quarter to six, despite the presence of menacing black clouds in the north, an amiable, well-wishing, albeit jocular crowd was waiting outside Judge Flitkins' office.

Suddenly somebody yelled, "Here he comes on his buckskin mare!"

There, sure enough, just crossing the railroad tracks, came the bridegroom-to-be. As he drew nearer it could be seen he was wearing a Prince Albert coat that almost fitted him. In this get-up, complete with clean duck breeches, boots, patched hat and black string tie, he was, to say the least, a striking figure.

And now, from the café, which stood in the middle distance between the railroad tracks and the justice of the peace's office, Miss Dilsey Dunnington, vivid with paint and spangled with beads, switched out of the front of the café just as, a second later, Ruby, carrying a black-snake whip coiled under her sweater, slipped out the back.

As Dilsey approached the intersection, hurrying toward the crowd, the spectators saw Powderhorn give heel to the buckskin mare. Pounding on at a gallop, he overtook Dilsey in the middle of the street. Leaning far out of the saddle, he swept her up in his strong right arm and galloped her up to the red brick front of Judge Flitkins' office.

The crowd cheered so spiritedly that even Dilsey, her clothes rumpled, accepted these plaudits, and the sweeping action that had brought them on, with coy pleasure.

The first man to meet them, when they dismounted, was Sam Creadick. He was holding a brand-new pearl-gray hat in his hand.

"Please excuse my temper for bustin' your hat," Sam said. "I'm ashamed of my bad manners. This hat, just your size, is a Seven-X sombrero, bought and paid for by your friends and neighbors as a wedding present. Because I treated you so ornery here a while back, I asked to have the honor of presenting it to you to prove there warn't no hard feelings left in me." He handed Powderhorn the hat, adding, "Here's wishing you and that frisky, bright-sorrel gal o' yourn a heap o' fun in life."

Where Powderhorn would never have accepted anything personally from a man who'd done to him what Sam Creadick had done, this present was from the town. And a fifty-dollar Seven-X sombrero, presented by the town he loved and served, meant to Powderhorn what a red hat means to a new cardinal or a general's stars mean to a soldier. Powderhorn had, in a sense, been knighted. A lump, big and hard as a dirt-dauber's nest, came into his throat.

"Golly Moses!" he managed to say. "Thanks!"

"Put it on!" cried the crowd.

He complied. And it looked just right on his head.

A cheer went up.

"This way, Miss Dunnington," Powderhorn said to Dilsey, and the crowd opened up before them.

As they walked through the open double doors, Judge Flitkins put down his crossword puzzle and said, "Well, I wasn't expectin' no celebrities. But hit certainly looks like we got 'em."

"Aw, judge," Powderhorn said, dropping his eyes.

Dilsey Dunnington tittered.

"Well," Judge Flitkins said, "let's call in a couple of witnesses from the crowd and get the wedding started. . . . Got the ring, Kavanaugh?"

"Such as it is, judge."

"Well, I guess we're ready to go," his honor observed.

He began the ceremony. When he reached the point where he asked, "Can any o' you folks show just cause why this man and this woman should not be joined in matrimony?" there was a disturbance in the back of the crowd. Mayor Loren Bradshaw burst into the room.

"What's your objection to these folks aweddin', Mr. Mayor?" Judge Flitkins asked.

"Disaster has struck!" the mayor shouted wildly. "Every cow and horse and hog in Hackberry is stampeding down the main street. A Brahman bull just butted Harvey Bredt's surrey horse through the plate-glass window of the newspaper office. Fifteen hogs have raided the feed store. My own son's pet billy goat, may the Lord forgive us, has butted the back door of the post office open. Done et up nearly all the mail that come in on Number Three. . . . Kavanaugh Flinders, do your duty, and do it this very second!"

All eyes fastened upon Powderhorn. He was, at this moment, the most important man in town, its defender against an invasion. But he did not lose his head. He asked Dilsey to wait for him down at the house, where he would call for her as soon as possible, so the wedding could be continued. Then, after he had swung into the saddle, he began appointing deputies and grouping them into committees, one in charge of the capture of horses and mules, a second for cattle, and a third for hogs. A captain was named for each committee. There was also a small committee of scouts, charged with the duty of reconnaissance.

"Now, men," he said, as Lee or Eisenhower or Napoleon might have said, "we'll keep Judge Flitkins' office open and use it as general field headquarters. Folks can phone in their reports and complaints here. I'll keep in touch. Civilians will please keep off the streets, and all children in the house. Till that Bremmer bull is penned, I'll go with the cow committee. Now, committees all, ride!"

And they were off with a clatter of hoofs.

Powderhorn's chief concern was that Brahman bull, which, if not handled just right, might well kill somebody. A scout rode up, reporting the bull to be grazing on the vacant lot beside the dentist's office.

"Well, don't nobody bother him," Powderhorn ordered. "Drive all the loose cows to that tooth dentist's office. In a herd, that Bremmer may behave hisself."

As this work went on, Powderhorn kept the bull under personal surveillance. As he watched and waited, a flight of geese passed overhead, going south in a hurry. *Hope we can get that rascal penned before the norther gets here,* Powderhorn thought. *Sure can't be long now.* He was prompted less by the prudent geese and the towering black cloud bank in the north than by the fact that his infallible old bunions were killing him. The weather, they informed him, was due to change any minute now.

Half an hour later, the cattle and that ton-heavy Brahman bull had been drifted into the corrals of the Hackberry livestock-auction barn.

Other pens were filled with horses and swine, whose owners could come after them in the morning.

Powderhorn had just finished counting noses and snouts—had learned he'd clear the princely sum of sixty-three dollars in fees—when, with such appalling force that the auction barn sagged and three sheets of galvanized iron sailed off the roof, the norther hit. That first gust, he figured, must have been blowing forty miles an hour.

When Powderhorn and his committees, leaning into the icy wind, had made their way to the Bluebonnet Café, he invited all hands to be his guests at that most popular of Hackberry entertainments, an "oystcher" supper, to take place as soon as he'd fetched Dilsey back to Judge Flitkins' office and the wedding ceremony had been completed.

Just then Skeet Clymore burst into the restaurant. "Trouble's done broke out in a new place!" he yelled. "This blue norther was just too much for Powderhorn's house!"

Powderhorn grabbed him by the shirt. "Skeet," he cried, "you don't mean hit . . . hit blowed down!"

"I do mean it, Powderhorn. Blowed flitter flat."

This was very nearly a mortal blow. Powderhorn slumped in a chair. Almost instantly he leaped back to his feet.

"Where's Dilsey?"

"Under the house. And Steve Baker, too. Tried to drag 'em out by myself, but the roof was too heavy. Had to come up here for help."

Powderhorn's terror and agony had now reached the ultimate pitch.

"Cancel the oystchers!" he cried, and ran out the door, his committees hard on his heels.

The first thing they saw when they turned their flashlights on the flattened house was a broken lariat tied to the roof, the other end of which had been made fast to the big post-oak tree at the back door. Then, beneath the wreckage, Dilsey and Steve could be heard groaning and moaning.

Once they'd been lifted from the debris, Steve Baker tried to speak, but fainted dead away. Dilsey, her wedding dress dragging the ground in slivers and with a currycomb tangled in her skirt, was in better condition.

"Oh, you poor little darling Dilsey!" Powderhorn wailed.

For a moment, Dilsey, slightly cattywampus due to the fact that the falling roof had broken the high heel off her right slipper, simply stood

127

there and looked at Powderhorn with glazed eyes, the left one, as it happened, now blackened.

"Oh, speak to me, little precious, broke-up bride!" he implored.

By way of reply, Dilsey picked up a one-by-four pine plank, swung it with whistling power, and split it over Powderhorn's head.

As he settled to the earth, Miss Dilsey Dunnington paid her respects to Hackberry and its people in language both vivid and charged with emotion. Among other things, she said that Hackberry was not even a fit place in which to raise a decent calf, and that she meant to load hers in her trailer at daybreak and head back to Lampasas.

The next morning early, Powderhorn dropped into the kitchen of the Bluebonnet Café, his body wrapped in his old World War I khaki overcoat, his head tied up in a rag. Ruby was cleaning the top of the stove.

"Hi, Ruby."

"Mornin', Kav. . . . A little coffee?"

"Be mighty good against this weather."

"Steve ain't here this morning, naturally. Won't be for a couple of days. How about some sausage and eggs on the house?"

"Reckon you ought to?"

"Sure. And a stack of buckwheats . . . just for good measure."

"Well, the Lord knows, Ruby, I don't want to be rude."

She dropped three thick pats of sausage into the skillet.

"I reckon," Powderhorn commented, inhaling the first warm, curling smell of frying sausage, "folks was right about the bracing on the house. But what I can't figure is how all that livestock got loose and broke up the weddin'."

Into a second skillet Ruby poured buckwheat batter from a white porcelain pitcher which had blue piping around the lip.

"It's purely a mystery, Kavanaugh. The good Lord knows, of course, but can be counted on, I rest assured, not to spill the beans." Still watching her cooking, she asked, over her shoulder, "Discouraged about your house, Kav?"

"I'm having to stand a mighty lot o' funning."

"Well, you recollect that my poor dead daddy who sits on high used to be a carpenter, don't you?"

"As good a one as ever drove a nail."

128

"Well, after you left Bug Tussle and moved to town, I used to help him. Near about do a man's work."

"I never knowed that."

"Well, I did. Didn't seem to be much call for female carpenters, though, so I give it up and commenced cooking." Ruby turned the pancakes. "Your heart broke about Dilsey?"

"It's kind of hard to go on loving a girl that uses your head to split kindlin' on. And yet," he added dreamily, "I'll swear, she had one of the finest shocks of red hair that ever hit this town."

"That's kind of a weakness of yours, ain't it, Kav?"

"Ever since a long time ago, Ruby, it always seemed like I was meant to have a redheaded wife."

"I know, Kav. Heard you say it many's the time."

"And the awful part is I don't learn no sense. I still want one worse than anything on earth."

"Honest, Kav?"

"Hit's true, Ruby, gospel true."

Ruby smiled like the sun at dawn. She pulled off her boudoir cap. Her hair was as red as the firebush that grew in Powderhorn's yard. His eyes bugged out so far you could have roped them with a grapevine.

"Why, Ruby! It's just like Myrtle's was . . . and Dilsey's too!"

"It was due to be, Kav. It came out of the selfsame bottle those other girls used. Put it on last night after I heard about Dilsey bustin' that plank over your head. Kind of thought today might find you looking for a new lady friend."

"Take off that cook apron, honey. At last," Powderhorn Flinders said, full of sudden and exciting understanding, "the truth has broke into this old hard head o' mine. Let's go knocking on the county clerk's door and get us a set of licenses. You and me can make out in the tent till we get our house rebuilt."

Ruby's heart was listening to rhapsodic music that echoed all over heaven.

"Not," she said dreamily, "until you've had your breakfast. It's hot and waiting for you. Here, Kav," she said softly, sinking on her stool, her eyes alight as she wiped the grease from her hands, "try some of these molasses."

"Well," said Powderhorn lovingly, beaming, "if you insist . . . Miss Ruby Redhead Flinders."

KATHERINE ANNE PORTER, Texas' greatest contribution to the short story, was born at Indian Creek, Brown County, May 15, 1894. She herself is authority for the statement that she began to write stories before she was four years old. One of the reasons for her exceptional position among short-story writers is, no doubt, the fact that she did not try to publish until she was thirty and that she destroyed whole trunkfuls of manuscripts. Another reason is her admirable independence as an artist. Though widely read in the works of other writers and though often compared, favorably, with Katherine Mansfield, she is imitative of no one and is a member of no literary school. As she puts it, "I knew no other writers and had no one to consult with on the single issue of my life."

The events of Miss Porter's outer life are not very important to the student of her writing. She was educated in Southern convent schools. She lived for a time in Dallas and Fort Worth. The World War I influenza epidemic nearly finished her off. Like her great-great-great-grandfather, Daniel Boone, she spent fifteen years (1920–37) at what she calls wandering about, in Europe and Mexico, earning a meager living from editing and journalistic writing. She helped popularize Mexican art in this country, and her first published stories, in *Asia* and *Century*, were on Mexican subjects. She has been twice married and twice divorced. She held Guggenheim fellowships in 1931 and 1938, and a Book-of-the-Month Club fellowship in 1937, awarded "for the precise and delicate art of her stories," and a Library of Congress fellowship in regional American literature in 1944. Though on record as saying that writing can't be taught, until 1949 she was writer-in-residence and lecturer on literature at Stanford University. She was awarded the first gold medal of the Society for Libraries of New York University in 1940 for her book *Pale Horse, Pale Rider*. She has been given the durable monument of a master's thesis on her work (by Hazel Moss Irby, University of Texas, 1951). And, finally, her native state has honored her with the new A. Harris award, Texas' own Nobel Prize, for a nationally significant career in the creative arts.

Few literary reputations of such stature are based upon so slender a published production. Miss Porter's books, of short and not so short stories, are *Flowering Judas* (1930), which won her a high place among American writers of the short story, *Hacienda* (1934), *Noon Wine* (1937), *Pale Horse, Pale Rider* (1939), and *The Leaning Tower, and Other Stories* (1944). The novel which has been perennially expected from her, in 1940 tentatively called *Promised Land* but in 1942 *No Safe Harbor,* has not yet appeared. She translated the Mexican picaresque novel *The Itching Parrot* (1942) and edited and translated a collection of French songs (1933). Something of the quality of her mind may be inferred from the fact that for twenty-five years she has been working, off and on, on a study of the New England Puritan divine, Cotton Mather.

The strands of Miss Porter's inner life, her heritage and memories, however, are of utmost importance, for it is of these that she has woven some of her best writing, that about Texas and Louisiana. Her true grandmother, who came to Texas from Kentucky, probably sat as model for the formidable Miss Sophia Jane of nine of the stories, a matriarch who "planted five orchards in three states." "All my past," the author has said, "is usable." Another group of stories focuses on Miss Sophia's granddaughter, Miranda, who bears more than a family resemblance to the author herself. The story here included, "The Grave," which first appeared in the *Virginia Quarterly Review,* treats the nine-year-old Miranda's approach to adolescence, with both beauty and wonder.

The Grave

THE GRANDFATHER, dead for more than thirty years, had been twice
disturbed in his long repose by the constancy and possessiveness of
his widow. She removed his bones first to Louisiana and then to Texas
as if she had set out to find her own burial place, knowing well she
would never return to the places she had left. In Texas she set up a
small cemetery in a corner of her first farm, and as the family connection grew, and oddments of relations came over from Kentucky to settle,
it contained at last about twenty graves. After the grandmother's death,
part of her land was to be sold for the benefit of certain of her children,
and the cemetery happened to lie in the part set aside for sale. It was
necessary to take up the bodies and bury them again in the family plot
in the big new public cemetery, where the grandmother had been buried.
At last her husband was to lie beside her for eternity, as she had planned.

The family cemetery had been a pleasant small neglected garden
of tangled rose bushes and ragged cedar trees and cypress, the simple
flat stones rising out of uncropped sweet-smelling wild grass. The graves
were lying open and empty one burning day when Miranda and her
brother Paul, who often went together to hunt rabbits and doves,
propped their twenty-two Winchester rifles carefully against the rail
fence, climbed over and explored among the graves. She was nine years
old and he was twelve.

They peered into the pits all shaped alike with such purposeful ac-
curacy, and looking at each other with pleased adventurous eyes, they
said in solemn tones: "These were graves!" trying by words to shape
a special, suitable emotion in their minds, but they felt nothing except
an agreeable thrill of wonder: they were seeing a new sight, doing some-

From *The Leaning Tower and Other Stories,* copyright 1944, by Katherine Anne
Porter; reprinted by permission of Harcourt, Brace and Company, Inc.

thing they had not done before. In them both there was also a small disappointment at the entire commonplaceness of the actual spectacle. Even if it had once contained a coffin for years upon years, when the coffin was gone a grave was just a hole in the ground. Miranda leaped into the pit that had held her grandfather's bones. Scratching around aimlessly and pleasurably as any young animal, she scooped up a lump of earth and weighed it in her palm. It had a pleasantly sweet, corrupt smell, being mixed with cedar needles and small leaves, and as the crumbs fell apart, she saw a silver dove no larger than a hazel nut, with spread wings and a neat fan-shaped tail. The breast had a deep round hollow in it. Turning it up to the fierce sunlight, she saw that the inside of the hollow was cut in little whorls. She scrambled out, over the pile of loose earth that had fallen back into one end of the grave, calling to Paul that she had found something, he must guess what. . . . His head appeared smiling over the rim of another grave. He waved a closed hand at her. "I've got something too!" They ran to compare treasures, making a game of it, so many guesses each, all wrong, and a final showdown with opened palms. Paul had found a thin wide gold ring carved with intricate flowers and leaves. Miranda was smitten at sight of the ring and wished to have it. Paul seemed more impressed by the dove. They made a trade, with some little bickering. After he had got the dove in his hand, Paul said, "Don't you know what this is? This is a screw head for a *coffin!* . . . I'll bet nobody else in the world has one like this!"

Miranda glanced at it without covetousness. She had the gold ring on her thumb; it fitted perfectly. "Maybe we ought to go now," she said, "maybe one of the niggers 'll see us and tell somebody." They knew the land had been sold, the cemetery was no longer theirs, and they felt like trespassers. They climbed back over the fence, slung their rifles loosely under their arms—they had been shooting at targets with various kinds of firearms since they were seven years old—and set out to look for the rabbits and doves or whatever small game might happen along. On these expeditions Miranda always followed at Paul's heels along the path, obeying instructions about handling her gun when going through fences; learning how to stand it up properly so it would not slip and fire unexpectedly; how to wait her time for a shot and not just bang away in the air without looking, spoiling shots for Paul, who really could hit things if given a chance. Now and then, in her excitement at seeing birds whizz up suddenly before her face, or a rabbit leap across her very toes, she lost her head, and almost without sighting she flung her rifle up and pulled the trigger. She hardly ever hit any sort of mark. She had no proper sense of hunting at all. Her brother would be often completely disgusted with her. "You don't care whether you get your bird or not," he said. "That's no way to hunt." Miranda could not understand his indignation. She had seen him smash his hat and yell with fury when he had missed his aim. "What I like about shooting," said Miranda, with exasperating inconsequence, "is pulling the trigger and hearing the noise."

"Then, by golly," said Paul, "whyn't you go back to the range and shoot at bulls-eyes?"

"I'd just as soon," said Miranda, "only like this, we walk around more."

"Well, you just stay behind and stop spoiling my shots," said Paul, who, when he made a kill, wanted to be certain he had made it. Miranda, who alone brought down a bird once in twenty rounds, always claimed as her own any game they got when they fired at the same moment. It was tiresome and unfair and her brother was sick of it.

"Now, the first dove we see, or the first rabbit, is mine," he told her. "And the next will be yours. Remember that and don't get smarty."

"What about snakes?" asked Miranda idly. "Can I have the first snake?"

Waving her thumb gently and watching her gold ring glitter, Miranda lost interest in shooting. She was wearing her summer roughing outfit: dark blue overalls, a light blue shirt, a hired-man's straw hat, and thick brown sandals. Her brother had the same outfit except his was a sober hickorynut color. Ordinarily Miranda preferred her overalls to any other dress, though it was making rather a scandal in the countryside, for the year was 1903, and in the back country the law of female decorum had teeth in it. Her father had been criticized for letting his girls dress like boys and go careering around astride barebacked horses. Big sister Maria, the really independent and fearless one, in spite of her rather affected ways, rode at a dead run with only a rope knotted around her horse's nose. It was said the motherless family was running down, with the grandmother no longer there to hold it together. It was known that she had discriminated against her son Harry in her will, and that he was in straits about money. Some of his old neighbors reflected with vicious satisfaction that now he would probably not be so stiffnecked, nor have any more high-stepping horses either. Miranda knew this, though she could not say how. She had met along the road old women of the kind who smoked corn-cob pipes, who had treated her grandmother with most sincere respect. They slanted their gummy old eyes side-ways at the granddaughter and said, "Ain't you ashamed of yoself, Missy? It's against the Scriptures to dress like that. Whut yo Pappy thinkin about?" Miranda, with her powerful social sense, which was like a fine set of antennae radiating from every pore of her skin, would feel ashamed because she knew well it was rude and ill-bred to shock anybody, even bad-tempered old crones, though she had faith in her father's judgment and was perfectly comfortable in the clothes. Her father had said, "They're just what you need, and they'll save your dresses for school. . . ." This sounded quite simple and natural to her. She had been brought up in rigorous economy. Wastefulness was vulgar. It was also a sin. These were truths; she had heard them repeated many times and never once disputed.

Now the ring, shining with the serene purity of fine gold on her rather grubby thumb, turned her feelings against her overalls and sockless feet, toes sticking through the thick brown leather straps. She wanted to go back to the farmhouse, take a good cold bath, dust herself with plenty of Maria's violet talcum powder—provided Maria was not present to object, of course—put on the thinnest, most becoming dress she owned, with a big sash, and sit in a wicker chair under the trees. . . . These things were not all she wanted, of course; she had vague stirrings of desire for luxury and a grand way of living which could not take precise form in her imagination but were founded on family legend of past wealth and leisure. These immediate comforts were what she could have, and she wanted them at once. She lagged rather far behind Paul, and once she thought of just turning back without a word and going home. She stopped, thinking that Paul would never do that to her, and so she would have to tell him. When a rabbit leaped, she let Paul have it without dispute. He killed it with one shot.

When she came up with him, he was already kneeling, examining the wound, the rabbit trailing from his hands. "Right through the head," he said complacently, as if he had aimed for it. He took out his sharp, competent bowie knife and started to skin the body. He did it very cleanly and quickly. Uncle Jimbilly knew how to prepare the skins so that Miranda always had fur coats for her dolls, for though she never cared much for her dolls she liked seeing them in fur coats. The children knelt facing each other over the dead animal. Miranda watched admiringly while her brother stripped the skin away as if he were taking off a glove. The flayed flesh emerged dark scarlet, sleek, firm; Miranda with thumb and finger felt the long fine muscles with the silvery flat strips binding them to the joints. Brother lifted the oddly bloated belly. "Look," he said, in a low amazed voice. "It was going to have young ones."

Very carefully he slit the thin flesh from the center ribs to the flanks, and a scarlet bag appeared. He slit again and pulled the bag open, and there lay a bundle of tiny rabbits, each wrapped in a thin scarlet veil. The brother pulled these off and there they were, dark gray, their sleek wet down lying in minute even ripples, like a baby's head just washed, their unbelievably small delicate ears folded close, their little blind faces almost featureless.

Miranda said, "Oh, I want to *see*," under her breath. She looked and looked—excited but not frightened, for she was accustomed to the sight of animals killed in hunting—filled with pity and astonishment and a kind of shocked delight in the wonderful little creatures for their own sakes, they were so pretty. She touched one of them ever so carefully, "Ah, there's blood running over them," she said and began to tremble without knowing why. Yet she wanted most deeply to see and to know. Having seen, she felt at once as if she had known all along. The very memory of her former ignorance faded, she had always known just this. No one had ever told her anything outright, she had been rather unobservant of the animal life around her because she was so accustomed to animals. They seemed simply disorderly and unaccountably rude in their habits, but altogether natural and not very interesting. Her brother had spoken as if he had known about everything all along. He may have seen all this before. He had never said a word to her, but she knew now a part at least of what he knew. She understood a little of the secret, formless intuitions in her own mind and body, which had been clearing up, taking form, so gradually and so steadily she had not realized that she was learning what she had to know. Paul said cautiously, as if he were talking about something forbidden: "They were just about ready to be born." His voice dropped on the last word. "I know," said Miranda, "like kittens. I know, like babies." She was quietly and terribly agitated, standing again with her rifle under her arm, looking down at the bloody heap. "I don't want the skin," she said, "I won't have it." Paul buried the young rabbits again in their mother's body, wrapped the skin around her, carried her to a clump of sage bushes, and hid her away. He came out again at once and said to Miranda, with an eager friendliness, a confidential tone quite unusual in him, as if he were taking her into an important secret on equal terms: "Listen now. Now you listen to me, and don't ever forget. Don't you ever tell a living soul that you saw this. Don't tell a soul. Don't tell Dad because I'll get into trouble. He'll say I'm leading you into things you ought not to do. He's always saying that. So now don't you go and forget and blab out sometime the way you're always doing. . . . Now, that's a secret. Don't you tell."

Miranda never told, she did not even wish to tell anybody. She thought about the whole worrisome affair with confused unhappiness for a few days. Then it sank quietly into her mind and was heaped over by accumulated thousands of impressions, for nearly twenty years. One day she was picking her path among the puddles and crushed refuse of a market street in a strange city of a strange country, when without warning, plain and clear in its true colors as if she looked through a frame upon a scene that had not stirred nor changed since the moment it happened, the episode of that far-off day leaped from its burial place before her mind's eye. She was so reasonlessly horrified she halted suddenly staring, the scene before her eyes dimmed by the vision back of them. An Indian vendor had held up before her a tray of dyed sugar sweets, in the shapes of all kinds of small creatures: birds, baby chicks, baby rabbits, lambs, baby pigs. They were in gay colors and smelled of vanilla, maybe. . . . It was a very hot day and the smell in the market, with its piles of raw flesh and wilting flowers, was like the mingled sweetness and corruption she had smelled that other day in the empty cemetery at home: the day she had remembered always until now vaguely as the time she and her brother had found treasure in the opened graves. Instantly upon this thought the dreadful vision faded, and she saw clearly her brother, whose childhood face she had forgotten, standing again in the blazing sunshine, again twelve years old, a pleased sober smile in his eyes, turning the silver dove over and over in his hands.

WINIFRED SANFORD

WINIFRED MAHON SANFORD was born in Duluth, Minnesota, March 16, 1890. After graduation from the Duluth Central High School, she attended Mount Holyoke College for a year, 1908–1909, and the University of Michigan, from which she received her B.A. degree in 1913. She taught school for a short time. Then, in 1916–17, she went to New York for a year's work at the Library School of the New York Public Library. In 1917 she married Wayland Hall Sanford, a lawyer. She came to Texas in 1920, living in Wichita Falls until 1931, after that, in Longview and Dallas. She is a member of the Texas Institute of Letters.

Mrs. Sanford's career as a writer began in 1925 with the publication of her short story "Wreck" in the old *American Mercury*. In 1926 four of her stories, in the *Mercury* and *Woman's Home Companion,* were given two-star ratings. During the twenties and thirties she contributed both fiction and articles to various periodicals. A novel, which has never been published, attracted the favorable attention of H. L. Mencken.

Although her total output has not been large, Mrs. Sanford unquestionably deserves a place in this anthology for her excellent study of the effect of newly discovered Texas oil on the life of a simple farm woman. "Windfall," which will remain something of a classic in the literature of the oil fields, has been twice reprinted.

Windfall

ALTHOUGH THE WELL had come in soon after midnight, and it was now the middle of the afternoon, Cora had not seen it. At first she was afraid she would be in the way. Afterward, she was too busy in the kitchen, for beside her own family she had the crews to feed, and six or eight oil men who couldn't take the time to drive thirty miles to town for their meals. And immediately after dinner, the girls, who were sometimes willing to help her, went off to the well and left her alone with the work. "I'll go down when I finish the dishes," Cora promised herself.

By the time the work was done, however, she was tired, soiled and sweaty, and the pasture was full of people who had driven in to see the well. She would have been ashamed to go down as she was. "I'll get cleaned up after a while, and then I'll go down," she thought, as she threw the scraps to the chickens gathered around the doorstep.

With the empty bucket in her hand she stopped for a moment in the doorway, under the newspaper fringe which rattled in the hot wind, and gazed into the far corner of the pasture. She could not see the well from the house; she could see only the mast of the drilling machine and the shiny new storage tank rising above the cluster of cars and people. Luke, she knew, was there, and her three girls, and her two boys, and most of her neighbors, for it was Sunday, and no one was working in the fields.

She went through the kitchen and into the bed-room. It was fully as hot as the kitchen, but it was dark, except for the pattern of the sun on the cracked window shade, and there was a bed to lie upon. Cora sat down on the edge of it and took off her house slippers. Her

Reprinted from the *American Mercury*, June, 1928; copyright 1928 by the author and used by her permission.

bare toes felt as though they had been glued together with the heat. She stretched them, and rubbed them with a towel she found on the floor; then she lay down on the crumpled sheet with her hand on her cheek.

Now and then, while she rested, she rubbed the side of her nose, or the corner of her mouth, or her neck. She was very tired, and this was the first time she had had the bed to herself since the drillers had come, three weeks ago, and had taken the other bed-room and the other two beds. The girls had moved in with her, and the four of them had lain, night after night, across the bed in a row, with their feet hanging over the side, while Luke and the boys had slept on pallets spread down on the kitchen floor.

Cora got up after a few minutes and began to put the room in order. The girls had gone off without making the bed or picking up their clothes, and Cora had to hang their pink nightgowns behind the curtain in the corner, and stuff their stockings in the dresser drawers, and empty the slop jar, which had stood all day full of dirty water, and wipe out the bowl and the soap dish before she could bathe herself.

The cool water made her feel a little better. She sat as long as she dared with her feet in the bowl, but she knew she must hurry if she were to see the well before supper, so she dried herself, after a moment, and put on her clean underwear, and sprinkled a very little of the girls' talcum powder on her neck and arms.

When she had put on her black shoes and stockings and her gray gingham dress, she took her sunbonnet from its nail in the kitchen and went outside. The chickens were still scratching about in the yard, and stepping into the muddy patches where she had emptied the slop jar. They came running up to her, but she shooed them away. She crossed the yard, passed the barn, skirted the wheat stubble, and entered the pasture.

Cars were standing everywhere, like shiny-backed beetles, in the sun. She could smell the hot leather, and the grease and the paint. When she came nearer, she saw the people—the city people, first, spreading rugs in the shade of their sedans, and drinking ice water from thermos jugs, and eating sandwiches and reading the Sunday papers. A little farther on she saw the country people—the men with their suspenders crossed on their backs, and the women with their flowered hats and their black shoes and stockings.

Cora did not really want to speak to any of them. She was always timid in a crowd, and conscious of her sunbonnet and her gingham dress, and lately, since she had lost her teeth, she was ashamed for anyone to see her mouth. They saw her, however, and would not let her pass.

"Say," they said, all of them looking her up and down, "you won't be speaking to us, Mrs. Ponder, now you've got a well on your place. You and Luke will be too good for us poor folks."

Cora stood shame-faced, with her fingers over her mouth. "Oh, I don't know," she said. She was very much embarrassed. "I come down to see it myself."

But she could not see it just then, because the men were in the way. There were oil men from town, with khaki breeches stuffed into their high boots, and East Indian helmets perched on their heads; there were farmers with creases in diamond-shaped patterns on their necks; and there were men in overalls, dodging the others while they worked with pieces of iron pipe.

"When they move to one side," she thought, "then I'll go over and see it."

Meanwhile she must find her girls. She didn't like to have them running around in a crowd like this with nobody to look after them. It wasn't right. They were dancing, when she found them, some time later, dancing on the grass with boys she didn't recognize. There was a phonograph playing, and they were dancing . . . on Sunday afternoon! Cora was uneasy, and yet she didn't have the heart to stop them. They looked so pretty with their curly heads and their bright dresses and their silk stockings and their fancy kid slippers. She watched them for a time, standing beside an empty automobile, but if they saw her, they gave no sign of it.

She walked back to the country women at last, and sat down with them on the grass, pulling her skirt carefully over her knees. "I wouldn't mind seeing that oil with my own eyes," she said. Yet she did not like to intrude where the men were gathered. They were all laughing and talking and spitting on the ground, and she knew they would be uncomfortable if she joined them. They would clear their throats, and mumble good afternoon, and touch their hats. And Luke would frown at her.

She saw Luke, now, hobbling around and smiling foolishly at his neighbors, as though this well were some joke he had played on them. And she saw Whitney, her younger boy, in his bare feet and dirty overalls, helping the men with the pipe. The older boy was nowhere to be seen. Cora sighed, because she was afraid he had gone off somewhere with one of the girls. She had seen him change his shirt, after dinner, and shave, and oil his pompadour, but she hadn't dared to ask him where he was going. He wouldn't have answered her, probably, if she had.

The women among whom she was sitting began to ask her questions. They wanted to know what she would do with the money from the well. Cora answered them with her hand over her mouth, "I don't know," she said, feeling her face grow red. "I don't rightly know what we'll do." She did not like to speak of her teeth, and yet she could think of nothing else she particularly wanted. "We might get a phonograph for the girls," she said at last.

The women were astonished. "Why, haven't you got a phonograph, Mrs. Ponder? You haven't! Nor a radio, neither! Well, what do you know!"

"We might get a radio, too," said Cora.

"Those girls of yours will sure spend the money, Mrs. Ponder; you can leave it to them."

Cora stiffened at that. "I'd be glad for them to spend it," she said. "I've never been one to begrudge things to my children."

They shook their heads at that, and said it wasn't always a good thing for children to have too much. "They don't have the respect for you they should have, Mrs. Ponder."

Cora looked at the ground. "I know," she said; "I know." She was beginning to wish she had not come down to the well. She might have known the women would be like this. And yet what they said was true enough. She had spoiled her children, and often she was sorry and ashamed. She ought to have made them help today with the work. She ought to have made them stop dancing . . . on Sunday, too, where everyone could see them. And it was true, what they said, that the girls would have had more respect for her, instead of always being ashamed of her. And yet . . .

142

"They'll want that you should move into the city; that's what they'll want," said one of the women.

Cora winced, because that very thought had been troubling her all day. "It's not likely that we'll be moving to the city," she said.

"They'll want a fine house in the city, Mrs. Ponder," said another woman, "and lots of parties and dancing."

Cora did not answer, and presently they left her alone.

She had nothing to do. She watched a red ant travel through the grass with a bit of wheat in his mouth. She watched a cricket scamper past on his high stilts. Finally, she pulled a blade of dusty grass and sucked it, and watched the cars stream into the pasture from the main road. There were Fords filled with farm boys, and smart roadsters from the city, and trucks with the dust as thick as moss on their greasy wheels. They left the gates open and drove where they liked, breaking down the limbs of the mesquite, and staining the grass with drippings of black grease. The crowd was everywhere, trampling the cotton in the next field, climbing through the barbed wire fences, peering into the barn, chasing the chickens in the yard, and marching into the house, even, to use the telephone.

Cora saw the people from the next farm drive up in their touring car, with the idiot boy gaping on the back seat. When they climbed out he followed them about like a foolish dog, grinning at everyone he met. From the back, in his new gray suit and his straw hat, he looked like anyone else; it was only when you saw his face, or his gait, that you suspected.

A few minutes later she saw Jasper Gooley drive up in his blue and yellow coupé. She had known Jasper when he was a boy on his father's farm, long before anyone knew there was oil under the cotton. Old Mr. Gooley had been the poorest of them all. All his life he had lived in a one-room shack, with no paint on its boards, and no grass in the yard, and no trees—not even a red cedar to break the wind in the winter or to give a little shade in the summer. It was just a bare shack standing on posts, so that the chickens could run underneath to get out of the sun.

Jasper was a boy then, like her Whitney. Cora used to see him lazily chopping cotton, in ragged overalls and a torn Mexican hat. Once she had passed him, on her way home from town, lying on his back in the ditch, where it was shady, and he had looked up at her and laughed. That was before he was old enough for girls.

143

Cora wondered sometimes what would have happened to Jasper if there had not been oil on his father's land. He would have had to stay at home, then, and run the farm, and make a living, and no doubt he would have settled down like his neighbors, with a wife and a family. Instead of that he had rented the farm to tenants. The very week after his father's death, Jasper had rented the farm and had gone to the city. People shook their heads now when they spoke of him. They said that he was wild, that he drank, and that he always had one woman or another on the seat beside him when he drove on the country roads. They said he had had an affair with a married woman in town, which had cost him ten thousand dollars in cash. Perhaps it was true, and perhaps it wasn't; Cora didn't know.

At any rate he had a woman with him now, a large blonde woman in a red hat. Cora saw her squint in a little mirror while she dabbed powder on her nose. She saw Jasper's Panama hat, and his fat hands resting on the wheel, and his puffy cheeks; and when he climbed out of his car, backward, she saw his blue and white striped seersucker trousers, and his white silk shirt, and his white shoes.

She was glad when Jasper passed her by without speaking, for she never knew how to act with city people, or what to say to them. It suited her much better to follow them at a little distance as they made their way toward the well. Now that Jasper had brought a woman among the men, she didn't mind going nearer.

She could see the pipe now, sticking up from the ground, and bending over at the top, and she thought she saw a black stream flowing into the tank below, but Jasper stepped in front of her, before she could be sure. She stood behind him, one hand supporting her elbow and the other supporting her cheek under her sunbonnet, waiting for him to move.

She felt a little guilty. She knew that Luke would think she ought to go back where she belonged, yet she did want to see the oil. She wanted to see what it looked like. She felt as she did sometimes at funerals, when she wanted a last look at a face she had known, yet hated to push herself forward.

She was feeling more and more out of place when she saw Whitney coming toward her, stepping over pipes and wrenches, and elbowing the crowd. Even in his old clothes, she thought proudly, he was the best looking of her children. The others were all a little too thin and sharp-featured, but Whitney was going to be broad and handsome, and sure of himself. He came up to her now, before everyone, not caring what they thought.

"Say, mama," he said, "did you see the oil, did you?"

"No, son, I haven't seen it yet."

"Come on, then, and look at it."

He took her straight up to the tank. "Look in there, mama," he said.

Cora glanced quickly about her to see if anyone disapproved before she dared to lean over the rim.

"See it?" asked Whitney.

She saw it . . . thick black oil, with a dirty scum on the top. The smell of it made her feel sick at her stomach.

"I see it, son; I see it."

Just then a sudden stream gushed from the mouth of the pipe, green in the sunlight. Whitney took her hand and held her finger in the stream.

"You taste it, mama," he said, eagerly.

Cora touched her finger to her tongue. It tasted like kerosene, and she had to spit it out on the grass.

"It's oil, mama," said Whitney. "See?"

"Yes, son, it's oil."

He wanted to tell her all about it. "They think it's going to make a hundred barrels," he said. "And they're going to drill another one over yonder where you see the stake."

"Yes, son, yes."

"And after that they're going to drill to the south. They're going to drill a lot of them."

"I see."

Cora was beginning to feel very uncomfortable. She felt conspicuous, standing here where everyone could look at her, with no teeth in her mouth, and the oil still greasy on her finger. She had to stoop, at last, and wipe it off, secretly, on her stocking. Even then a little of it remained, black under her nail.

She was really glad, at last, to find an excuse to back away from the men. She saw part of a newspaper impaled on a mesquite thorn, beyond the well. She walked over to it, without attracting anyone's attention, and picked it up. Then she saw a scrap of shiny brown paper and a wad of tinfoil, and beyond that, in a clump of cactus, a piece of

145

sandwich wrapping, streaked with yellow salad dressing. There was an empty bottle lying under the wrapping, and bits of broken glass shining here and there all over the pasture. "Tomorrow," thought Cora, "after the washing is finished and on the line, I'll bring a bucket and gather it up before the cattle get into it."

On the top of a little rise, not far from the house, she stopped and looked back at the well. Luke and Whitney, she saw, were talking to Jasper Gooley. Jasper had his left hand on the shoulder of the woman he had brought with him from town; and as Cora watched, he crossed one white foot over the other and put his right hand on Whitney's shoulder. Whitney stood tall under his weight. Cora wondered, with fear in her heart, what Jasper was saying to her son.

JOHN WATSON

JOHN CHERRY WATSON was born in Smithville, Bastrop County, July 18, 1909, and has lived most of his life in the East Texas farm country of which he usually writes. After graduation from the Smithville High School, he took his B.A. at Southwest Texas State Teachers College, San Marcos, in 1933. His master's thesis at the University of Texas, where he took most of the course work required for the Ph.D., is "Women in the Life of Lord Byron" (1935).

How Watson felt about his first teaching job can probably be guessed from his story "The Man Teacher," in the *Southwest Review*. As he points out, he has taught (mathematics as well as English) in every type of educational institution in Texas, from a one-man rural school to the state university. Formerly on the English staff at Texas Agricultural and Mechanical College, he spent 1947–48 on a Eugene F. Saxton Memorial Fund fellowship awarded by Harper and Brothers. The result was *The Red Dress* (1949), his first novel, which in Aunt Dode and Uncle Deck Cherry is a testament to the strength and beauty of rural life.

Then followed a series of short stories, a number of them humorous, first in quality magazines such as the *Southwest Review*, *Harper's*, and the *Atlantic*, and later in *Collier's*, *Esquire*, and *Today's Woman*. Almost all of Watson's stories have been rated "distinctive" in *Best American Short Stories* of the year of their appearance. "The Gun on the Table" was reprinted in Herschel Brickell's *Prize Stories of 1948*.

Watson lives in Austin, where he is associate professor of English at the University of Texas, teaching creative writing and, with others, Mr. Dobie's course "Life and Literature of the Southwest." The scene of "Benny and the Tar-Baby" is the farm country "fifty or sixty miles east of Austin" which Watson employed in *The Red Dress* and in his second novel, which has been delivered to his publishers. The limitation of the narrative point of view to the boy Benny makes for pleasant ironies and for much of the story's humor. But in the background, always carrying through, is the author's preference for simple country rather than strident city life. It is not surprising that he has built his own stone house on Lake Travis.

Benny and the Tar-Baby

But if you shoot the Princess," I told Uncle Mark, "then the Tar-Baby will surely die. He will starve to death, because he ain't old enough yet to ketch on to how to eat grass and corn and stuff like his ma can. Seems like he ain't got the hang of it yet."

I explained it to Uncle Mark, but it didn't make no difference. He had his head set on shootin her. "That-air mare is a dangerous animal," he said. "She might up and kill somebody else. The colt will have to git along the best way he can."

"Maybe she didn't aim to do it," I told him. "Maybe it was an accident; she stepped in a gopher hole and stumbled, and he fell off and hit his head on the rock."

But he never give in. He just set there in the old rawhide-bottom chair by the cook-stove with his legs crossed and peeled them slithers of red cedar off of the little piece of stick with his pocketknife and let them fall on the floor around his feet. "Besides," he said, "a eight-year-old young'un ain't got no call to be buttin into grown folks's business. You better go 'long and shuck off to bed."

That was the next night after Papa got on Princess along about sundown and rode out in the pasture to look for Queen Mary because she never come up with the rest of the cows at milkin time and he knowed she was prolly out there on the gully some'eres with a fresh-born calf, waitin for it to get strong enough to walk up to the house with her. And Tar-Baby went along with them because he always follows his ma wherever she goes, like a feist dog that might follow you to town of a Saturday mornin. He'll fool around sniffin at a mesquite bush or smellin in the grass, makin out like he don't know you're gettin way

Reprinted from *Harper's Magazine*, December, 1947; copyright 1947 by the author and used by his permission.

ahead of him. Then here he'll come in a high lope, prancin and kickin up his heels and sail on past you and keep goin for maybe a hundred yards until he sees another bush or weed or something and he'll play like he's awfully interested in it and let you come on by and get ahead again.

Anyhow, they went on out in the pasture, Papa ridin bareback on the Princess and her carryin her head high and steppin like the ground might be covered with eggs, kinda watchin Tar-Baby out of the corner of her eyes, proud-like, because she knowed full well it wasn't air 'nother colt in the whole state of Texas as pretty as he was, much less as smart.

They wasn't gone more'n a half a hour or such a matter till Princess come back to the house with the bridle reins draggin and Tar-Baby cavortin around and runnin back and forth through them reins like he was playin some kind of a game. So Mama knowed it was something wrong and she made me stay there in the kitchen and watch the biscuits so they wouldn't burn while she footed it on out there in the pasture to see what was the matter. Then pretty soon *she* come tearin back to the house wringin her hands with a wild look out of her eyes, and I knowed they was something wrong too. But it wasn't Tar-Baby, because he was out there at the barn gittin his supper.

Mama come runnin across the back yard screamin like it might of been a pack of wolves sniffin at her coat-tail. "Benny," she said, "run git Mr. Roberts as quick as you can. Your pa has fell and hurt hisself."

So I didn't wait to ask no questions. I just run out to the lot and jumped on Princess because she still had the bridle on, and me and her went flyin down the big road to Mr. Roberts's place. But we didn't go too fast, because we didn't neither one of us want to run off and leave Tar-Baby. He's little and he can't go as fast as his ma can when she really lets herself out. Old Mr. Roberts never lost no time neither. He jumped on that chestnut horse of his'n that he works to the buggy and here we come lammin it back down that red clay road makin sounds like you hear in the movies of a Saturday night when the sheriff is chasin a cattle rustler.

Mama done already had the mules hitched up to the wagon when we got back and she just waited long enough to yell at me, "Run for the doctor, Benny," and they went high-tailin it on down across the pasture. I guess she was so worked up over the whole business she never realized till I got back what it was I had been ridin around on—over to Mr. Roberts's place and all the way to Oakville and back. Because by that time her and Mr. Roberts had done loaded him in the wagon and hauled him up to the house and put him in the bed. And Dr. Cunningham had beat me there by a long ways because he was ridin in a bran new Buick and I was ridin on Princess and her foolin along takin her own good time so Tar-Baby could keep up.

So things was kinda quieted down a little bit when we got back and I guess that's the first time she happened to think about it.

"Lordamercy, child," she said, "you been ridin that skittish mare all over Chaparral County and she just finished throwin your daddy off and bustin his head wide open on a rock."

When Dr. Cunningham got back to town that night he telephoned Uncle Mark and Uncle Wayne—that's Papa's two brothers that live in Austin. But they never come over till the next day because Austin's forty or fifty miles away and that's a fur piece. I guess they didn't want to go galivantin around anyhow on a dark night like that. So it must of been nearly dinner-time when they come drivin up in Uncle Wayne's new Chevrolet. I speck they had to find somebody to run their saddle shop before they could leave.

Uncle Mark hadn't no more'n hit the house good till he said he was goin to take the shotgun down off the deer horns and go out there and shoot her. And Mama said, "Not now, Mark. Not yet. He ain't even regained consciousness yet."

"He ain't never goin to regain his consciousness," Uncle Mark said. "That she-devil has done and killed him. And I'm goin to shoot her between the eyes with a load of buckshot if'n it's the last thing I ever do."

"It ain't no sense in that," Uncle Wayne said. "That ain't none of Sam's mare. She belongs with the estate. She's part yours and part mine. That was Pa's mare."

"Sho," Uncle Mark said. "All right. I'm goin to shoot my part. And I'll be bound you Sam would thank me for shootin his part if he was able to talk and realize what she has done went and done to him. You can do whatever you want to with your part."

"You're cuttin your nose off to spite your face," Uncle Wayne said. "She'd bring a nice piece of money if we was to sell her."

They argued around like that for the longest, and neither one of

150

them ever even mentioned what would happen to Tar-Baby. It looked like they never had even so much as realized that he hadn't learned how to eat grass yet. Both of them ought to of knowed it too, because they was raised on the farm right over there across the creek where Grandpa lived before he took sick and died two or three years ago. And they had handled horses a lot. So it ought not to of been necessary for me to have to tell them. But I told them that night when they was settin in there by the cook-stove and Uncle Mark was whittlin on the cedar stick and Uncle Wayne was chewin tobacco and spittin in the woodbox. "He will die," I told them, "if you shoot his ma, because he's too little. He can't hustle for hisself."

And Uncle Mark said, "You're gittin too big for your britches. Stickin your nose in places where it ain't got no business to be. You better go on to bed where you belong."

So I went on and made out like I was goin to bed. But pretty soon I come on back and snuck in behind the stove, because I had to find out what they was goin to do. I knowed Uncle Mark was the oldest and he usually always had his way about things. But I had to find out for sure.

I hadn't no more'n set down good till Mama come back in the kitchen with that little book in her hand that Papa used to write in at night. She handed it to Uncle Mark and he opened it and kinda flipped through the leaves and grunted. "Huh," he said. "So that's his set of books, is it?" I knowed then that I might just as well of gone on to bed because it wasn't nothin in that book about Tar-Baby. Papa hadn't even took the book down from behind the clock since way before the colt was born.

I knowed it wasn't goin to be nothin but just grown folks talk, but I was afraid to git up and leave because I didn't want Uncle Mark jumpin on me again. He wasn't payin no attention to me yet. He was lookin in the book. "Ever'thing's in a fine mess," he said. "This is a nice time for Sam to curl up his toes and hang up his harness and die."

"What's the matter?" Uncle Wayne said. And Uncle Mark closed the book and slapped it down on his knee. "Matter!" he said. "They's plenty the matter. How long is it now since Pa died and Sam started lookin after the place?"

"Must be two years, goin on three," Uncle Wayne said. "Why?"

"Because me and you's done been skunt out of no tellin how much money," Uncle Mark said. "Because Sam quit keepin books on the place about two years ago. They ain't a scratch in here to show how much was made on the last two crops. And Pa's cattle and the cord wood that's been sold off of the place."

"Sho now," Uncle Wayne said. "That's a pretty kettle of fish. Maybe Mollie knows about them transactions. Maybe she knows how much of mine and your money her and Sam has got in the bank and how many of our cattle's got mixed up with theirs."

"Yeah," Uncle Mark snorted. "Sho. Maybe she does. How about it, Mollie?"

And Mama said, "Couldn't we just wait till he gets well? Or at least until he comes out of the coma? He's got all them transactions in his head. He knows where ever penny is that belongs to the estate. I realize he's neglected to write them down, but he can tell you to the last cent what belongs to Grandpa's place. Couldn't we just wait till he regains consciousness?"

"He ain't goin to never regain consciousness," Uncle Mark said. "He might linger on a day or two, but he's a gone goslin. The doc said so hisself. It's a bone pressin in on his brain."

"We should of had a settlement a long time ago," Uncle Wayne said. "Like it is now, Sam's got his money all mixed up with ours. You can't tell what belongs to his place and what belongs to the old home place."

"You might as well count Sam out of this deal," Uncle Mark said. "What you mean is, Mollie's got a lot of mine and your money in the bank in her name. I don't know how you feel about it, Wayne, but I ain't aimin on losin my part."

"I don't know as I got air dime to give away to a widder woman neither," Uncle Wayne said. "I aim to git my part."

Well, I seen they was clean off the track. They wasn't none of 'm thinkin about what was goin to happen to Tar-Baby. Anyhow, it looked like his ma was safe until mornin at least, because Uncle Mark hadn't even got the gun down to see if it had any shells in it. So I oozed on out the door and went back to the shed-room and went to bed. And the next thing I knowed, the sun was shinin in my face.

It kinda skeered me at first. And then I realized that Uncle Mark wouldn't take the trouble to lead her far enough away from the house

152

so I couldn't hear the shot. So maybe she was still alive and Tar-Baby had done and got his breakfast all right. Anyhow, I knowed I better be crawlin out of the shucks and findin out what the score was. So I got up and put on my overalls and shirt and a sweater, because fall of the year was settin in and it was pretty fresh outside.

Mama was settin in there in the fireplace room where Papa was layin on the bed, and Grandma was settin in the wheel chair with that wild look out of her eyes and her hair not even combed yet. I looked all around and listened good before I asked her. "Where's Uncle Mark?" I said. Because I was afraid he might of got the gun and went off down to the barn.

"They left last night," Mama said. "They went back home so they could open up the saddle shop bright and early this mornin. You ready to eat your breakfast?"

Well, that sho made me feel good. "Yes ma'am," I told her. "I'm ready. I won't be but just a minute." And I went flyin out the back door and down to the barn as fast as I could pick 'm up and put 'm down. And sho 'nough, there he was, prancin around like nobody's business. And there was his ma, bitin off mouthfuls of grass and chewin it up as unconcerned like she never had even so much as heard of a man named Uncle Mark.

So I went back to the house and washed my face and set down to the table and I was feelin like a million dollars. But still I knowed it might not last. So I had to find out. "When they aimin to come back?" I said. "Tonight maybe?"

"No," Mama said. "Not unless your pa passes away. They'll want to have a settlement then."

Well, that made me feel mighty fine. I could of gone ahead to school. Because that was what really had me worried—me goin off to school and leavin Uncle Mark there and the shotgun on the deer horns with a whole box of shells on the shelf. But Mama said maybe I better just hang around the house and she would write a note to the teacher the next day. So it looked like ever'thing was goin to be all right until about the middle of the evenin when this satchel-packin city bird come drivin up to the front gallery and got out and come in.

He hadn't no more'n got in the house and set down good till he told Mama that Mr. Mark and Mr. Wayne Garwood had sent him over.

When I heard that, my pulse beat ris a notch or two, because I thought maybe they had hired him to shoot the Princess, or maybe kill her in some kind of a citified way, like with an electric wire or poison gas.

But pretty soon I could tell it was just the same old stuff—all about the cattle and crops and cord wood on our place and how some of it had maybe creeped across the creek from Grandpa's place, because Grandpa had died two or three years ago and they had moved Grandma over to live with us and Papa had been lookin after the stuff over there and hirin a bunch of hands to work the crops.

"They are goin to sue you," the man said. "They have retained me to fix up the papers and file the suit." And Mama said, "I can't help it. It ain't nothin I can do. But can't they even wait to see if he is goin to live or die?"

"You don't understand," the man said. "They will enter suit right after the funeral. They've got an open and shut case." And Mama said, "Yes, I reckon they have. But why did you come and tell me about it? What do they want me to do?"

"It might be we could settle it out of court," he said. "Maybe if you would write them out a check for two or three thousand dollars. Maybe we could agree on a sum. But of course you would have to wait till after the funeral. Then the boy would come in for his part. You couldn't touch a thing—not even Mr. Samuel's bank account—until you had got yourself bonded and legally appointed your son's guardian. You couldn't sell a cow, nor a pig even, until you had done that."

"I don't know," Mama said. "I don't know if we even got a dime in the bank. Sam always handled the money matters."

So pretty soon I seen it wasn't nothin but grown folks talk. He hadn't come to shoot her or electrocute her or poison gas her. Like as not he hadn't never even heard of a mare named Princess, let alone knowin she had a coal black colt named Tar-Baby. So I went on out to the barn to give her some feed and watch him stick his head in the trough with her and blow his nose and kick up his heels and caper around like he was somebody come.

That night Elmer Doolittle and Uncle Jimmy Hancock come over after supper. Uncle Jimmy ain't really my uncle. He ain't even no blood-kin. He's a old old man that owns the store down at the cross-roads and ever'body in Chaparral County knows him and calls him Uncle Jimmy. But they don't nobody call Elmer Mr. Doolittle. I don't know why, because he's as old as Papa and he owns a sight of land in the Bend.

Anyhow, they hadn't no more'n got set down good till Elmer wanted to know where's Mark and Wayne. And Mama told him they went home about ten o'clock last night because they had to run the shop and make saddles and cowboy boots and belts and stuff. "You mean they went off home after I left?" Elmer said. "I thought they was here to stay. Who set up last night?" And Mama told him she did.

So one thing led to another and pretty soon they got to talkin about that same stuff again. Mama told them how the money and cattle and cord wood and crops had got all mixed up between the two farms and how the lawyer from Austin had come over and set a spell with her. But I didn't pay no attention to it, because by that time I had done and heard it three or four times.

Finally I thought they had got done talkin about it, because Elmer and Uncle Jimmy told Mama they had come to set up all night and they made a big pot of coffee and told her to fix off to bed. They told me too, but I wasn't a bit sleepy. So she helped Grandma git her nightgown on and git out of the wheel chair and into the bed and then she said good-night and turned in too. But I stayed there by the fireplace because Uncle Jimmy knows a lot about the Indians and the Alamo and the Texas Rangers and I thought maybe he might git wound up like he does sometimes down at the store and tell about how it was in the old days.

"That's pretty good," Elmer said. "She's been takin care of their own invalid mammy for nigh onto three years. Now they can't wait till Sam's in his grave to hire a shyster lawyer from Austin to come over here and try to beat her out of the last red cent she's got. If that don't take the rag off the bush."

"Sho," Uncle Jimmy said. "That's gratitude for you. Me and you better saddle over to Silver City tomorrow and talk to old Cap'm Jenkins. He's the best lawyer in the state of Texas. He'll build a fire under that city slicker's tail."

So there we was again—back on the same old subject. And I was just about ready to give up and go on to bed. But it was something Elmer said that made me stay. "No," he said. "They've got a good case against her and they know it. And besides, it ain't but one thing that

155

will ever satisfy me. I'll prize up Chaparral County and mortgage every acre of land I've got to do it." And Uncle Jimmy said, "What's that?"

"It's to see him git well," Elmer said. "To see him rise up out of that bed and take that shotgun down off of them deer horns and shoot both of them square between the eyes with a load of buckshot."

"Sho now," Uncle Jimmy said. "If we only could."

Well, maybe you think that didn't make me set up and listen. Because I didn't see why Elmer wanted Papa to shoot Tar-Baby too. It wasn't his fault. He didn't even have no hand in it.

"He needs a specialist," Elmer said. "A man that can perform a delicate operation on a cook-table and take that piece of bone off of his brain. So he can git well and git up out of that bed and load that gun and aim accurate and pull the trigger."

"Sho," Uncle Jimmy said. "That's what he needs."

"That's Raymond Morgan," Elmer said, "that was born and raised right here in the Bend. You recollect Ray, don't you?"

"I recollect him," Uncle Jimmy said. "I hear tell he's done and gone to New York now."

Elmer cut hisself a chew of tobacco and put it in his right-hand jaw like he had done figured it all out. "That's right," he said. "He's a brain specialist. I reckon it's more folks in New York with something the matter with their heads than it is in Texas. I reckon it'll take a heap of money to git him down here on a airplane, but I'm goin to personally foot the bill myself."

"Won't them boogers rare up on their hind legs when they hear about it!" Uncle Jimmy said. "They'll figure that money creeped across the creek from the old man's cattle and crops and cord wood."

"Sho," Elmer said. "It'll be a sight to see. And the only pay I'll ever expect will be a ringside seat at the shootin."

"Folks around in the Bend says Ray Morgan ain't never found hisself no wife yet," Uncle Jimmy said.

"That ain't neither here nor there," Elmer said. "A doctor don't need to work in double harness. I reckon a single man can handle a knife just as well as a married man."

"He used to spark Mollie like it was pretty serious before she up and married Sam," Uncle Jimmy said. "Folks always said she kinda give him the run-around while he was off at school."

"Sho," Elmer said. "Yes. I see what you mean. It would be a temptation. Mollie's still mighty young and pretty."

"A slip of the knife," Uncle Jimmy said, "a nice funeral, and a few months to wait. He'd have her right back in his lap again."

"We can lessen the temptation a right smart," Elmer said, "if we stand behind him with a six-shooter and kinda steady his nerve. If his hand slips, I'd have to tend to them other two. I might just as well make it a crowd."

"It's your party," Uncle Jimmy said. "Go ahead on."

So Elmer said he was goin to town to use the telephone, and he went outside and cranked up his car and drove off.

Well, by that time I was layin down on the floor with my head on my old red houn'dog and I guess I was gittin pretty sleepy.

"Why don't you git up and pull your clothes off and go to bed right?" Uncle Jimmy told me.

So I got up and set down in the chair like grown folks. "I thought bein as Elmer's gone," I said, "maybe you'd tell me a story."

"Sho," Uncle Jimmy said. "All right. Which one?"

"The one about the Indians stealin your horses," I said.

"You've heard that one seventy-five or thirty times," Uncle Jimmy said. "You want to hear it again?"

"Yes," I told him. "Tell it like you always used to. And don't leave out none of it."

"Sho," Uncle Jimmy said. "If you'll go to bed then. Just that one."

"All right," I said. And he cut hisself a fresh chew of tobacco and rared back in his chair and told it. He didn't leave out a bit. And jeez, it was fine. And I went on back to the shed-room and pulled off my clothes and crawled in.

Things was pretty quiet the next day or two until Elmer come down to the lot where I was feedin Tar-Baby a little sugar. "You want to ride over to Austin with me?" he said.

"I b'lieve not," I told him. "You goin over to see Uncle Mark and Uncle Wayne?"

"No," he said. "Not today. That will come later. I'm goin over to meet the airplane comin in from New York."

So I changed my tune and went with him. And comin on back we had the doctor in the car with us—not Dr. Cunningham but the New

157

York doctor. We went by the hospital, and him and Elmer loaded in a bunch of junk and we come truckin on home. Once he looked at me and said, "Well, well, so this is Mollie's boy, is it?" And Elmer said, "Yes. It sho God is, and it's Sam's boy, and we got to git Sam up out of that bed because he's got to git that gun down off of them deer horns and practice up on his shootin lessons."

"You didn't mean Tar-Baby too, did you?" I said.

And Elmer said, "Who's Tar-Baby?"

"He's my colt," I said. "I guess he ain't exactly mine, though. Because the Princess used to belong to Grandpa but Grandpa died and now she belongs to Uncle Mark and Uncle Wayne and Papa. So who would Tar-Baby belong to?"

"That's pretty complicated," Elmer said. "But just as soon as we git a few matters settled, I speck things will be simplified considerable. It won't be nowhere near as many heirs to Tar-Baby."

"You had me skeered until we got out of Austin," I told Elmer. "I thought maybe you might be aimin to bring Uncle Mark back with us."

"No," Elmer said. "He'll come on over later. On the train, I guess. In the baggage car. Uncle Wayne too. I speck they'd have a hankerin to be planted in the peach orchard alongside their pa."

So we come on home and got out and went in the house. Elmer and Uncle Jimmy and the New York doctor went on in the fireplace room where Papa was, but they shut me out. I seen the six-shooters stickin out of Uncle Jimmy's hip pockets, so I thought maybe they had changed their minds. Maybe the doctor was goin to cure Papa and Uncle Jimmy was goin to let him use the pistols instead of the shotgun.

Anyhow, I went on down to the barn and put the bridle on the Princess and rode clean down to the back side of the pasture and Tar-Baby scamperin along with us.

Grown folks is funny. Because I never heard no more about the business for several days. The doctor had done left by that time and flew back to New York. Elmer and Uncle Jimmy had come over to set a spell and Papa was propped up in bed eatin a bowl of soup. It was Elmer that brought up the subject again. "Sam," he said, "you 'bout ready to crawl out of there and oil up your gun?"

And Papa said, "Yes. Near 'bout. I sho God ought to. I ain't even seen them two since the mare stepped in that hole and I busted my head."

"Because if you ain't goin to do it," Elmer said, "I am goin to personally shoot them both between the eyes and drag their carcass off out in the pasture for the buzzards to have a picnic on."

And then Mama ris up and put her hands on her hips. "You just as well to shut up, both of you," she said. "Because it ain't goin to be no shootin done around here. Them two saved Sam's life."

And Elmer said, "Well, I'll be durned. If it wouldn't take a woman to add up the whole business and come out with a answer like that."

"Sho now," Uncle Jimmy said. "I see what you mean, Mollie. And besides, Elmer ain't got no ringside seat comin, because Ray Morgan never charged him a cryin dime."

"Yes," Mama said. "Them two saved his life, sho as the world."

Well, I didn't see how Tar-Baby had done much of anything to help him save his life. And the Princess had done a right smart to help him lose it, even if she didn't mean to. But I never said nothin.

So she went ahead givin him his nourishment and pretty soon she learned him how to eat grass. That was maybe a month ago. And jeez, you ought to see him now!

MARY KING O'DONNELL

OF PIONEER STOCK, Mary Paula King was born on a farm near Angleton, Brazoria County, March 2, 1909. Her father was an oil driller in the days that followed the coastal-field boom. For three years Miss King attended the University of Texas. Upon leaving school, she worked at a variety of jobs in Houston and then, in 1936, moved to New Orleans.

There she met and married a novelist and short-story writer, the late Edwin P. O'Donnell, who helped launch her literary career. Her first novel and first short stories, of which the present story is one, were written here. For her prospectus of a novel about an oil town, she was awarded a Houghton Mifflin literary fellowship. This novel, *Quincie Bolliver* (1941), marked her as a promising young writer.

At O'Donnell's death in 1943, his widow moved to San Francisco, where she wrote her second novel. *Those Other People* (1946), signed Mary King O'Donnell instead of Mary King, is an interestingly experimental novel about one day in the life of a great many people in a large city (New Orleans). In San Francisco the author married Michael Quin, journalist and radio news commentator. Since his death in 1947, she continues to make California her home, residing in Olema, a small town within commuting distance of San Francisco. In 1951 she married Steven Charter, an agricultural engineer. She has two daughters, Colin, age seven, and Quincy, age two.

Mary King O'Donnell has published but few short stories; their quality, however, has been such as to attract attention. Those that have been rated "distinctive" include "The Honey House" and "Chicken on the Wind," both of which first appeared in the *Southern Review;* "The White Bull," which appeared in the *Yale Review;* and "A Pair of Shoes," which appeared in *Good Housekeeping.* "Chicken on the Wind," in which the author's delicate fancy is foot-loose and free as the wind, is a fine example of a kind of writing all too rare in the American short story—uncondescending warm human folk comedy.

Chicken on the Wind

SOLDIER BASCOM sat on his front doorstep waiting for his wife Bertha to return from the Post Office.

The sun had set. The long summer twilight was deepening. Soon the water in the canal would be as dark as the sky. A south wind, heavy with the pungent odors of fencerow weeds basted all day in the hot sun, blew damp and cool off the rice field. From their watery doorways the frogs began to question and affirm, one voice joining another until the combined sound lifted and swelled across the flat land.

"Listen the little suckers!" Soldier said aloud, admiringly.

He could see Bertha standing with a group of people in the lighted front of Lee Bird's General Store and Filling Station. The bus bringing the mail was not due for half an hour.

Soldier and Bertha lived in a freight car run off on a spur track up against the big rice barn. The car had not been moved for a long time. Grass grew under it and weeds grappled its wheels. Close beside it, under a young chinaberry tree on the slope of the track embankment, were two wire chicken coops, a barrel chair, and a tub of fat-leafed geraniums in red bloom.

The two old people belonged to the town, and yet were strangers in it. Their strangeness might have been due to their living on wheels, to the dividing line of the highway which separated them from their neighbors, or to the fact that since theirs was the sole dwelling in the town to face east, they saw the sun rise through their front door instead of through their back door as did the others.

Soldier was watchman of the barn. He was a small man past sixty, with shoulders so curved forward over his breastbone that he

Copyright 1940 by the *Southern Review;* reprinted by permission of the author and publishers.

seemed to be trying to cover himself with himself. He took great pleasure in the barn. He drew from it a feeling of solidity and purpose. Whenever he had not slept well for the town dogs baying a 'coon or a 'possum back in the woods, or his morning coffee tasted bitter, or his fingers, stiffer than usual with rheumatism, lost small objects his eyes had trouble finding—whenever anything displeased him or made him unhappy—he went to the barn. There, squatting on his heels, with his shoulderblades set against the shady wall, he felt comforted.

It did not occur to him to share his thoughts with his wife. It did not occur to him that Bertha might have thoughts of her own.

Bertha had several thoughts she shared with nobody. The possession of these thoughts shaped her plump face to a strange sly mold when no one was looking; inside her, their voices clamored strongly for public acknowledgement; but she held them silent and waited. Why she waited or for what, she did not know. But when she woke on a winter night to the powerful throbbing of a fast freight on the main track, or watched on summer evenings the canal water flood silently over the rice fields, she felt that some day, something would happen, and then she would talk.

Soldier slanted his eyes down the highway and saw the bus lights coming. The bus stopped, and the crowd followed the mail sacks into the store. Soon Bertha came out and crossed the highway carrying a letter. By the swing of her skirt she was a woman with news. She toiled up the embankment and dropped into the barrel chair. Soldier waited until she got her breath and then said, casually,

"Now who'd be writin' us a letter d'you suppose?"

"Shoo!" Bertha said abstractedly to a stray dog that had come up and was nosing her skirt. "Go way! go on home, you! I got no time for dogs!"

"We got a letter, eh Bertha?"

"His ways is strange . . . strange indeed . . . after all these years!"

"Strange? Whose years?"

"You remember my uncle Sennet Thompson, my mother's brother that married and took out life insurance and his wife died?"

"Can't say I recall."

"Well, it don't matter. He's dead, praise the Lord! Rest him in peace," she added piously. "It was noble of him."

"I don't know," Soldier said mildly, "seems to me everybody dies, come sooner or later."

"You're an old fool! He named me for his money. Four thousand insurance I got right here in this letter, it says!" Soldier sat up excitedly.

"For a fact? Why didn't you say so? Sittin' there clammed shut on four thousand dollar! Well! What'll we do with it?"

"It's my money! Mine alone!"

The words were out. The two old people looked at each other with hostile eyes, and then, embarrassed, looked away. Soldier began to fiddle with his pocket knife, opening and shutting the blades. Bertha snipped dead leaves from the geranium. She cleared her throat. She was too excited to remain long silent.

"Oh Sojer, don't it seem past studyin' about? Me, with four thousand dollars all my own that never had more than ten dollars and sixty cents in these hands at one time?"

"What d'you aim to do with it?" Soldier asked slowly.

"I don't know yet. I got to think."

"Maybe we could buy a car and take a little trip? You'd like that, wouldn't you, Bertha?" His voice was diffident.

"Money like this is a gift from God. I got to think."

Two days passed. Soon after breakfast on the third morning, Bertha, parting the curtains to stare at the scattered houses across the highway, made her announcement.

"I aim to build me a church!"

Soldier had been pointing the end of a match to pick his teeth. His hand stopped with the sliver halfway to his mouth. His mouth hung open with astonishment.

"What say?"

"I aim to build me a church," Bertha repeated firmly.

"What?"

"A church, I said! Are you deaf? There's no church here, no sign of one. I aim to get established. I'm sick of livin' in a travelin' freight car likely to take out home for Rock Island any minute, day or night. It ain't right for a woman my age to live over wheels. Three years I lived here and no woman has set foot inside my front door—not as I blame 'em."

"Why, Bertha, I never knew you felt that way about it! You never said. I thought you liked it here, the same as me."

163

"You know right well I didn't like it! You and your barn! Time and again I said 'Look at us livin' like cattle or hogs in a pen, livin' in a freight car, respectable people, gettin' on in years!' Time and again I said—and it's God's own pity it ain't happened—'Like as not they'll forget we're livin' here and run a herd of steers in over us some night, or a train'll back up and hook onto us, and no tellin' where we'll wake up!' You know I said it, Sojer Bascom, and me eatin' my heart out with shame for livin' in a freight car. But you never listened, you never cared! Any old place is good enough for you—not an ounce of pride you got, I always knew it! Look at us, respectable people, livin' in a freight car!"

"It's been mighty comfortable. Seems to me we managed to be right respectable in it."

"Certain things a man can't get through his head, let him live to be a hunnerd and he never gets some things through his head! You got no pride! It's true, I see it now, you got no pride!"

"Hey, hold on a minute, gimme time to push in a word! What I can't see is where you plan to live if you quit livin' in this freight car and use up all your money on a church. Whyn't you build a house? That would be sensible. Or a hamburger stand and a little shack alongside it? You'd get a good highway trade. You plan to live in the church? Who'll preach for it when you do get it built?"

"I'll have a house every woman in this townsite'll step inside, and be glad to. Yes, and every man too!"

"Woman, you gone clean crazy with the heat!"

"It won't be no ordinary kind of church. I've thought it all out these two days. It'll have pews in the back where young people can do their courtin' in the house of God like it should be, not where they go now. I seen what's goin' on around here. It's nice and shady in that barn of yours, ain't it, and sacked rice is plenty soft? I ain't blind like you think I am, and I'll clear the grounds for picnics and dig barbecue pits and sell soda-pop, and as for preachin', the Lord'll raise me up a preacher, He'll tend to that. Look what He done already!"

"Raise you up trouble!" snorted Soldier. "The Lord ain't no hand in it! This idea come straight from the devil hisself!"

"You'll see!"

"But where'll we live?"

"Never you mind, the Lord'll take care of His own, and furthermore I ain't tellin' a soul. Let 'em wonder and talk like it's good for 'em. 'The

164

Lord sent it,' I'll say, and it's the truth. You can live where you please. Me, I'm livin' in the back of my church till I take up collections, and then maybe I'll build a house."

"Collections?" Soldier jumped to his feet. Bertha looked at him calmly.

"Don't go jumpin' around like a flea on a hot griddle, you'll upset your stomach."

"A lot you care about my stomach!"

"Well, I do own a few other things on my mind now you mention it."

"Now, Bertha, now listen!" Soldier's voice became conciliatory. "Try and look at it my way, see? Now what right you got to take people's cash in church without bein' a preacher to build a house? It ain't honest! Besides, you'll make us both a laughin' stock for the whole county!"

"It's my money. My mind's made up. I thought and I prayed."

"Prayed! It's wicked vanity makes you want to own a church. You ain't no hand for good fortune, Bertha. Seems you can't bear up under it."

"Forty years I put up with your shiftless ways and look where it got me—livin' in a freight car! Well, I'm through!"

All day Soldier went about in a deep study. After supper he tried approaching the situation from a different angle.

"You'll have land to buy and it'll cost you plenty. You won't have no money left to build a church. Besides, where'll you keep your chickens? In the churchyard?"

"I've already talked to Mr. Lee and he'll let me have that acre at the edge of the grove down the road at a good reasonable price. As for the chickens, we'll see."

"You ain't even got the money yet, all you got is a letter!"

"I'll get the money. I aim to catch the bus into Houston tomorrow and go see the lawyer. Every man, woman and child in this townsite'll set foot in my house."

"I won't set foot in it!"

"I guess I can stand it if you don't!"

Before Soldier fell asleep his anger subsided and he felt sorry and hurt. Bertha had completely excluded him from her plans. In the morning she did not speak to him. She dressed in her Sunday clothes, polished her spectacles, and put a fresh handkerchief in her purse. As she prepared breakfast she hummed cheerfully. Soldier's eyes followed her

165

wistfully. She had been a good wife. She was a big fine woman, almost as big and fine as the barn, in her own way. What was to be done about it all? Still ignoring him, Bertha broke into a hymn, a rapt expression on her face which dismayed and infuriated the old man.

The bus was due at eight forty-five. While Bertha watered the geraniums and fed the hens she kept an eye on the clock. Last of all she unlatched the door of the big red Wyandotte rooster's coop and left him free to run. This rooster's name was Bobo. He was Bertha's pet, but Soldier did not like him. The rooster, with the run of the house, had developed impudent and untidy habits from which Soldier's best shoes had suffered more than once.

"Red bastid!" Soldier muttered under his breath, as the rooster stalked majestically from the coop, stood on his toes, stretched his wings, and crowed. Aloud, seeking to make talk, he said,

"You're mighty fond of that fowl, ain't you, Bertha?"

"So what if I am?"

"Oh nothin', Bertha. It just come to me he must be gettin' along, gettin' pretty old for a chicken I expect. Now, how old would you say he was?"

"Old enough to have some sense."

"Now look here—it's you, not me!"

"He was a handsome fella, yes he was!" Bertha crooned, stooping to set a pan of scraps before the rooster.

"You think more of that chicken than you do of me," Soldier said angrily.

"Maybe I do. Times he seems almost human—and look how proud he walks!"

From that day on Bertha was too busy to cook and Soldier got his own meals. The insurance money came. With it Bertha ordered lumber and hired workmen. She tucked up her skirt and strode around the building site in rubber boots, bossing the men. Her round cheeks grew red with sunburn, her gray hair curled like pine shavings under an old felt hat of Soldier's. When she was not working her eyes wore a faraway expression. Once she even said something about visions, but Soldier silenced her with a look. She ate at the Open Hand Cafe next door to the filling station, and offered this treat to Soldier also, but he declined. He spent most of his time sitting in the doorway of the rice barn where he could watch without being seen. He went to the store only for food and tobacco. He felt ashamed and lonely. He was miserable.

As the skeleton of the church began to rise, a warm odor of resinous pine floated across the road to Soldier. All day he smelled it, and the more days he smelled it the angrier he grew. At least, he was angry in the daytime. At night, when Bertha came home and crawled under the mosquito bar beside him, he didn't care what she did with her money if only she would be as she used to be. When daylight came again, and with it the repeated sight and smell of wasted lumber, his anger returned and he would not have replied had she spoken to him.

When the walls were halfway up the work slowed down. Bertha could find no hands to help her except when field work was over in the evening. The August days grew hot and hazy. In the canal the river water dropped. The tin side of the big barn reflected a blistering heat into the freight car. Bertha lost weight. For some time no words had passed directly between the two old people; they were enemies in silence; and then each began addressing slyly to the rooster remarks meant for the other's ears.

"Look at 'er!" Soldier would say derisively. "Did you see her tryin' to hammer in that nail? Can you beat it? She'll have a church, nothin' will do her but a church. Tired of livin' alongside me, she says, so she'll try a church, give picnics, she says. Didn't have no fun with me so she'll try a church. Makin' herself ridiculous, but I won't share in it, not a finger . . . to hell I say!"

"He's jealous, that's all! Wicked, jealous old man, selfish and stubborn!"

"Ashamed of herself, that's why she wants a church. Done somethin' she's ashamed for. Tell her the sooner she moves out and quits sleepin' alongside me, the better it'll be."

"Tell him, just wait! He'll see!"

When the church had a roof on it, Bertha moved in with all her belongings, leaving the freight car strangely empty.

"When you get over bein' stubborn you can come live with me," she said, speaking directly to him for the first time in days. "I don't aim to be unreasonable, I just got an idea. It's cool over to my place, and I don't know but I'll make a house of it yet because it seems a shame to waste all that cool space on the trash around here. . . . Yes, I may turn it into a house and take in boarders . . . and again I may not."

Soldier slung his mosquito bar under the chinaberry tree and slept outdoors. He was very lonely, and he wondered if Bertha were lonely too. People watched the new building curiously, speculating among themselves.

"It ain't like any house I ever seen," said one.

"More like a stable or a dairy barn with all them windows," said another.

"He don't help her atall. I wonder why?" said a third.

"Your wife's puttin' up a mighty nice house," Lee Bird said to Soldier one morning in the store.

"I hear she come into some money," said Mrs. Bird. "I guess you keep pretty busy over to the barn?"

"I keep pretty busy," said Soldier.

So far, nobody suspected that Bertha's building was a church. Maybe if he swallowed his pride and moved in with her, thought Soldier, she would change her mind. He was still debating this question with himself when the steeple arrived. It came crated, on a truck from Houston. When Soldier saw it he abandoned hope. It looked like a pretty tall steeple, and its use was unmistakable. For two days it lay on the ground before men could be found to raise it. Once it was established, the meaning of Bertha's new building was plainly apparent to the countryside for several miles around.

A buzz of talk and laughter followed. At first Bertha threaded her way among the comments unscathed and proud, even taking some advantage to herself. Over her shoulder she loosed hints. Soldier could not be seen. Unnoticed, he crept into the barn and stayed there, coming out only for meals. Something in his soul had been violated. Now the church steeple was the last object folded into the dusk, the first to emerge with daylight. Pointed and proud, it dominated the flat landscape. The rice barn was insignificant beside it.

The weather turned squally and work on the church rested. Bertha fretted at the warping lumber that lay in useless piles on the ground. From her enforced idleness was born another idea. The church must have a name. She painted the sign herself and nailed it over the door.

THE SCATTER SUNSHINE CHURCH
COME ONE   COME ALL

This invitation was a mistake. Lumber began to be stolen, and words and pictures chalked by children on the flat clean surfaces of the walls. Grimly Bertha cleaned the walls and carried the lumber inside. She did not ask Soldier for help. The old man kept his peace. He was beginning to feel sorry for her, but every time he looked at the church he cringed.

The steeple had been up for a week when one morning around nine o'clock Lee Bird's radio gave out storm news. Teeny Bird, who was ten years old, ran out in the road waving her arms, shouting "Hooray, hooray, there's a storm comin'!" Excited talk followed the announcement.

"I knew it! I said to Fanny yesterday, 'This is hurricane weather! Somethin' queer in the air,' I said to her, 'I can't draw breath!'"

"Where'll it strike? Do they say?"

"Anywheres between Galveston and Brownsville, they say. They don't know exactly where yet."

"Now don't you all get worked up," Lee Bird said. "Nothin' to do but board up and lay low if she comes, but she ain't come yet. Miles of coast to light on, and she ain't picked us yet. They'll keep us warned."

Soldier went home worried. He stood in the barn door and took stock of the weather. A nervous north wind was shingling the rainy sky with darker slate-colored clouds. Under them the earth lay flat and unshining, grown suddenly unimportant, somehow, as an old plate with the gloss rubbed off. He lifted his eyes again to the moving sky. After dinner he returned to the store for news. As he walked up the steps a group of people burst through the door and began running and calling.

"It's coming, the storm's coming! Headed inland at Port Aransas! Due to strike around ten tonight!"

Bertha was one of the group. She passed Soldier and hurried down the road to her church. He followed and caught up with her. They stood together, looking silently at the new pine building. Bertha's mouth drooped, her shoulders drooped also. She looked old and tired and bony. Soldier put his hand on her shoulder.

"You better come on home tonight," he said. She shook off his hand.

"I'm stayin' right here."

"It's shackly-built. You better come home."

Bertha's lips quivered. "That's as good-built house as any here. Don't nobody know how good a house that one is ... don't nobody appreciate it. ..."

"It's too high-up off the ground."

"I'm not comin'. Go on home yourself."

"Well, if you won't come, catch a ride into town—plenty people leavin' will give you a ride—or take the bus."

"I'll stay in my church, and I'm not going to board the windows and ruin my good pew lumber with nail holes either. I ain't skeered of a little wind!"

By dusk the wind had sloped to the northeast and flattened to an even blowing. There was something deliberate about it that Soldier didn't like. The sky was a black scoreboard smudged over with dirty chalk. Trees and bushes that had bent over and sprung up, now leaned all one way under a steady pressure. The rain tasted like salt. A smell of salt was in the air. Flocks of gulls and summer duck beat over to the shelter of the woods. A flock of cranes passed. Soldier watched the scurrying. People concerned for their possessions were tying them up, nailing them down, or running away with them. Where to? Everything upon the land seemed impermanent and unanchored. A steady stream of cars passed through the town on their way from the coastal resorts. A great exodus was taking place in which he had no part. The barn door bolted, nothing remained for him to do but to wait.

At eight o'clock Soldier could stand his loneliness no longer. He put on his slicker and stepped outside. The wind was blowing a gale, slashing the rain to a fine mist. He dug his feet into the muddy ground, and shading his eyes, stared anxiously toward the church. He could make out the dim spike of the steeple in the blowing oak branches, but could see no light. The town was deserted except for an occasional belated car that swayed past, headlights blurred by rain. The townspeople who remained waited behind barred doors and windows.

Leaning hard on the wind, Soldier crossed the track and made his way up the highway toward the church. Through a back window he saw Bertha cooking supper on the kerosene stove. The two chicken coops, covered with sacking, were near the Bible stand. He called and banged on the window, and finally Bertha heard him and came and put her face against the pane.

"No, I won't come!" she screamed. "You go on back before you get blowed away, you old fool! I'll crawl out on the prairie and grab holt of a seeny-bean bush before I pass a storm in that freight car and get blown clean to Jericho!"

"Come stay in the barn!"

"I won't!"

Soldier turned home. The wind hit him broadside and blew him into a shallow ditch. He crawled out soaked to the skin. Small movable objects were beginning to fly past him: papers, shingles, pieces of tin, the wooden bread box from in front of Lee Bird's store. He screamed words that he himself could not hear, but they eased his helpless anger at the woman and the wind. ". . . go away . . . stay away . . . old fool, fool woman you . . . chickens and churches . . . it might as well, I wouldn't care . . . you might as well . . . see if I care!" The wind made a sounding cave of his open mouth, shrieked in and out, tearing the words off his tongue.

He reached the barn and tried to pry open the door, but his strength was no match for the wind which bore against him. He cursed himself for his useless trip, and dropping on his stomach, made his way into the freight car. The car was protected by an angle of the barn from the worst of the wind. Inside it was strangely quiet. He wiped the water from his eyes and looked around. The flame of the lamp shivered and danced. He blew it out, and feeling in the dark, wrapped himself in a blanket and lay down on his cot. The car rocked and teetered. The wind seemed to be turning. Everything was getting wet. The rain seemed to drive through the very walls. An oak branch ripped through the small window, and rain followed in a sheet. Soldier crept under his cot.

The world belonged to the wind. Once, during the night, Soldier thought of Bertha, but as a person he had known a long time ago, a woman long dead. No such wind could pass and not take something away with it. He did not hear the crash that was the roof of the barn settling down over the freight car.

Toward morning he crawled from under his piled-up furniture and clawed across the leaning floor to see if the stove were in any shape to make a cup of coffee. The wind was gone. The inside of the car was black as an inkpot. He felt for matches, and finally found one in his pocket that would strike. The lamp chimney was smashed, but he coaxed oil up the wet wick and by this wavering light examined the stove. It was tipped against the wall, but he managed to straighten it enough to get a fire going. With a cup of hot coffee in his stomach his mind cleared and he remembered Bertha and the necessity for finding out if she were dead or alive. He felt in the cupboard for a dry biscuit, but all food had been soaked to a pulp.

He pried open the wedged door of the freight car and dropped to the ground. In his mind he had already found Bertha and she was dead. He could feel no sadness, only a dazed relief at the wind's cessation. He could not even feel sorry about the barn. The metal eyelets of his soaked shoes bit into the tender flesh of his insteps. Bedraggled and shivering, stiff with rheumatism brought on by the wet, he crept along under the broken roof of the barn on hands and knees toward daylight. He came to a sack of rice, split open, bleeding grain. From behind it sounded a weak clucking. He felt around, and his fingers closed on the warm wet body of a chicken. It was Bobo. The wind had evidently blown him down the road from the church just before the barn roof fell. Bobo's pride was gone, he was shrunken and miserable. Conciliatory sounds came from his throat.

"That'll learn you to answer me back!" Soldier grunted, as he wrung the rooster's neck.

He returned to the car. In a few minutes he had dismembered Bobo and put him down to simmer on the stove. Again he started out to find Bertha.

He reached the open, carefully avoiding the tangled wires that lay beside the railroad track, and rose to his feet. In the watery dawn the world seemed to have been twisted strangely awry by a slap from some great hand. Three wet skunks picked their way down the sandy spit in the middle of the road. A bedraggled house cat looked at him wildly and bounded away. Soldier looked toward the grove where Bertha's church had been. Splintered branches covered the ground. The church steeple was gone. The body of the church itself was off its blocks, tipped forward on its front end like a hog rooting for acorns. Sudden fear gripped the old man.

"Bertha!" he shouted, splashing down the road, "Bertha, where are you?"

Breathless he reached the church and peered through one of the broken windows. Nobody was inside, not even the hens. Bertha was gone.

"Bertha, Bertha, answer me!" Soldier wrung his hands. Small whimpering sounds came from his throat.

"Hoo-o-e-e, Bertha!"

He began to search the grove, climbing painfully over fallen branches, wading in water thigh-deep in ditches. The rice field had disappeared under a lake. Two hundred yards from the church he saw the steeple floating in the canal. He was conscious of other people moving about. One of them hailed him, but he did not reply.

When he saw her he could not believe at first that it was she. He remembered a bigger woman. She stumbled toward him, a tiny bent old woman, plastered with mud and leaves. They met and clung, laughing and weeping.

"I thought you was dead," Soldier said.

"I thought you was dead too."

"My barn's gone . . . most of it. . . ."

"So's my church."

"The steeple's safe in the canal, other side the track. I seen it as I come by."

"Oh . . . the steeple . . ."

"Where was you in all that wind?"

"Holdin' to a seeny-bean on the prairie like I said I would. The danged church took to jumpin' like a Hi-lifed cat so I crawled through a window and got out in the open."

"It was a terrible wind. A mercy we're both alive."

"It was a mighty wind."

"The Lord was lookin' out for us, Bertha."

"Praise God, He was lookin' after us."

"Bertha, will you come home with me and take some nourishment? I got a fire goin'."

"Reckon I might as well."

Clinging together they waded down the road and passed under the fallen barn roof into the freight car.

"Kind of cozy, eh, old woman? Here, wrop up in this blanket till I get you somethin' warm to eat, stop that shiverin'."

"What's that I smell?"

Too late Soldier tried to hide the feathers. He had forgotten Bobo.

"What you got there?" Bertha asked sharply. She stopped huddling herself in the blanket and reached for the pan Soldier held behind his back.

"Nothin', Bertha, honest! Nothin' atall!"

173

"It's entrails and feathers, red feathers! What's in that cookin' pot?"

"Nothin' but a nigger duck hit the barn in the night, and I brought him in and potted him."

"Duck nothin'! Them's Bobo's feathers! I'd know 'em anywhere. You killed him!"

"No, honest now, Bertha, it's Bobo all right, but he was layin' out dead under a tractor wheel, been there all night I expect, dead like I found him."

"Don't tell me! A drownded fowl dead all night won't show blood like I see on them feathers! You wrang his neck! You always hated him!"

"Bertha, wait a minute. . . ."

". . . and you ain't even man enough to admit it!"

"You always liked him better than me!"

They glared at each other, the pan of bloody feathers and entrails between them.

"Hello, hello in there! Are you all right?" shouted a voice from the road.

"All safe!" shouted Soldier in reply.

"Sure you don't need any help?"

"All safe!" shouted Soldier again.

After a minute Bertha sighed and dipped her hand into the steaming pot. She drew it out, blew on her fingers, and stared dazedly around the wrecked car. Soldier fished out a wing and a drumstick, her favorite pieces, and offered them silently.

They both began to eat.

DILLON ANDERSON

DILLON ANDERSON was born at McKinney, Collin County, July 14, 1906. After attending Texas Christian University briefly, he took his B.S. degree from the University of Oklahoma in 1927, and a LL.B. from the Yale Law School in 1929, in which year he was admitted to the Texas bar. Since then he has been a corporation lawyer in Houston, after 1940 a member of the firm of Baker, Botts, Andrews, and Parish. During the war he was a colonel in the General Staff Corps, receiving the Army Commendation Ribbon and the Legion of Merit.

Throughout the years Anderson has been a very busy man. His business ventures are not only substantial but far flung. On money from the Union National Bank, Houston, and carrying a briefcase from Foley Brothers (he is chairman of the Foundation), the young director can say good-bye to the Houston Chamber of Commerce and go by the Houston Transit Company over Texas Bus Lines to inspect the Galveston Electric Company—without ever leaving one of his directorates. All this, plus a wife and three daughters, has not kept Anderson from pulling his full share of Houston's civic and social load. He is a director of the Houston Fat Stock Show and Livestock Association, the Houston Symphony Society, and a leader in other local activities; yet he has time for a number of social clubs.

Obviously, Anderson is not really oppressed by the complexities of modern urban existence. Perhaps one reason he is not is that he has invented Clint Hightower and his friend Claudie, who from the point of view of social responsibility are Anderson's opposites. It was hardly necessary for him to say, on the jacket of *I and Claudie* (1951), that these adventures, which had appeared in the *Atlantic* and *Collier's,* "are in no sense autobiographical." What he added, however, doubtless explains his as well as the world's interest in these charming rogues: "but sometimes I am sorry they are not. Clint and Claudie are not go-getters, boosters, or pillars in anybody's community. They don't entertain people they don't like. They are free from amenities, protocol, and taxes." "Forty Years of Firewood" is not a part of *I and Claudie,* which won the Texas Institute of Letters–McMurray Bookshop award, but a further adventure of the resourceful pair. We hope there will be many more.

175

Forty Years of Firewood

Some of the tales Old Man Nate Pinkney told me and Claudie went all the way back to the days of the Indian fights. His pappy had been an Indian fighter from one end of the Red River Valley to the other, and when he told us about his pappy's forays against the Choctaws, I figured some of them would have made Joshua in Canaan look like Nedrick in the First Reader. Old Man Nate would talk about Indian fights at the drop of a hat; he was always ready. I and Claudie were just as ready to listen, too, during the rainy spell we spent on the Pinkney place near Midlothian, Texas, since free meals went with the listening. We propped one end of our trailer house on a cedar stump in Old Man Nate's front yard, and since we did not have a car to pull it, we sort of settled down there. From the first we found the fare of grits, sowbelly, black-eyed peas, and Indian fights was agreeing with us. Also, it did not call for any manual labor on our part.

I borrowed a book on Indian wars from the old man, and every day while Claudie helped him with milking the cows and feeding the stock, I read up on Indian trouble all the way from Florida to Canada. I figured I might as well learn about both sides of these fights, but from what the book said, I could tell that the Indians had always been in the wrong.

The weather faired off the third afternoon we were parked there, and that was the day we learned that there was at least one Indian still around. It was a warm, cloudy evening, and we'd had supper with Old Man Nate on his back porch before moving out into the chairs under a big umbrella china tree in his back yard. He was telling us for the second time in two days about his pappy's Choctaw fight at Pilot's

Copyright 1951 by Dillon Anderson, trustee; used with permission of the author. First published in the *Southwest Review*, Autumn, 1951, this story also appears in *Claudie's Kinfolks*, published in October, 1954, by Little, Brown and Company.

Knob, when we looked up and saw a tall man and a short woman walking along the bois d'arc hedge toward the house. They were followed by two lean, hungry-looking brindle hounds.

"Who's that?" I asked, breaking in on the story.

"That's Sheb Sprunt and his Indian wife, Josie," he said. "Sheb rents the south eighty acres of my place." Then he went on with his yarn, but he lost Claudie, since Claudie never knew before what Indians looked like, except from copper cents and cigar stores.

Sheb and Josie stopped about ten steps away from us and stood there close together by the cistern. Sheb was a scrawny, skinny, young fellow wearing dirty brown britches and a washed-out duckin shirt. He had an odd squint in one eye. Josie's skin was about the color of bock beer by lamplight, and her eyes were inky black. She was what I'd call squatty and square in the way she was set up. You could almost see corners through her faded calico dress.

"Mr. Pinkney," Sheb called out, "me and Josie want to go to the reservation tomorrow. 'Zit all right with you if we do? We'll be back Saat'dy night or Sunday."

"It's a pity," the old man said, "that you can't wait until the crops are laid by."

"Josie's brother's gonna be made chief of the Waxahachie Tribe, and he writ her to come." Sheb had made his speech. He turned and nodded to Josie, who grinned and showed her teeth. They were square and very white.

"How are you figurin' to go?" Old Man Nate asked.

"We thought if we could go in your car we'd take orful good keer of it."

"That's what I was afeared of," the old man answered, turning to us as if to let us in on his bother. "That Indian reservation is way down below Gruntsville—must be over a hundred miles—but I reckon I've got to let 'em go." He turned and told them they'd have to put some cylinder oil in the car before they went, then he turned back to us and polished off a few more Choctaws before it got good and dark.

When he had finished, I said: "Mr. Pinkney, I think I and Claudie had better go on back to the trailer house and get us a good night's sleep. That sounds like a long trip to the Indian reservation."

"You ain't going, too, are you?" the old man wanted to know.

"Yes," I told him. "That car of yours will handle the trailer, I believe.

177

We'd better be moving on. We don't want to wear our welcome out here, and I know Claudie wants to see them Indians."

Next morning, bright and early, Claudie found some spare bailing wire in the barn and hooked the trailer house on behind Nate's battered-up old Dodge sedan. I told Sheb to drive slow, since there was a mean wobble that cropped up in the trailer at about twenty-five. Then, before Josie got in the car with him, I told her not to let Sheb drive too fast. She said, "Sheb bad driver; can't drive fast," and with that to think about we climbed into the trailer and Sheb pulled out.

On the way Claudie fussed some about leaving. He said, "I'd like to see them Indians, all right, Clint, but that's the nicest place we ever left without being run off."

"Claudie," I told him, "I sometimes think you haven't got any more ambition than a dadburned mule. Can't you see it's time to get a move on? We've been listening to Old Man Nate and eating his food for nearly a week. But it's been a rainy week; too wet to work in the fields. The weather is clearing up today, ain't it?"

"Yes," Claudie answered, "the weather is fairin' off."

"All right," I told him. "There you are. You don't think we could eat like that in dry weather without working, do you? Manual labor, too."

"My old man allus said a rollin' stone don't gather no moss," Claudie grumbled.

"There you go, Claudie," I told him. "Stubborn, too, like a mule. Man cannot live by moss alone."

It was after noon when we reached Gruntsville, and from there we drove east a few miles through the deep piney woods to where a big sign said: "Waxahachie Indian Reservation ½ Mi. North." We followed a dusty woods' road north, with the branches and brambles scuffing and rattling against our trailer house, until we came to a little clearing.

All around was thicket. The undergrowth of palmetto, Cherokee rose and briars was so heavy you couldn't see ten feet outside the clearing. The trees were tall and thick; pine, magnolia, hickory, and beech, and here and there a sprinkling of dogwood.

The clearing was no bigger than an acre or an acre and a half; a number of cars were parked in it, and a lot of people and a few grunting razorback hogs milled about. Mostly the people weren't Indians, though; they were Texans. Also, the Texans seemed to have things in charge. Several grown Indians and a lot of little Indians were huddled here and there, hovering around the fringe of something that you could tell was about to take place.

There was a new platform over on one side of the clearing, all covered with red, white, and blue bunting, and alongside it a big earthen crock. FREE LEMONADE, it said on a sign, and the Texans were drinking the lemonade.

On the platform stood seven very uncomfortable-looking Indians, all dressed up in hot, heavy-looking robes and feathers. Josie said the one in the middle was her brother Joe Eaglebeak, and I noticed Joe had that same square look about his face and person that Josie did. However, all the other Indians did too. The headpieces with all the feathers in them were much too big for these Indians, and you could see only the lower part of their faces—all except Joe Eaglebeak. He had shoved his feathers back to where they sat at an angle on his head like some of the hats the English women wear in the horse race pictures. The platform Indians all looked sweaty and tired in their hot, heavy Indian suits.

I sidled up to one of the Texans, a big, bald fellow dressed in a seersucker suit, who seemed to be having something to do with what was going on. I said, "The feathers don't fit them Indians very well, do they?"

"You are looking at all of the Indian costumes we could find in Houston," he told me, without even looking my way. "Matter of fact," he explained as he walked off, "we needed three more because we've got ten Indians on the Council."

Then he climbed up on the platform and said in a big voice that it was two o'clock and things were going to start. Everything got quiet, and some people took a lot of pictures of the seven Indians in the feathers and the big Texan in the seersucker suit. They said it was for the newspapers.

As everybody gathered in close around the platform, the big seersucker Texan said they were going to have a double-header. They were going to inaugurate a new Chief, Joe Eaglebeak, and they were going to break ground for the new gymnasium that the government was building for the Waxahachie Tribe. The Texans cheered and even gave out a few Indian war whoops; then the Indians out on the edge of the crowd cheered too. Josie cheered, seeing as how Joe Eaglebeak was

179

her brother, but the seven Indians up on the platform were too bogged down in feathers and robes to do anything but stand there and sweat. Joe Eaglebeak grinned and nodded his head every time his name was mentioned, and I noticed that his teeth were big and white, like Josie's.

While they were making a Chief out of Joe Eaglebeak, I asked another one of the Texans who was standing around just who the big shot in the seersucker suit was.

"That's B. Roger Blight," he told me. "He's a big political boss from Tyler."

"What's he doing way off down here?" I asked him.

"He's the contractor that's going to build the gymnasium," the Texan explained.

When they got around to the gymnasium part of the program, Mr. Blight said there would have to be a very ceremonious ground-breaking. He called on Joe Eaglebeak to go over in the far side of the clearing and start digging at a place marked with a little stake. They gave Joe a spade, and he began to dig while the State Senator, an old man with a long haircut, made another speech. They took some more pictures of the Senator speaking and Joe digging, then everybody but the Indians started leaving. The Texans took the feathers and robes along with them, and the next thing I knew I and Claudie and Sheb Sprunt were the only people left except the Indians. There weren't over seventy-five members of the tribe around, counting the children and the real old ones. They were chattering and making a big to-do over Josie. According to Sheb, she was about everybody's cousin in the whole tribe.

The Texans had left the jar of lemonade, and the Indians all moved over to get what was left. Then somebody asked where Joe Eaglebeak was. In the crowd around the platform nobody had noticed that he wasn't drinking lemonade. We looked over at the far side of the clearing, and there was Joe, still digging. Nobody had told him to stop.

Late that afternoon we went with Sheb and Josie down a little trail in the woods to Joe Eaglebeak's place. It was not over fifty yards from the clearing. Joe and his wife, Joey—who looked a whole lot like him —lived in an old, run-down, two-room house that swayed low on the east side where some of the supports were gone. I noticed that there were porches on all four sides of Joe's house, so I said, "Lots of porches you've got here, Chief."

"Need much porches," Joe said. "Porches good for sit. In winter Joe Eaglebeak follow sun around house. In summer follow shade."

Right beside Joe's place was about two-thirds of a nice big, new-looking frame house. It must have been twice as big as Joe's house—leastaways, it would be when finished.

"Nice new place you're building there, Chief," I remarked.

"Not building," Joe said. "Tearing down. Don't like inside smell of new house. Old house best."

"Why did you build the new house, then, Chief?" I asked him.

"Don't build new house," he told me. "Government build new house. Good for firewood. Last maybe one year for firewood. Joe Eaglebeak chop no trees while government house last. Time to eat."

We all sat down to supper on one of the porches with Joe and his wife, Joey; and they fed us cold possum and corn pone. When the food was put out on the table, little Indians showed up from everywhere. They swooped on and off the porch like a flock of teal, and as they'd pass the table, they'd grab handfuls of food.

After supper Joe Eaglebeak said, "Time for radio," and went in the house. Then the radio came on full blast. It boomed; it rattled the windows; it made the house shake on the east side where it was swaying; it drowned out everything else. We could see Joe inside as he worked turning knobs. He got all sorts of music and talk about soap, skin lotions, politics, and cigarettes, but he never turned it down. It even seemed to get louder, and finally Joe came back to where we were sitting on the porch with Joey. He grinned and said something, but it was lost in the roar of the radio.

'Long about sundown I yelled at Claudie and told him I thought we'd better get back to the clearing. Joe walked with us up the trail, and as soon as we got out from under the blanket of radio racket, I turned to Joe Eaglebeak and said, "How's the game around here?"

"Plenty game," Joe said.

"Lived here all your life, Chief?" I asked him.

"Except in German war," and as he said it, Joe's skin seemed to tighten up across his face. He almost looked like a different Indian. "In German war," he went on, "Government draft Joe Eaglebeak to Oklahoma. Private Eaglebeak in Fort Sill, Oklahoma, twenty months. No game in Oklahoma."

I explained to Claudie about the Field Artillery School in Fort Sill;

181

then I asked Joe, "Did you learn to shoot cannons there, Chief?"

"Nope," Joe said. "Joe no shoot cannons. Keep horselot clean in Oklahoma. War not good for Joe Eaglebeak." Then he turned back toward home, and I and Claudie went to the trailer house and turned in for the night.

The next morning, about daylight, Sheb and Josie came to tell us goodbye, and before they left we got them to pull our trailer house over to the edge of the clearing. We knew we'd need the shade. As the old Dodge disappeared up the woods' road, I almost felt stranded again and blue. In the early morning light the clearing looked pretty bleak and dreary. The bunting on the platform was all limp in the dew, and some rusty-colored hogs were rooting around the hole Joe Eaglebeak had dug. It didn't look like a very good place even for an Indian gymnasium.

For breakfast we didn't have anything but coffee, and no cream for that until Claudie caught a stray cow grazing close by and milked her. The sun wasn't very high when it started getting so hot and muggy that the air quivered across the clearing. There were lots of flies and gnats about. When I began to feel a little itchy about the armpits, I checked up on myself and found that I was alive with wood ticks. So was Claudie. I don't know many things that will get a man's dander down further or faster than a passel of wood ticks in the early part of the day. I could tell that Claudie's spirits needed a prop, so I explained that I had things all figured out for us.

"We'll be in on the ground floor when the contractor starts to build the gymnasium," I told him. "We might even both get jobs timekeeping, or straw bossing, or something that does not take any manual labor."

Along about nine or ten o'clock we saw a big black sedan come into the clearing from the north, and when it pulled up even with our trailer house, out hopped a fat citizen with a thick, chubby face and little eyes set very close together. He wasn't any Indian either; he didn't even look like a Texan. He said he was looking for the Waxahachie Chief, and I pointed to the trail leading toward Joe Eaglebeak's house.

After he had gone, Claudie said that he did not like this fat guy's looks one bit.

"I don't either, Claudie," I told him. "I'm afraid he ain't our kind of folks." Then, while Claudie fixed us some breakfast, I sat in the shade of the trailer house and thought a while about a number of things; but mainly I thought about how badly stranded we were, particularly in case we needed to make a quick move for one reason or the other. We needed a car in the worst way.

In an hour or so I and Claudie noticed that the lemonade stand was going again full blast, and the Indians were all gathering again around the platform on the other side of the clearing. They were being spoken to once more, and we could see from where we were that the speaker was the fat fellow with the close-together eyes who had come in the black sedan. We couldn't hear what he was saying, but he seemed to have his heart more in it than the speakers had the day before. He was waving his arms in the air like a man fighting bees, while the Indians all stood around listening and scratching themselves.

"Wonder if these Indians have a speakin' every day?" Claudie asked me.

"I don't know," I said, "and I don't much care, but I hope they don't cut out that daily lemonade. Let's go have some."

Just as we got over to the platform, the Indians all took a vote on something or other. "All in favor hold up their hands," the fat speaker said, and the Indians all held up their hands. We drank our fill of lemonade as the meeting broke up.

Pretty soon we saw what the meeting had been about. Indians started boiling out of the woods on all sides. They went over to the black sedan where the fat man handed them signs on long sticks, and they started marching single file around the clearing. The signs said:

B. ROGER BLIGHT
IS UNFAIR TO AMALGAMATED ASSOCIATION
OF HELPERS, HOD CARRIERS AND
BUILDING TRADE APPRENTICES,
LOCAL 1131.

The Indian pickets, as they walked by the trailer house, all looked very mad and warlike.

Pretty soon a big truck filled with sand came down the road from the north. It stopped at the edge of the clearing where the Indians were marching. The driver got out and said it was the damndest picket line he'd ever seen, but he wasn't going to cross it. Then another truck came and stopped the same way; then another and another, until by sundown the trucks were backed up all the way to the Gruntsville road turnoff.

183

It was nearly dark when Mr. Blight, wearing a fresh seersucker suit, turned up. He walked by the stopped trucks and came to the trailer house where I and Claudie were sitting watching the pickets. He was in an awful fret. His face and the back of his neck were as red as a turkey gobbler's wattles, and his eyes were all bloodshot.

"So you've organized the Indians," he said as he walked up to me with his hands on his hips.

I called Claudie to come and said: "Take it easy, Mr. Blight. A haughty spirit goeth before destruction. Why weren't you fair to the Amalgamated?"

"I'm not unfair to the Amalgamated," Mr. Blight said. "I never heard of any union in here until an hour ago when they told me my trucks were tied up."

By this time Claudie was standing there, about a foot taller than Mr. Blight, so I said: "Now, Mr. Blight, if you will be so kindly, I'll thank you to have a civil tongue in your head. Let's get things clear. We didn't organize these Indians."

"Oh, yeah?" he said, but I could see that Claudie's size and my firm, polite way were telling on him.

"Certainly not," I said. "Maybe we can unorganize them, though. I know a lot about Indians, and my associate, Claudie here, does too."

"What's your name?" he asked. He was getting a lot more friendly.

"Clint Hightower, and I think that I can help you with these Indians if you will let yourself cool off a little," I said.

"Well," Mr. Blight explained, as he eased up in the tone of his voice, "this is sure one hell of a mess. You see, I agreed when I got this contract that I'd use Indians for common labor. Now the Union has tied up all my labor and my building material, too."

"Let's get down to business," I said. "Do you want these Indians unorganized or not?"

"What's your price?"

"Well," I said, "I and my associate have us a nice trailer house, as you can see, but we do not have any car to pull it. We're getting awful tired of hitchhiking rides for it."

"Do you mean—?" he started and choked, turning red in the face again.

"I mean," I said, "we want a car that will pull this here trailer house."

"Why, I'd see you in hell first. The law—," he choked again.

"You keep forgetting, Mr. Blight, that we didn't organize the Indians. We only want to unorganize them," I explained.

"But—," he said, and I broke in:

"If there is a strike on this time tomorrow, we don't get anything. If there ain't, we want a car."

"You have made a deal," he told us and left. But he was still mad.

It was pitch dark by the time Mr. Blight left. Claudie fired up a lantern, and we went down the trail to Joe Eaglebeak's house. We found him sitting on a stump in the yard smoking a corncob pipe and listening to the radio. It was on full blast.

"Chief," I yelled as loud as I could to make him hear me above the radio, "tune that thing down; I want to talk to you." Joe went inside and turned it down a little.

"Joe," I asked him when he came back, "who was that fat fellow in the black sedan?"

"Union organizer," Joe said.

"I thought so," I told him. "Who's head man in the new Union?"

"Joe Eaglebeak, President," he answered.

"Good for you, Joe. I'm proud of you. Tell me about the Union. What all do you know about it?"

"Not much." Joe lit his pipe again and sat down as he said it. "You know much about unions?"

"Oh sure; they're a lot like the Army, Joe," I told him.

"Union like Army? Army not good for Joe Eaglebeak."

"A great deal like the Army," I went on; "and another thing: that big, fat fellow in the black sedan sounded just like a top sergeant to me."

"Sergeant?" Joe dropped his pipe in the grass as he got up. "Sergeant?" he said it again to himself, and fighting lines showed up around his mouth. "Sergeant no good."

"Joe," I said, "it looks to me like you are going off somewhere again to clean horselots. You may like it, but how about the other Indians?"

"Sergeant no good," Joe kept saying to himself as he looked for his pipe in the grass; then, when he found it, he struck out for the tall timber. I and Claudie walked back up the trail to the clearing.

The next morning when the fat organizer came to the clearing in his black sedan, the Indians were waiting for him. There were forty or fifty of them milling around him about a minute after he got there. They all had their picket signs, but they weren't marching any more. This time the Indians were doing the talking, and above it all I could hear them yell, "Sergeant no good." The fat man didn't have a chance. One of the Indians hit him over the head with a picket sign; then there was an awful mixup, with Indians pushing and shoving and chattering like a bunch of women at a rummage sale.

I got Claudie to go with me, and we ran over to the crowd. We dug the organizer out the way football umpires dig out the man with the ball. He was pretty badly ruffled up when we got him in the clear, and Joe Eaglebeak had hold of him by the coat collar. I asked Joe to turn loose and get things quieted down so I could talk. "This ain't a fair fight, Joe," I said. "You Indians have this good man outnumbered." Then I turned to the organizer and said: "I don't believe these Indians like you very much, but the way they are treating you is too much for my sense of fair play. I and my assistant here want to help you, Mister, but not in any Indian fight."

He was too out of breath to talk, but with all the Indians standing around and muttering at him he seemed to be almost persuaded that it was about time to leave. Then I said, "I'm afraid I can't promise to hold them off much longer."

That was enough for him. He bolted for the car, but when he did the Indians swarmed after him again. It was all I and Claudie could do to hold those Indians off, but with some help from Joe Eaglebeak we did, and the man in the black sedan sloped for the Gruntsville road. The Indians all went off down the trail that led to Joe's house.

After the dust and the Indians had cleared away, the trucks all came into the clearing, and the drivers started unloading sand and gravel and lumber. Mr. Blight came along after a little while, and he was the most relieved customer I'd seen since the time we pulled Claudie's Uncle Zeke out of the bear trap back in Alabama.

"You fellers didn't take long," he said.

"I think I'd like a red automobile," I told him. I figured I'd better strike while the iron was hot.

"Let's get a green car," Claudie put in.

"We'll take red, Mr. Blight," I said. "Maybe we can get a red one with a little green trimming somewhere on it."

About this time we looked over toward the trail leading to Joe Eaglebeak's house, and there came the Indians again. Joe was in the lead. They went over to the platform, got the UNFAIR signs, and started to march around the clearing. All the truck drivers quit, folded their arms, and stood there watching the pickets. Mr. Blight looked at me like you'd look at some carcass the dogs had drug up from the creek.

"There they go again," Claudie said—as stupid a remark as I'd heard him make all day.

I went over to Joe Eaglebeak, who was leading the picket line. I took him by the arm and said, "Chief, what the hell's up? I thought we'd fired that fat organizer."

"Fired organizer," Joe said and kept on marching. I marched along with him until we were even with the trailer house, then I asked Joe to come in for a minute so we could talk things over. The other pickets marched on while Joe went in with me.

Inside, Joe sniffed and looked around; then a nice friendly look came across his face—almost like that of Indians on calendars. He said, "Joe Eaglebeak like inside smell of trailer house."

"O.K., Joe, and thanks," I said, "but what the hell's going on out there?"

"Joe Eaglebeak big Union chief now," Joe stated. "Indians strike."

"Listen, Joe," I said, "you're fixing to louse this gymnasium job up if you don't watch out. What the devil is it you are striking for this time? What do you want?"

"Big house in Florida for Joe Eaglebeak."

"Florida?" I said. "What do you know about Florida?"

"Know from radio," Joe said. "Union chiefs get Florida houses."

"Wait a minute, Joe," I argued.

"Blonde bathers, too, for Union chiefs in Florida. Bathe squaw in ocean," Joe went on.

"Do you know anything about the game in Florida, Joe?" I asked him.

"Never thought of game." Joe looked a little stunned at this.

"Well," I said, "there's no more game there than there is in Oklahoma."

Joe looked pretty hard hit, and I went on while I had him bothered. "Joe," I said, "I once knew a wooden Indian who used his head more than you are using yours right now."

This seemed almost to hurt Joe Eaglebeak's feelings, and he got up and started to leave. He was talking to himself, but all I could hear was, "Bathe naked squaw in ocean."

187

"Hold it, Joe," I yelled, remembering a chapter from Old Man Nate's book on Indian fights. "There's one more thing about that house you want in Florida. There's a war on over there, you know."

Joe sat back down, and I saw the skin tighten up on his face again. He said: "War in Florida? No more war for Joe Eaglebeak. Had war in Oklahoma."

"Of course you did," I said. "Now you listen to me, Joe. Did you ever hear of the Seminole Indians?"

"Seminoles? Sure," Joe grinned and nodded.

"All right," I went on, "the Seminole Indians have got them a war on over in Florida. It's been going on a hundred years or so. Big Chief Osceola started war. No peace treaty yet."—I found I was beginning to talk a little like Joe.—"No war in Texas; plenty game here, too. Big Texas house is what you want, Joe. Government calls it gymnasium. Let them build it. If you don't want to live in it, you've got forty years of firewood."

"Forty years of firewood?" Joe asked.

"Of course, Joe," I told him. "Forty years anyhow."

"Forty years enough," Joe said.

"Now you are talking, Joe," I said. "Let's burn up them picket signs."

"Indians burn platform, too," Joe said. "But, first, Indians need smart fellers' help to build gymnasium. Indians make no mistake if Clint and Claudie work too."

"You don't need us, Joe," I argued. "I'm no good at manual labor."

"You no work, Indians no work; Indians strike." Joe took hold of the picket sign and started to raise it up.

"Hold it, Joe," I said. "Claudie will work on the gymnasium. I might be a straw boss or something."

"You no work, Indians strike," and he said it like an Indian that comes from a long line of fighting Indians.

"O.K., Joe, you win," I told him. "I and Claudie will both work on that damn gymnasium." Joe nodded and grinned until all his square teeth showed. We shook hands on it.

We had a big bonfire that night in the clearing. We burned the platform and all the picket signs. We all drank our fills of lemonade that B. Roger Blight fetched from Gruntsville. He brought it in a red Ford coupe with green wheels. It was second-hand, but it would run. He handed me the registration on the car, made out in my name, but I saw that the blank headed "Occupation or Business of Owner" was not filled in.

"What goes here?" Mr. Blight asked me.

"Just put it down 'manual labor,' " I told him.

J. FRANK DOBIE

If Texas ever had a truly native writer, that man is J. Frank Dobie. True, he has been outside the state often enough—to study at the University of Chicago, summer of 1909; to take an M.A. at Columbia, 1914; to keep an appointment with the A.E.F., 1917–19; to lecture on American history at Cambridge University, where he was awarded an honorary M.A., 1943–44; to teach for the Information and Education Division of the United States Army at Shrivenham American University in England and lecture to troops in Germany and Austria, 1945–46; to study at the Huntington Library, 1948–49; and to go foot by foot all over the Southwest which he knows, loves, and shares with others.

Otherwise, Dobie's booted feet, while they weren't in the stirrups, have stood firmly planted on Texas ground. He was born on a ranch in Live Oak County, "altogether out of reach of bookstores and libraries," September 26, 1888. He was given his first schooling by his mother and a ranch governess. Putting on his first pair of shoes—patent leather they were—he went to Georgetown, where in 1910 he received his B.A. from Southwestern University. In the summers of 1910 and 1914 he worked as a reporter on the *San Antonio Express* and the *Galveston Tribune*. He kept school, first as principal at Alpine, 1910–11; at Southwestern, 1911–13; at Oklahoma Agricultural and Mechanical College, 1923–25; and at the University of Texas, off and on, from 1914 to 1947. In one of the important "off" seasons, 1920–21, he managed his uncle Jim Dobie's two-hundred-thousand-acre ranch. In others, 1930–31, 1932–33, 1934–35, he held Rockefeller and Guggenheim fellowships. From 1945 to 1948 he was a member of the United States National Commission for UNESCO.

Through all these years Dobie has collected Texas and Southwestern natural history and legends. Since 1924 he has been a contributing editor of the *Southwest Review*. He was secretary and editor of the Texas Folklore Society for about twenty years, resigning in 1943. His own books—the stack of cards on which his name is entered in the card catalogue of the University of Texas Library is more than an inch thick—include *A Vaquero of the Brush Country* (1929), *Coronado's Chil-*

190

dren (1930), *Tongues of the Monte* (1936), *Apache Gold and Yaqui Silver* (1939), *The Longhorns* (1941), *Guide to Life and Literature of the Southwest* (1943, 1952), *A Texan in England* (1945), *The Voice of the Coyote* (1949), *The Ben Lily Legend* (1950), and *The Mustangs* (1952).

Although Dr. Dobie (Southwestern awarded him an honorary D.Litt. in 1931) has made a contribution of immense value in his writings, he has been of service to the arts in Texas in at least two other ways. First, several thousand Texans have a greater understanding and appreciation of their heritage from taking his famous course at the University of Texas, "Life and Literature of the Southwest." Second, he has been one of the hardest-stinging gadflies to keep Texas from being smug about such achievement as she has made in the arts. For example, consider his remark that "the number of worthless books classified as Texasana is large and the rate of their increase is indecent."

Coronado's Children is not a volume of short stories but a collection of legends—as the subtitle puts it, *Tales of Lost Mines and Buried Treasures of the Southwest*. As such, it would not need to be represented in this collection. Dobie's method is such, however, that "Midas on a Goatskin" meets a test insisted upon by one group of critics of the modern short story—that it reveal character in a "moment of illumination," similar to what James Joyce calls an "epiphany." When the narrator concludes, "I don't know, but it seemed to me then, and it seems to me still, that there are many ways of living worse than the way of this village scavenger with a soft goatskin to sit on," the tale has become essentially a short story.

Midas on a Goatskin

*High on a throne of royal state, which far
Outshone the wealth of Ormus and of Ind.*
—Paradise Lost

He's the second sorriest white man in Sabinal," my host said. "The sorriest white man keeps a Mexican woman without marrying her, but Dee Davis lawfully wedded his *pelada*. He's town scavenger, works at night, and sleeps most of the day. He'll probably be awake 'long about four o'clock this evening and more than ready to tell you the kind of yarns you want to hear."

We found Dee Davis just awaking from his siesta. He occupied a one-roomed shack and sat on a goatskin in the door, on the shady side of the house.

"I'm a great hand for goatskins," he said. "They make good settin' and they make good pallets."

I sat in a board-bottomed chair out on the hard, swept ground, shaded by an umbrella-China tree as well as by the wall. The shack was set back in a yard fenced with barbed wire. Within the same enclosure but farther towards the front was a little frame house occupied by Dee Davis's Mexican wife and their three or four half-breed children. The yard, or patio, was gay with red and orange zinnias and blue morning-glories. Out in a ramshackle picket corral to the rear a boy was playing with a burro.

"No, mister," went on Dee Davis, who had got strung out in no time, "I don't reckon anything ever would have come of my dad's picking up those silver bars if it hadn't of been for a surveyor over in Del Rio.

Reprinted from *Coronado's Children;* copyright 1930 by the author and used by his permission.

"You see, Dad and Uncle Ben were frontiersmen of the old style and while they'd had a lot of experiences—yes, mister, a lot of experiences—they didn't know a thing about minerals. Well, along back in the eighties they took up some state land on Mud Creek and begun trying to farm a little. Mud Creek's east of Del Rio. The old Spanish crossing on Mud was worn deep and always washed, but it was still used a little. Well, one day not long after an awful rain, a reg'lar gully-washer and fence-lifter, Dad and Uncle Ben started to town. They were going down into the creek when, by heifers, what should show up right square in the old trail but the corner of some sort of metal bar. They got down out of their buggy and pried the bar out and then three other bars. The stuff was so heavy that after they put it in the buggy they had to walk and lead the horse. Instead of going on into town with it, they went back home. Well, they turned it over to Ma and then more or less forgot all about it, I guess—just went on struggling for a living.

"At that time I was still a kid and was away from home working for the San Antonio Land and Cattle Company, but I happened to ride in just a few days after the find. The Old Man and Uncle Ben never mentioned it, but Ma was so proud she was nearly busting, and as soon as I got inside the house she said she wanted to show me something. In one of the rooms was a bed with an old-timey covering on it that came down to the floor. She carried me to this bed, pulled up part of the cover that draped over to the floor, and told me to look. I looked, and, by heifers, there was bars as big as hogs. Yes, mister, as big as hogs.

"Nothing was done, however. We were a long ways from any kind of buying center and never saw anybody. As I said in the beginning, I don't know how long those bars might have stayed right there under that bed if it hadn't been for the surveyor. I won't call his name, because he's still alive and enjoying the fruits of his visit. My dad was a mighty interesting talker, and this surveyor used to come to see him just to hear him talk. Well, on one of these visits he stayed all night and slept on the bed that hid the bars. One of his shoes got under the bed, and next morning in stooping down to get it he saw the bars. At least that's the explanation he gave. Then, of course, he got the whole story as to how the bars came to be there and where they were dug up.

" 'What you going to do with 'em?' he asked Dad.

" 'Oh, I don't know,' Dad says to him. 'Nothing much, I guess. Ma here figgers the stuff might be silver, but I don't know what it is. More'n likely it's not anything worth having.'

" 'Well,' says the surveyor, 'you'd better let me get it assayed. I'm going down to Piedras Negras in my waggin next week and can take it along as well as not.'

"The upshot was that he took all the bars. Two or three months later when Dad saw him and asked him how the assay turned out, he kinder laughed and says, 'Aw pshaw, 'twan't nothing but babbitting.' Then he went on to explain how he'd left the whole caboodle down there to Piedras Negras because it wasn't worth hauling back.

"Well, it wasn't but a short time before we noticed this surveyor, who had been dog poor, was building a good house and buying land. He always seemed to have money and went right up. Also, he quit coming round to visit his old friend. Yes, mister, quit coming round.

"Some years went by and Dad died. The country had been consider'bly fenced up, though it's nothing but a ranch country yet, and the roads were changed. I was still follering cows, over in Old Mexico a good part of the time. Nobody was left out on Mud Creek. Uncle Ben had moved to Del Rio. One day when I was in there I asked him if he could go back to the old trail crossing on Mud. The idea of them bars and of there being more where they come from seemed to stick in my head.

" 'Sure, I can go to the crossing,' says Uncle Ben. 'It's right on the old Spanish Trail. Furthermore, it's plainly marked by the ruins of an old house on the east bank.'

" 'Well,' says I, 'we'll go over there sometime when we have a day to spare.'

"Finally, two or three years later, we got off. First we went up to the ruins of the house. About all left of it was a tumble-down stick-and-mud chimney.

"Uncle Ben and Dad, you understand, found the bars right down the bank from this place. Just across the creek, on the side next to Del Rio, was a motte of *palo blanco* trees. The day was awfully hot and we crossed back over there to eat our dinner under the shade and rest up a little before we dug any. About the time we got our horses staked, I noticed a little cloud in the northwest. In less than an hour it was raining pitchforks and bob-tailed heifer yearlings, and Mud Creek was tearing down with enough water to swim a steamboat. There was nothing for us to do but go back to Del Rio.

"I've never been back to hunt those bars since. That was close to forty years ago. A good part of that time I've been raising a family, but my youngest boy—the one out there fooling with the burro—is nine years old now. As soon as he's twelve and able to shift for himself a little, I'm going back into that country and make several investigations."

Old Dee shifted his position on the goatskin.

"My eyes won't stand much light," he explained. "I have worked so long at night that I can see better in the darkness than in the daylight."

I noticed that his eyes were weak, but they had a strange light in them. It was very pleasant as we sat there in the shade, by the bright zinnias and the soft morning-glories. Pretty soon Dee Davis would have to milk his cow and then in the dark do his work as scavenger for the town. Still there was no hurry. Dee Davis's mind was far away from scavenger filth. He went on.

"You see, the old Spanish Trail crossed over into Texas from Mexico at the mouth of the Pecos River, came on east, circling Seminole Hill just west of Devil's River, on across Mud Creek, and then finally to San Antonio. From there it went to New Orleans. It was the route used by the *antiguas* for carrying their gold and silver out of Mexico to New Orleans. The country was full of Indians; it's still full of dead Spaniards and of bullion and bags of money that the Indians captured and buried or caused the original owners to bury.

"Seminole Hill hides a lot of that treasure. They say that a big jag of Quantrill's loot is located about Seminole too, but I never took much stock in this guerrilla treasure. But listen, mister, and I'll tell you about something that I do take consider'ble stock in.

"Last winter an old Mexican *pastor* named Santiago was staying here in Sabinal with some of his *parientes*. He's a little bit kin to my wife. Now, about nine-tenths of the time a sheepherder don't have a thing to do but explore every cave and examine every rock his sheep get close to. Santiago had a dog that did most of the actual herding. Well, two years ago this fall he was herding sheep about Seminole Hill.

"According to his story—and I don't doubt his word—he went pirooting into a cave one day and stepped right on top of more money than he'd ever seen before all put together. It was just laying there on the

195

floor, some of it stacked up and some of it scattered around every which way. He begun to gather some of it up and had put three pieces in his *jato*—a kind of wallet, you know, that *pastores* carry their provisions in—when he heard the terriblest noise behind him he had ever heard in all his born days. He said it was like the sounds of trace-chains rattling, and dried cowhides being drug at the end of a rope, and panther yells, and the groans of a dying man all mixed up. He was scared half out of his skin. He got out of the cave as fast as his legs would carry him.

"An hour or so later, when he'd kinder collected his wits, he discovered three of the coins still in his *jato*. They were old square 'dobe dollars like the Spanish used to make. As soon as he got a chance, he took them to Villa Acuna across the river from Del Rio, and there a barkeeper traded him three bottles of beer and three silver dollars, American, for them.

"Well, you know how superstitious Mexicans are. Wild horses couldn't drag old Santiago back inside that cave, but he promised to take me out there and show me the mouth of it. We were just waiting for milder weather when somebody sent in here and got him to herd sheep. Maybe he'll be back this winter. If he is, we'll go out to the cave. It won't take but a day."

Dee Davis rolled another cigarette from his supply of Black Horse leaf tobacco and corn shucks. His Mexican wife, plump and easy-going, came out into the yard and began watering the flowers from a tin can. He hardly noticed her, though as he glanced in her direction he seemed to inhale his smoke with a trifle more of deliberation. He was a spare man, and gray moustaches that drooped in Western sheriff style hid only partly a certain nervousness of the facial muscles; yet his few gestures and low voice were as deliberate—and as natural—as the flop of a burro's ears.

"What I'd rather get at than Santiago's cave," he resumed, "is that old smelter across the Rio Grande in Mexico just below the mouth of the Pecos. That smelter wasn't put there to grind corn on, or to boil frijoles in, or to roast goat ribs over, or anything like that. No, mister, not for anything like that.

"It's kinder under a bluff that fronts the river. I know one ranchman who had an expert mining engineer with him, and they spent a whole week exploring up and down the bluff and back in the mountains. I could of told them in a minute that the mine was not above the mouth of the Pecos. If it had of been above, the trails made by miners carrying *parihuelas* could still be seen. I've peered over every foot of that ground and not a *parihuela* trace is there. You don't know what a *parihuela* is? Well, it's a kind of hod, shaped like a stretcher, with a pair of handles in front and a pair behind so two men can carry it. That's what the slave Indians carried ore on.

"No, sir, the mine that supplied that smelter—and it was a big mine —was below the mouth of the Pecos. It's covered up now by a bed of gravel that has probably washed in there during the last eighty or ninety years. All a man has to do to uncover the shaft is to take a few teams and scrapers and clear out the gravel. The mouth of the shaft will then be as plain as daylight. That will take a little capital. You ought to do this. I wish you would. All I want is a third for my information.

"Now, there is an old lost mine away back in the Santa Rosa Mountains that the Mexicans called El Lipano. The story goes that the Lipan Indians used to work it. It was gold and as rich as twenty-dollar gold pieces. El Lipano didn't have no smelter. The Lipans didn't need one.

"And I want to tell you that those Lipan Indians could smell gold as far as a hungry coyote can smell fresh liver. Yes, mister, they could smell it. One time out there in the Big Bend an old-timey Lipan came to D. C. Bourland's ranch and says to him, 'Show me the *tinaja* I'm looking for and I'll show you the gold.' He got down on his hands and knees and showed how his people used to pound out gold ornaments in the rock *tinajas* across the Rio Grande from Reagan Canyon.

"Now that long bluff overlooking the lost mine in the gravel I was just speaking about hides something worth while. I guess maybe you never met old Uncle Dick Sanders. I met him the first time while I was driving through the Indian Territory up the trail to Dodge. He was government interpreter for the Comanche Indians at Fort Sill and was a great hombre among them.

"Well, several years ago an old, old Comanche who was dying sent for Uncle Dick.

" 'I'm dying,' the Comanche says. 'I want nothing more on this earth. You can do nothing for me. But you have been a true friend to me and my people. Before I leave, I want to do you a favor.'

197

J. Frank Dobie

"Then the old Indian, as Uncle Dick Sanders reported the facts to me, went on to tell how when he was a young buck he was with a party raiding horses below the Rio Grande. He said that while they were on a long bluff just south of the river they saw a Spanish cart train winding among the mountains. The soldiers to guard it were riding ahead, and while they were going down into a canyon out of sight, the Comanches made a dash, cut off three *carretas*, and killed the drivers.

"There wasn't a thing in the *carretas* but rawhide bags full of gold and silver coins. Well, this disgusted the Comanches mightily. Yes, mister, disgusted them. They might make an ornament out of a coin now and then, but they didn't know how to trade with money. They traded with Buffalo robes and horses.

"So what they did now with the rawhide sacks was to cut them open and pour the gold and silver into some deep cracks they happened to notice in the long bluff. Two or three of the sacks, though, they brought over to this side of the Rio Grande and hid in a hole. Then they piled rocks over the hole. This place was between two forks, the old Comanche said, one a running river walled with rock, and the other a deep, dry canyon. Not far below where the canyon emptied into the river, the river itself emptied into the Rio Grande.

"After the Comanche got through explaining all this to Uncle Dick Sanders, he asked for a lump of charcoal and a dressed deerskin. Then he drew on the skin a sketch of the Rio Grande, the bluffs to the south, a stream with a west prong coming in from the north, and the place of the buried coins. Of course he didn't put names on the map. The only name he knew was Rio Grande del Norte. When Sanders came down here looking for the Comanche stuff, of course he brought the map with him and he showed it to me. The charcoal lines had splotched until you could hardly trace them, but Sanders had got an Indian to trace them over with a kind of greenish paint.

"Uncle Dick had some sort of theory that the Comanche had mistook the Frio River for the Rio Grande. Naturally he hadn't got very far in locating the ground, much less the money. He was disgusted with the whole business. Told me I could use his information and have whatever I found. I'm satisfied that Devil's River and Painted Cave Canyon are the forks that the Indians hid the *maletas* of money between, and the long bluff on the south side of the Rio Grande where they poured coins into the chinks is the same bluff I've been talking about."

Dee Davis got up, reached for a stick, squatted on the ground, and outlined the deerskin map that Uncle Dick Sanders had shown him. Then he sat down again on the goatskin and contemplated the map in silence.

It was wonderfully pleasant sitting there in the shade, the shadows growing longer and the evening growing cooler, listening—whether to Dee Davis or to a hummingbird in the morning-glories. I did not want the tales to stop. I remarked that I had just been out in the Big Bend country and had camped on Reagan Canyon, famed for its relation to the Lost Nigger Mine. I expected that Dee Davis would know something about this. He did.

"Now listen," he interposed in his soft voice, "I don't expect you to tell me all you know about the Lost Nigger Mine, and I know some things I can't tell you. You'll understand that. You see I was *vaciero* for a string of *pastores* in that very country and got a good deal farther into the mountains, I guess, than any of the Reagans ever got. You may not believe me, but I'll swear on a stack of Bibles as high as your head that I can lead you straight to the nigger who found the mine. Of course I can't tell you where he is. You'll understand that. It was this away.

"One morning the Reagans sent Bill Kelley—that's the nigger's name —to hunt a horse that had got away with the saddle on. A few hours later Jim Reagan rode up on the nigger and asked him if he had found the horse.

" 'No, sah,' the nigger says, 'but jes' looky here, Mister Jim, I'se foun' a gold mine.'

" 'Damn your soul,' says Jim Reagan, 'we're not paying you to hunt gold mines. Pull your freight and bring in that horse.'

"Yes, mister, that's the way Jim Reagan took the news of the greatest gold mine that's ever been found in the Southwest—but he repented a million times afterwards.

"Well, as you've no doubt heard, the nigger got wind of how he was going to be pitched into the Rio Grande and so that night he lit a shuck on one of the Reagan horses. Then a good while afterwards when the Reagans found out how they'd played the wilds in running off, you might say, the goose that laid the golden egg, they started in to trail him down. No telling how many thousands of dollars they did spend

199

trying to locate Nigger Bill—the only man who could put his hand on the gold.

"I've knowed a lot of the men who looked for the Lost Nigger Mine. Not one of them has gone to the right place. One other thing I'll tell you. Go to that round mountain down in the *vegas* on the Mexican side just opposite the old Reagan camp. They call this mountain El Diablo, also Niggerhead; some calls it El Capitan. Well, about half way up it is a kind of shelf, or mesa, maybe two acres wide. On this shelf close back against the mountain wall is a *chapote* bush. Look under that *chapote* and you'll see a hole about the size of an old-timey dug well. Look down this hole and you'll see an old ladder—the kind made without nails, rungs being tied on the poles with rawhide and the fibre of Spanish dagger. Well, right by that hole, back a little and sorter hid behind the *chapote*, I once upon a time found a *macapal*. I guess you want me to tell you what that is. It's a kind of basket in which Mexican miners used to carry up their ore. It's fastened on the head and shoulders.

"Now, I never heard of a *macapal* being used to haul water up in. And I didn't see any water in that hole. No, mister, I didn't see any water.

"As I said, as soon as my boy gets to be twelve years old—he's nine now—I'm going out in that country and use some of the knowledge I've been accumulating."

Dee Davis leaned over and began lacing the brogan shoes on his stockingless feet. It was about time for him to begin work. But I was loath to leave. How pleasant it was there! Maybe Dee Davis is "the second sorriest white man in Sabinal." I don't know, but it seemed to me then, and it seems to me still, that there are many ways of living worse than the way of this village scavenger with a soft goatskin to sit on, and aromatic Black Horse tobacco to inhale leisurely through a clean white shuck, and bright zinnias and blue morning-glories in the dooryard, and long siestas while the shadows of evening lengthen to soften the light of day, and an easy-going Mexican wife, and playing around a patient burro out in the corral an urchin that will be twelve *mañana*, as it were, and then— Then silver bars out of Mud Creek as big as hogs—and heaps of old square 'dobe dollars in Santiago's cave on Seminole Hill—and Uncle Dick Sanders' gold in the chinks of the long bluff across the Rio Grande—and somewhere in the gravel down under the bluff a rich mine that a few mules and scrapers might uncover in a day—and, maybe so, the golden Lipano out in the Santa Rosas beyond—and, certainly and above all, the great Lost Nigger Mine of free gold far up the Rio Bravo in the solitude of the Big Bend.

Dee Davis is just one of Coronado's children.

FRED GIPSON

Frederick Benjamin Gipson was born on the farm near Mason, Mason County, where he now lives. How he spent his boyhood is clear from nearly everthing he has written. While he worked at picking cotton and tending livestock, he was absorbing the sights and sounds and smells of farm and other outdoor life in the Texas Hill Country. He attended the University of Texas, where he studied under that potent team, Dobie and Boatright, being graduated in 1937. While still a student he published his first story, "Hard-Pressed Sam," in the *Southwest Review*, to which he has given credit for greatly assisting him as a writer.

A student of journalism, Gipson worked for three years as a newspaper reporter, part of the time on the *Denver Post*. In 1940, however, he returned to Mason and decided to face the lean years that lie ahead of a beginning free-lance writer. The first year he earned only $155. Then he began to enjoy a steady if not handsome income from pulp westerns, from stories which were perhaps too good for the magazines that published them.

Impressed with Colonel Zack Miller's tales of the great 101 Ranch, Gipson recorded them in his first book, *Fabulous Empire: Colonel Zack Miller's Story* (1946), which sold over twenty-five thousand copies. Throughout his career Gipson has devoted himself to the subjects that he knows best, boys and coons and dogs and hunting and all the rest of Texas rural life. In 1949, Harper and Brothers published *Hound-Dog Man*, which was a Book-of-the-Month Club selection, won the Texas Institute of Letters–McMurray Bookshop award, and passed the final test (alas) of the contemporary novel, success as a paper-backed reprint.

The Home Place (1950) continues the rich, fresh, homespun idiom which is its author's best vein. Full of boys and dogs, close to the Texas earth, it, too, was a club choice. Sears, Roebuck's People's Book Club sold it to Twentieth Century–Fox before publication. Austin folk are still talking about the high jinks that recently accompanied the Austin opening of the resulting motion picture, *Return of the Texan*. Gipson's latest book is *Cowhand* (1953), the story of Fat Alford, a working cowboy quite different from Gene Autry.

Fred Gipson's work represents no literary escapism or dwelling on

202

the romantic past and pastoral present for cultish reasons. Through the boy in "My Kind of a Man," here printed, Gipson asks serious questions about the relative worth of town and country, competitive and simple, life. The answers, of course, are those the author himself has found and lived out. He took his stand when he gave up his job in Denver and made the return to Texas. After his success, when asked when he would be gallivanting off to Hollywood or New York, he replied: "New York? I can't even take Dallas. Mason County is the only place for me." So he lives on his home place, writes, farms, and brings up his boys right, with plenty of dogs.

My Kind of a Man

WHEN I WAS a patch-seated kid, Charlie used to come by our house.

Charlie lived with four hound-dogs over on Wolf Branch. He had a chicken-coop shack there under the elms and pecans. It sat so low in the creek bottom that sometimes Charlie had to move out for an hour or two while the flood waters of Wolf Branch moved in. But that wasn't often.

Charlie kept chickens and ducks and lots of times a pet coon or two. And the squirrels that lived in the hollows of the same trees his chickens roosted in had the run of the shack.

I was always glad when Charlie came by our house, but Mom wasn't. In the first place, Charlie's hounds would beat him there by anywhere from five to ten minutes. One would make directly for the slop bucket and run his head into it. Another would make the rounds of all Mom's feed pans and clean up the sour milk and stale bread she had put out for the chickens. The third was an egg-sucker and knew where all the hens' nests were. And the fourth made for the kitchen, hoping there would be a pan of cornbread set out to cool.

It used to hack me terrible when Mom flew into that bunch of hounds with a stick of stove wood. They'd howl so pitiful and run off with their tails clamped to their bellies. And Charlie, he'd come up looking kinda sheepish and quarreling at the dogs to show that he'd tried to raise them different.

Mom didn't like Charlie's state of bachelorhood or his precarious way of living. She held that a man was duty bound to woman and should settle down and provide for a family. She used to scold me for wanting to prowl with him.

Reprinted from the *Southwest Review*, Autumn, 1944; copyright 1944 by the author and used by his permission.

"Do you want to grow up and live wild," she'd scold, "with a passel of old pesky hound-dogs underfoot? Never doing nothing but roving the woods? Just living from hand to mouth?"

And I'd say: "No'm, I guess not."

But I was lying. The truth was that I could think of no better way of living—out in the woods where there were no cotton patches to hoe, no corn to weed, no hot sand to burn my bare feet. I couldn't see anything wrong with it.

Charlie *was* ragged most of the time. Winters, he had to wear two and three pairs of pants so that the holes wouldn't match and let the cold air in. He hobbled around in old castoff shoes, and the skunk scent he acquired in the winter trapping season never quite left his clothes all summer. But he was my kind of man. He could tear off a piece of oak leaf and hold it against the roof of his mouth with his tongue, and blow on it and call a fat turkey within gun range at gobbling time. And he could imitate a lovesick hen quail's call till half the rooster quails in the country would be whistling and strutting and dragging their wings all about us. One time he came by with a swarm of wild bees, big as a sack of corn, hanging to a persimmon branch he'd cut off. And the bees weren't stinging him.

But Mom said Charlie was shiftless; he wouldn't work. He'd never have any money, Mom said. She wanted me to be like Cullen Morten, the banker, who owned the finest house in town. The banker was a "respectable citizen," Mom said. He'd helped to build the town.

I didn't want to build a town and, although I did sometimes think it would be mighty fine to have a whole house stacked full of gold and silver, I knew Charlie didn't think much of Cullen Morten.

"He's got a watch-chain belly," Charlie said scornfully one time. "His tongue'd be hanging out of his mouth a foot by the time he'd follered a pack of real coon hounds half an hour!"

Charlie was as lean-flanked as one of his own hounds; he could run with them all night.

Charlie wouldn't even sell that pompous banker a hound pup. I saw him try to buy one from Charlie once.

Cullen Morten drove out to Charlie's shack in his big, shiny automobile and tried to buy the pup for one of the brothers of his lodge who lately had taken a fancy to fox hunting. They were pretty pups, blue and white spotted. I wanted one myself, only Mom wouldn't let me have it.

But Charlie wouldn't sell. Cullen Morten offered him five dollars, then finally fifteen. But Charlie just stood around fingering a hole in the seat of his pants and reckoned he didn't figure on selling none of them pups. Figured to make coon dogs out of them. He said his old dogs were getting as cranky and hard to manage as old people. Hardly fit to take into the woods any more.

Next week Charlie gave that hound pup to Horsefly Sanders, a neighbor kid who wanted it bad but had no money to buy it. Me and Horsefly trained the pup with Charlie's hounds that weren't fit to take into the woods any more. A year later a wild boar hog down in the brush thickets along Comanche Creek, opened a slit in the dog's belly a foot long with one slash of his tusk.

Me and Horsefly cried some that night. Charlie was along and shot the pup to stop its suffering. He tried to comfort us, too. He claimed a dog that was fool enough to tie into a old boar hog like that wasn't worth his feed, anyhow. He said he'd give us another pup when the old bitch littered again.

Me and Horsefly were pretty sure that Cullen Morten would never give us anything. We thought Charlie was all right.

Then came a night when I found out for certain. Charlie came hobbling up to the house just in time for supper that evening. He usually came in time for a meal when he came. He was coatless and his wiry frame shivered in the raw air. He said he'd stuffed his coat and a chunk of firewood in the opening of a hollow post oak that grew on a ridge above the cattle tank in Jim Frenzel's pasture. There was a big boar coon in that hollow. The two hounds he had with him, Red and Bulger, had run the coon in that hollow. The coon couldn't get out now till we got back with an axe to cut him out. We sure could have us a big coon fight, Charlie said.

Mom told me I couldn't go. She said I was too little. She said I'd scuff up my new winter shoes and they had to last me till time to go barefooted next spring. She said I might get rattlesnake bit. Anybody but a woman would have known the rattlesnakes were denned up now, along with the skunks and possums and ringtail cats that help to keep them warm. She said I had to get my lessons. Mom didn't want me to go see that coon fight with Papa and Charlie. She thought Charlie was a bad influence.

But I went. I raised a big howl, and wouldn't eat my supper till Papa got Mom off in another room and talked her into letting me go. He claimed he'd watch out for me. Mom was pretty grim, but I went to see the hounds fight the boar coon.

A big-bellied moon was climbing up over the mesquite ridges when we left the house. Frost was fuzzing the grass and the dried cow chips along the trail. You'd never think just an old dried cow chip could be pretty till you've seen one all fuzzy with white frost, and the moonlight shining down on it, making it glimmer like a crust of diamonds.

Papa carried the lantern. Charlie carried the axe. I didn't have anything to carry. I just chased along, all excited and asking questions. I never had seen a coon fight before.

Once, Red threw up his muzzle and drifted into the black shadows of a scrub-oak thicket. A moment later his trail cry lifted—a loud, ringing, deep-toned bay. It made you think of the new church bell the Methodist ladies had taken up a collection for during the cotton-picking season. The bell sure did sound pretty; but old Red did, too.

Charlie called Red back, though. Said he was trailing a possum. Said he could tell by the sound of Red's voice. We didn't have time to fool with a possum trail tonight, Charlie said.

The frost got to biting my fingers and toes. But I was plenty warm inside my new ducking coat that had a red blanket lining. That coat, out of a Dallas mail-order house, had cost me a blind pig I'd fed all fall. You can't get much cold in a new blanket-lined coat that's cost you a whole pig—even if the pig was blind.

We walked a long time across the rolling Texas hills. Finally, Charlie pointed out a post oak on top of a ridge and said the coon was trapped in it. My heart set up a wild hammering, and my toes and fingers tingled with fresh, warm blood.

The moon was big as a wagon wheel and it hung in the top of the post oak. The tree laid a long, black lane of shadow down the slope toward us. The hounds bounded ahead along that lane of shadow and set up a loud baying when they reached the tree. Our coon was still there, all right.

Red was mighty anxious to get at that coon. He'd back off and take a running start and do his best to jump to the first fork of the tree.

207

Finally, he made it. He stood on the lowest branch and reared up on his hind legs and whined and gnawed at the edges of the hole where Charlie had stuffed his coat. Red was a good coon hound, Charlie said. He said that Red had plenty of grit and would tackle anything that traveled on four feet, but he liked coons best. He said he thought sometimes that Red had more grit than sense.

I sure did wish I had a coon dog like Red.

Papa lit the lantern so Charlie could see to use his axe. They made me hold Bulger, so he wouldn't maybe run up and get his head chopped off. Charlie showed me how to sit beside Bulger and hold his forelegs. That way Bulger couldn't get loose till they had the coon ready.

The post oak was just a hollow shell; it cut easy. Charlie's axe went through to the hole the first blow. The second, and we heard the boar coon growl. Bulger let out a big bawl then and went to jerking hard. He nearly got loose, too. He dragged me two or three feet before I could stop him. Then he shut up and stood with his mouth open, panting. Water dripped off the end of his tongue onto my bare neck, and he gave my back a hard switching with his tail.

"He sure puts up a big war talk, don't he?" Charlie said. He was talking about the coon.

"He'll likely back up every word he's saying when we turn him out," Papa said, grinning.

Me, I didn't say anything. I just held my breath and shivered all over, and hung onto Bulger's forelegs.

When Charlie finally knocked a hole in the bottom of the tree, he must have hit the coon. We heard a loud squall, and the next minute the coon was sticking his head out and growling into the lantern light.

I couldn't hold Bulger then. He leaped for the coon, bawling and dragging me with him. I lost my holds and slid on my face. Old Red tumbled down out of the tree and landed beside me, roaring like a bull. The coon squalled again and came charging out to meet them. Red and Bulger tied in, and the whole biting, slashing tangle of them rolled over me, smothering me. With the rank hot scent of blood and angry animals in my nostrils, I knew for an instant the paralyzing terror of being torn to death by savage animals.

Charlie jerked me to my feet, then tore out down the sharp incline of the brush-tangled slope, yelling to Papa. "Head 'em, Beck! Head 'em! Don't let 'em git in that tank!"

The lantern had been knocked out, but in the moonlight I could see Papa plain, leaping through the brush and yelling. Charlie was following, waving his axe and yelling some more. I couldn't see the fight; but I could hear the brush popping, the dogs yelping and growling, the coon squalling.

Down below was water trapped behind a dirt dam thrown up across a spring branch. The pool was bright in the moonlight, its smooth surface shiny as a looking-glass. A black, raging whirl of dogs and coon rolled out of the brush toward the water and dropped in. The mirrored surface of the water shattered into a million silver blades that licked out, spreading in ever-widening circles.

"He'll drown 'em!" Charlie hollered. "He'll climb on their heads and hold 'em under!"

Fear for myself was all gone now. I was frozen with fear for the hounds. It tied my insides all up in knots and made me weak and sick. Then I ran down through the brush. It was thick brush and it dragged at my clothes. It tore a big snag in my new blanket-lined coat, but I didn't notice. I ran a prickly-pear thorn right through one of my new shoes and it stuck in my big toe. I didn't stop.

But I couldn't do anything when I got down to the edge of the water. There just wasn't anything a little old scared boy could do.

Charlie had stumbled out into the water, following the fight. The water was waist deep to him right at the bank. It was getting deeper every step. Charlie had his axe drawn back; he aimed to cave that boar coon's head in if he ever got a chance. He was hollering: "You, Red! Turn him loose, Bulger! Git outta there!"

Charlie was bothered about his coon hounds.

But Red and Bulger, they couldn't hear. They were flailing the water with their feet, whipping it into a white froth, trying to keep their heads above the surface. But the squalling coon was climbing on them and shoving them under. Old Red and Bulger couldn't hear Charlie calling them out.

Charlie got hold of Bulger's hind leg and dragged him loose from the coon. He waded to the bank, pulling Bulger behind him. Bulger was howling the way he howled when Mom lit into him with a stick of stove wood. Bulger didn't want to be pulled out of that fight.

Charlie reached Bulger's hind leg to Papa and told him to hold tight, not to let him get back in there with that coon. Then he hurried out into the water with his axe again. He had to try and save Red.

Bulger watched Charlie go and howled his frustration. He pulled and strained and howled, but Papa wouldn't let him go. He got so excited—Bulger did—that he whirled and snapped at Papa's hand. But Papa was quick. He jerked his hand out of reach and grabbed Bulger by one of his long ears. Old Bulger couldn't get at him then and he knew it. He hushed his racket and lay down, whimpering and whining. He sounded just like a spoiled baby crying, Bulger did.

Red and the big boar coon were out in the middle of the tank by now. They were just two black, rolling shapes out in the bright water. They were biting and snarling and squalling and clawing. But the coon had the bulge. That big varmint was riding Red under, strangling him. That old coon could pancake himself on the water and float like a cork; he was used to it. Red wasn't half a match for him. Not out there in that deep water. Red had killed many a coon in his time, but he was sure taking a whipping now.

It made the hair crawl on the back of my neck to listen to that fight. It made me choke up inside and my eyes sting. Old Red, out yonder fighting that big boar coon in deep water where he didn't have a chance!

And Charlie—him wading out to the rescue! The water was up to his chin now. And him still going!

Then Charlie was swimming—swimming with one hand and holding the axe with the other—still hollering to Red, telling him to come out of there.

But Red couldn't hear. He wouldn't have listened if he could. Red had tackled himself a big boar coon; he'd fight it to the finish. He'd hang and rattle, Red would. Red was a coon-fighting hound.

I wished Mom could have been there and seen Charlie swimming out there to save Red. She'd have known then that Charlie wasn't just a no-account rake. She'd have known he was a brave man. Only a brave man would swim right into the face of a big boar coon just to save a hound-dog. Charlie was noble. I felt it, deeply. I squatted there on the bank and shivered and hoped I'd grow up and do something as brave and noble sometime.

The big boar coon had Red under again when Charlie reached them. Charlie drew back and struck with his axe. But it wasn't much of a blow.

You can't swing an axe in swimming water—you can't brace yourself. You've got no power. Charlie struck and went under. The coon squalled and went under. Red bobbed to the top, coughing and churning the water. The coon came up and climbed right back on Red. Charlie came up and knocked him off again.

"Look out, Charlie!" Papa called. "He's after you now!"

Sure enough, the coon was swimming for Charlie's head. He was mighty mad, that coon was, and he bared his white teeth in the moonlight and growled. His fur was turned all wrong-side-out, and he was ready to fight anything in sight.

"Better get out of there, Charlie," Papa warned. "That coon's fixing to drown you both!"

"Turn Bulger loose!" Charlie gasped. "He ain't drownded us yit!"

He hit the coon and went under again. The coon swam back and got on top of Red's head.

Bulger hit the water with a splash and a roar. He headed for the fight, swimming fast. But Bulger used his head this time. He didn't tie right into that coon like Red. Maybe he didn't have as much nerve as Red, but he showed more sense. He swam up and jerked the coon off Red's head, then fell back out of reach. When the coon went back to climb on Red again, Bulger pulled him off a second time. When he made for Charlie, Bulger grabbed him and shook him. Then he turned him loose and the coon made a grab for Bulger, and Bulger, he hit out for shallow water, swimming fast, with the coon right after him.

Charlie followed, swimming on his back. He had to swim reading-the-Bible style like that because he had an axe in one hand and Red's tail in the other. Red was petered out; he never could have made it to the bank by himself.

Bulger worried the coon out into shallow water and then he lit into the varmint. He was savage now, Bulger was. He'd been held out of that fight too long to suit him. He aimed to make up for lost time.

Charlie's feet hit bottom. He stood up, gasping for air. I ran out into the water in my new shoes and dragged Red to the bank by his tail. Mom would sure prize up a row about wetting those shoes, but I couldn't help it. Old Red was about to drown, and I had to get him out.

Charlie got his wind, and then he kicked Bulger and the big boar coon apart. He swung his wet axe aloft. It glistened in the moonlight and the water ran down the handle and streamed off Charlie's arm in a silvery spray. He struck once. The coon fight was over.

Bulger dragged the dead coon ashore, still shaking it and growling. Charlie staggered out on the bank, the water running from his clothes and gurgling in his shoes. He flung himself down on the grass and lay there, blowing and heaving. Papa ran into the brush and started gathering wood for a fire. Red grunted and got to his feet. He shook himself, popping his long ears against his head and showering my new blanket-lined coat with a spray of muddy water. Then he went over and licked Charlie in the face. He knew who'd saved his hide, old Red did.

Charlie cussed him and shoved him aside. But Charlie was laughing when he did it, and it looked like Red was laughing with him.

Papa got a roaring fire built up. Charlie stripped to the skin and hung his wet clothes on a hackberry bush to dry. He was shaking all over and his teeth rattled. He stood as close to the fire as he could get, toasting his hide till it got pink.

I looked the other way, mostly; I wasn't used to looking at naked people.

Charlie reached into his wet pants and pulled out a roll that made me forget my embarrassment. It was a roll of green-backs, big as my fist, all tied up with fodder twine. He undid the string and handed me the money.

"Lay it out to dry," he said, and in that instant I knew just how wrong Mom had been about coon hunters. Charlie was rich!

"That's my fur money," he said. "A hundred and thirteen dollars. Takes a lot of coon hides to bring a hundred and thirteen dollars. I come might nigh letting that boar coon drown me'n old Red out yonder, thinking about all that money I was packing!" He grinned at Papa.

I laid the money out on the ground, each banknote by itself. I put rocks and sticks and pieces of dried cow chips on each one, so it wouldn't maybe blow into the fire. I laid it out and then stood back to stare at it. A hundred and thirteen dollars!

That was more money than I had ever seen. That was more money than you could make hoeing cotton and corn in a million years. I bet that was more money than even Cullen Morten had stacked up in his bank. Nobody but a coon hunter could have that much money!

Charlie's dead now and his chicken-coop shack has been rotted down for years. But on frosty, moonlight nights, when I hear the long, lonesome baying of some coon hound drifting across the ridges, I like to think that following that hound is the ghost of old Charlie—hobbling along in old misfit shoes that hurt his feet, but covering more ground than many a man with a good horse between his legs.

In a way, I'm glad he's not here any more. I'd sure hate to face him now with the watch-chain belly I've developed behind Cullen Morten's cashier window.

Sometimes I wish Mom had let me grow up to be a coon hunter like Charlie.

WILLIAM GOYEN

Born in Trinity, April 24, 1918, William Goyen grew up in Houston. He attended the Rice Institute, from which he received the B.A. in 1937 and the M.A. in 1939. In 1941 he taught briefly at the University of Houston. During World War II he was for nearly four years an officer on an aircraft carrier.

A *Southwest Review* fellowship in creative writing assisted Goyen in the writing of his first novel, *The House of Breath* (1950), of which sections had appeared in the *Southwest Review* and other periodicals as early as 1947. The book, which is a series of sharply etched pictures from a dying East Texas town called Charity, won the Texas Institute of Letters–McMurray Bookshop award for the best first novel of 1950 by a Texan. It has been translated into German by Ernst R. Curtius, the translator of T. S. Eliot, James Joyce, and Ezra Pound. Critics agree that *The House of Breath* possesses unusual intensity and sensitivity and that its author represents a new poetic talent among the writers of the region. In 1950, also, Goyen translated from the French of Albert Cossery *The Lazy People* and *The Fertile Valley*. In 1951 he was awarded a Guggenheim fellowship which permitted him to travel both in this country and abroad.

The poetic is stressed still more in Goyen's *Ghost and Flesh* (1952), a series of eight highly lyrical "ballad-like tales." As do other serious modern writers, Goyen makes significant use of myth, and the texture of the whole book is compounded of the classical and medieval four elements, earth, air, fire, and water.

Goyen's short stories have appeared in *Accent, Harper's, Harper's Bazaar, Horizon, Partisan Review, Scribner's,* and the *Southwest Review.* "Her Breath upon the Windowpane," which was reprinted in *Best American Short Stories of 1951,* is the poignant heart-cry of the desolate spinster Hattie in her moment of self-illumination. Through her questioning on the meaning of existence, the author has lodged a forceful indictment of the spiritual poverty of modern urban as well as small-town life.

Her Breath upon the Windowpane

Aᴀꜰᴛᴇʀ ᴀ ʙᴜꜱɪɴᴇꜱꜱ ᴄᴏᴜʀꜱᴇ at Miz Cratty's Select Business College in Jacksonville, where I learned Gregg Shorthand and comtometer and typin, I came to the city, got this job with the S.P. rayroad, been here twenty-five years.

O my folks! Never should a left that town of Charity, I guess, but helped em there, every paycheck I got sent a tithe of it home to em, Mama and Papa and Willadean and Gilbert and Thrash.

Got Willadean through high school, struggled to get her finished only to see her marry a widower from up at Sanderson with three children.

Somethin in Charity ruined Willadean, prissed her all up and sent her straight to ruination. It was that CCC Camp out at Groveton did it; made a wicked girl out of Willadean. Then she worked at the C.O.D. Café, met all the wrong kind, the sawmill boys and the roughnecks from the oilfields and the just plain tramps of Charity.

Willadean O Willadean, I nursed you like my very own when you was little, washed you in winter by the cookstove, wiped off smut from your little hands twenty times a day, washed you and fed you and played with you under the shadetree and swang you in the tireswing, shook down pussimons and called doodlebugs and picked goobers—anything you wanted. Carried you on my hip round the place day in and day out till I pulled my side loose, made me slouched like I am today. Can still feel you astride my hip, clingin there like a little warm possum on to me wherever I went. Sometimes you was as heavy as a croakersack of roastinears, but I went on totin you, pullin my very insides out for you.

Guess I made a mistake in leavin em there in Charity, but it was up

From *Harper's Magazine*, July, 1950; copyright by William Goyen, 1950, and reprinted by his permission.

215

to the boys to help make the livin and I had this chanct for this job in the city. What in the world would they have ever done without me? It was always Hattie Hattie kin you come home to Charity this weekend cause the front porch is fallin in and we got to get it fixed and Papa is drawn double with rheumatism and Mama cain't squat even to gather eggs from the henhouse. Or Hattie Hattie come home on the bus soon as you get off on Saturday noon count of Willadean's in trouble by a drummer that came through Charity sellin Watkins Products.

Never had a life of my own, always workin and doin for others, till suddenly I'm an old woman, fifty, and an old maid, kissed once at the Charity Chatauqua by the best-lookin man of Charity County but never had time to follow it up, never had time to give to kissin and courtin, had to let him go, Huck Chandler uz his name.

Remember once I went in the C.O.D. Café after Willadean and what did I see but that young priss standin on her tiptoes on some scales that said upon them "Your wate and fate" and a young roughneck graspin her around the lower waist and both of em gigglin to beat the band. I could see Willadean's fate right there, didn't have to putt no penny in no machine to ask *her* fate. Well, I said to myself, Hattie you're a Christian and like a mother to Willadean, raised her from the cradle, nursed her and washed her and fed her and toted her like your very own, it's up to you to get her home and do some talkin to her. But I decided to just set down first without makin any fuss that might let her know I was there and to just watch this Miss Willadean. The C.O.D. Café was just full, people at the machines, all at the counter, ever seat at the tables was filled with somebody from the Charity sawmill or the CCC Camp out at Groveton or the oilfields, smokin and drinkin their beer and bottles of whiskey under the tables; and the nickelodeon was on the rampage, playin at the moment Ding Dong Bells. Miss Willadean was in her glory, I could see that; prissin in and out like a prissike at the tables, switchin here and there, laughin and cuttin up with the rowdies and singin right with the nickelodeon as she waited on them, "Ding Dong bells are ringin, but not for me. . . ." I was standin way back in a corner, alone in a corner of the whole world, and my heart breakin to see this Willadean I never knew about.

After a while I sneaked out and went on home with the dingdong bells ringin in my head.

Well when Willadean got off work and came home I took her to task for her actions in the C.O.D. Café and we had a family ruckus good and proper, Willadean shoutin "I've got a right to do as I *damned* please. When *you* start tellin *me* what to do, the fat's in the fire. Got me some good men friends here, as good as any you'll find in Houston or anyplace else—*you've* never had any, but *I'm* goin to—and right now my special one is Mr. Steve Cavanaugh who is an oil man with lots of money and a big Packard. . . ." And Mama said, "Hattie Hattie Willadean's pretty and popular in the town, not like you was, goin to church and Sunday school and doin all the chores on the place. Why are you so hateful? Times have changed and ways have changed in Charity, and Willadean has to have her some men friends, she's no little girl anymore. . . ."

That was all the thanks I got.

Well, when Willadean got married to the widower from up at Sanderson I never heard from her much anymore. And there was Gilbert to handle, pore crippled Gilbert up and grown and needin to have braces on his legs so he could walk, since he was paralyzed when just a little boy by the paralysis plague that hit all the children of Charity so hard and killed quite a parcel of em back in the woods. Sent Gilbert to doctors in Houston, paid for his braces, by the month, then sent him to a school up north in Illinois to learn watchmakin.

But there was nothin I could do with Thrash, just hung around Mama and sat on the front porch, never would do a lick a work, like a child, cuddlin close to Mama, warm and close in some dream.

O Mama and Papa and Willadean and crippled Gilbert and pore old Thrash, ever time I punched the timeclock at the S.P. it uz for you.

What of my time and life I didn't give to all them in Charity I give to the Church and the Young People in Houston. What times we had! Wienerroasts and barefooted hikes and hayrides and New Year's Watch Parties. Oh the programs we put on on Sunday nights at Epworth League! The fine speeches made by my boys and girls and the readin out of the Bible verses. The hymns we sang, all of em settin before me, young and bright, Clara Lou Emson, Joe David Barnes, Folner Ganchion, Conchita Bodeen, and all of em, singin loud and joyful "He Leadeth Me" and "I Will Be True, For There Are Those Who Trust Me" and our very favrite of all, "Blest Be the Tie That Binds." Just for a little while, not long, but just for a beautiful wonderful little while, they were all mine, bound to me and bound together, the only thing I ever had, in Fellowship Hall.

And then they all began to fall away. What ever stays, in this world? One by one, and in such a little while, they drew away and turned from me—to somethin they had found beyond me and the Epworth League that I could never find—and the Epworth League at the Methodist Church was never the same again.

It was, I am sure, because all of em went to college and I never had more'n a high school diploma and a business course. This made em take to other interests, the symphony concerts and college clubs, talkin atheism and biology and historical learnin that I never had. I knew they was thinkin "Hattie we've outgrown you," and on Sunday nights they went to dance at the Rice Hotel instead of comin to League, and on New Year's Eve they was all at the night clubs, and I watched alone. Except for a few old reliables like Sarah Elizabeth Galt who had a harelip, pore thing, and that kind of a sissy Raphael Stevenson, but both good Christians.

And then a college class was formed at the Methodist Church with Mr. Smart, a college graduate and a prominent lawyer, teachin em. Oh I'm sure he did a good job—but I ask you, is a college graduate a better Christian? Was Jesus a college graduate? These are some things to think about.

And now there's no one else to help or to call Hattie Hattie kin you come home, Hattie Hattie this and Hattie that. Mama and Papa's dead and buried away in Charity and Willadean's raisin her heathen family up in Sanderson and Gilbert's got a good watch-repairin business up north in Deetroit Michigan. And pore old Thrash is in a State Home in Orange where he is taken good care of but don't know nothin, nobody. I send things up to him and once I went up to see him on the bus, but he never knew who I was, he's gone, in another world.

I never go anymore, just cain't stand it.

Now all this has passed like a dream and I never go to Charity anymore, cept onct in a while for a funeral of an ole-timer and hear em all say to me, "I swan if tisnt Miss Hattie Clegg—Hattie, remember the old days?" As though I'd just come *home* to remember em on a week-end. . . . That bus I ride home to Charity on, to put flowers on graves at funerals, is a long ride between rememberin and rememberin with nothin but rememberin in between. Here I set in a room I rent from old Miz

Johnson in East End, an old maid left with a twisted face from the Bell's Palsey that struck me like a curse of the Lord six months ago when I was ridin the S.P. on my pass, goin to the Grand Canyon on the first vacation I ever took for myself past Charity Texis as a result of the three weeks they give me at the office for workin twenty-five years with the Southern Pacific. (I get to wear a gold button, now, with a 25 on it.) I don't even own my own washrags, everthin round me is rented.

Why? Why? Been a Christian all my life. Why, after all this, should I be twisted with a twisted face and no one in the whole wide world to call to me Hattie Hattie. . . . This is my reward.

There is a pane of glass between me and the world, seems like, and nothin in the world can ever get to me anymore, only press its nose up against the pane and look through at me. All the world seems flat-nosed against this glass (what breath blows this fog upon my pane?) and I am separated from everthin in the whole world and feel alone and lost and afraid, with no one needin me for anything, useless and twisted and no one dependin on me, callin Hattie Hattie Hattie.

CHARLES CARVER

THE AUTHOR of "Hanging Hollow," Charles Carver, was born near Philadelphia in 1915 and is a graduate of Yale University. He was in the publishing business in New York City until World War II, during which he served on mine sweepers in the Mediterranean and the Pacific.

In 1947 he moved to Waco, his wife's home, and devoted himself entirely to story-writing. His stories have appeared in *Collier's, This Week*, the *American, Liberty*, the *Christian Herald*, and elsewhere. They have been reprinted in England, Sweden, Australia, Brazil, Canada, and other countries.

"Hanging Hollow" is based, the author says "very roughly," on an event which occurred in a small ravine back of the author's home before the turn of the century. It is an example of the writing maxim that the material at hand is often the best source of inspiration. It is an example, also—the only one in this collection—of an interesting fictional development of this century, the short-short story, a genre which Carver has cultivated with considerable technical skill.

Hanging Hollow

Mary and I bought the old house near Drake's Hollow chiefly because of the trees. Even for Texas they were outstanding—a great walnut, two lusty pecans, and three tremendous black Spanish oaks, plus some plum and dogwood. In early spring, people would drive out from town, down one side of the hollow, across the aged plank bridge, and up the other side, just to look at the profusion of pink and white against the new green.

In winter, however, when the great limbs were bare and cold, a less wholesome brand of sight-seer visited the hollow, generally around dusk. They were the people who had heard about the hanging, who came to gape at the ancient trees and to wonder from which of the branches Ben Drake had swung at the end of a rope. The fact that the event had occurred in 1895 made no difference to them at all.

Though Mary and I are as literal as they come, I must confess that sometimes, especially on cold autumn evenings when the mist curled in the silent moonlight below the grotesque bleak limbs, it wasn't too difficult to picture the gruesome scene being re-enacted below us.

No matter how we tried to forget the affair, we couldn't, because even after fifty years the grim business at Drake's Hollow still kept the town split into two bitter factions: those who defended "the Judge," and those who hated him. For Tom Phillips, who had formed the posse which had tried and executed young Drake, was still very much alive, and as sour and picturesque an old character as there was in central Texas.

He was a real old-timer—drove longhorns up the cattle trails to market, won gun fights, became rich on cattle and cotton, and wound up a county legend who stalked around wearing the string tie, wing

Reprinted from *Collier's*, May 17, 1952; copyright 1952 by the author and used by his permission.

collar and broad black hat of another era. His son, Mason, was a chip off the same old block. He was a sharp lawyer with a finger in local politics. Father and son were in business together, the younger learning every sly trick in the book from his slippery old father.

The Judge's enemies claimed that, because of a girl, he'd framed Ben Drake on a charge of cattle rustling and persuaded a gang of hotheads to hang his rival without even time for a prayer. But prayer or not, Drake found breath enough for a dying man's curse, and he swore he'd wait in the hollow to even the score with Phillips. Then the rope choked him off, and the only sound as Ben's soul left his body was a last frightful jangle of his shining spurs.

Taking their cue from Ben Drake's curse, the Judge's enemies said that if Tom Phillips ever went near the hollow again he'd find Ben there, waiting to settle accounts. Considering the sad state of the rotting old bridge, their prediction became more ominous as the years passed. In fact, Phillips used the condition of the thing as a very logical excuse for detouring whenever business or pleasure took him north of town.

"Drive a car across that thing?" he would say. "I'm not that crazy. This town ought to do something about that trap. Need a new mayor around here, that's what we need!" and he'd be started on a caustic harangue.

The Judge's son, as arrogant and mean as the old man must have been in his own youth, took perverse pride in flouting the legend. He told the story of the lynching defiantly in public speeches, making a great joke of the matter by calling Drake the ugly duckling, and so forth. He drove at breakneck speed through the hollow, challenging the ghost to wreak vengeance if it could.

But the bridge never gave way, although it became more and more decrepit. Finally the city fathers had to take notice. Money for a new bridge was appropriated, and I suppose the little groups of people who stood about watching the workmen take up the rotten old planks felt pretty much the way Mary and I did—that we were watching a legend die. "If the story of the curse is true," I told Mary, "that ghost is going to have to hop into town to get the Judge. That new bridge will last a hundred years."

The new bridge was a beauty. Too nice, in fact, because after the bulldozers had churned up the ancient roadbed and the new concrete had set on the span, cars would roar down the hill, shoot across, and zoom up the far side recklessly, no longer held back by the weak old wood. . . .

It was sundown one evening, about six months later, that Mary and I heard a terrific crash in the hollow, which was less than two hundred yards from the house. I rushed outside and down to the scene. A new car lay twisted and shattered on its side against the concrete guardrail. The driver was dead.

I ran back to the house and called the police. I asked them to call the family of the victim; I didn't have the courage to do it myself.

They arrived in a little while—the police, and the ambulance, and the old man himself. I watched him, stern with grief, stand by while they took away his son. I thought he would follow, but he stood near the wreck as though he were reconstructing the accident in his mind.

The police, doing the same thing, were busy with cameras and a steel tape measure. After a while, one of them walked over to the Judge. "It was a tire, sir," he said. "It blew here"—he paced off several steps—"and he didn't have time to slow down before he hit the bridge."

The policeman was standing about twenty yards from the bridge, to one side of the road, and almost directly under the smooth black limb of a Spanish oak. The Judge's face was a white mask, but I felt a chill take my heart when his eyes flicked suddenly from the man to the limb, then back to the man again.

Another policeman had been inspecting the car. "Here's what did it," he said, and he pulled something sharp from the left front tire of the crumpled car.

The grader had evidently brought the object to the surface, for it was bent and pitted. The two policeman and I gathered close to examine it, and then we looked from one to the other in awe, the three of us wondering the same fearful thing.

For it was as though Ben Drake himself had come riding up from the dead and dug his spur into the old man's heart.

SYLVAN KARCHMER

Sylvan N. Karchmer was born in Dallas on the last day of 1914. After graduation from high school there, in 1930, he worked ten years as a clerk for an oil company. During World War II he saw active service with the armed forces in North Africa and Europe.

What he saw there made it impossible for Karchmer to return to stamping "O.K. to Pay" on invoices. In February, 1947, he entered the University of Texas, where he was an excellent general student and a very superior student of playwriting, under E. P. Conkle. He received the B.F.A. degree in 1949 and the M.F.A. in 1950. His master's thesis was the writing and production of a most impressive full-length play, *Stranger upon Earth*. He is now an instructor in creative writing at the University of Oregon and in summers at Banff, Canada, but gives Dallas as his permanent address.

Even while a graduate student of drama Karchmer found time to write distinguished short stories, which were soon published in principal little magazines. Very few writers surpassed his output in 1950. In *Best American Short Stories of 1951* five of his stories, including that offered here, were judged "distinctive." "A Fistful of Alamo Heroes" is more than an autobiographical sketch of how a clerk became a writer. It is a critical comment not only on the makers and readers of contemporary literature but upon the folkways of strictly contemporary urban Texas, of which our writers are often thought to have been neglectful. Humble, earnest, and dedicated to writing the best that is in him, whether it will make him rich or leave him poor, Karchmer is a writer of whom Texas will someday take due notice.

A Fistful of Alamo Heroes

M Y INTENTION WAS to do a little writing this afternoon, but just listen to the noise! Every kid in this neighborhood is playing under my window, and you never heard such shouting. In another five minutes I'll have to give up. Maybe it's nicer to daydream and not try to work at all. . . . But one of these days I'm going to live in a fine Georgian house; it will be set in the middle of an immense lawn, and I'm going to have all the peace and quiet I need. Then . . . you watch me write. Now I'm not talking through my hat. Really I'm not. You see next Tuesday my first book will be released and I'm depending on it to be the start of something . . . big!

It won't be a Literary Guild selection or sell a million copies, though Mr. Robinson, the publisher's agent, wrote me that if I'll follow his suggestions in regard to the plotting of my next book, he doesn't have any doubt it'll make me some real money. Mr. Robinson should know. He's been scouting material for twenty-five years; he didn't discover Hemingway or Faulkner, to be sure, but he's pleased over the fact that two of his own "finds" have made more for his firm than either one of these so-called literary giants. In a way he "found" me. It was like this. I noticed in the paper that he was in town scouting material. That was three years ago, when after a spell in Italy, Southern France, and sixteen months in a PW camp in Ossheim, Germany, I was back. Before the war I'd worked at the Transcontinental Oil Company, where my job was to stamp *O.K. to Pay* on accounts payable invoices. I could process more invoices than anyone else in the department, but when I got back I wasn't interested in stamping invoices; I lagged behind the other stampers. This was bad enough, because it kept me from a sorely-

Reprinted from the *University of Kansas City Review*, Summer, 1950; copyright 1950 by the author and used by his permission.

needed raise, but what was worse I discovered I didn't care. Nevertheless, I might have gone on stamping *O.K. to Pay* on invoices the rest of my waking life except that one morning I chanced to read in the paper that an old army buddy of mine named De Leon from South Texas had been shot while he was driving home.

I got to thinking about De Leon and what he'd been through in the war and how funny it was that this had to be the way things ended for him, and first thing I knew I was determined to put down some of these reflections in what I told myself would be a novel. Now mind you, when I started, I didn't have any clear notion what I was up to. All I knew was that I wanted to write about these things; it helped clear up the confusion in my own mind and at the same time it permitted me to see De Leon a little better. He had always puzzled me.

When Mr. Robinson came to town searching for new talent, I had already completed three hundred pages of my book, and acting on a hunch of my wife, I took the MS. to him. While he idly glanced at it, tweaked his ear, asked me some questions about myself and leafed through the sheets, I had a sinking feeling inside me. What was I doing here? What business did I have even trying to write? Why wasn't I back at my desk stamping invoices? I guess I lived a thousand years in that moment until Mr. Robinson very casually said that when I finished the whole thing to send it to his office. Within a few weeks I mailed the MS. to him; and then after three months, when I was beginning to think they'd chucked the whole thing into the wastebasket, here comes a four-page letter from Mr. Robinson. His editor wanted the novel and would I sign the enclosed contract . . . and then followed the four pages of projected changes. Oh boy, I thought, me, a nobody, a clerk for an oil company, a pfc in the army, and now an author! I skipped the four pages and wired my acceptance, and the next morning I did something I'd had in mind for a mighty long time: I told my boss I was quitting. I didn't even ask for a leave. I just quit outright. My wife and I figured we could live on our war bonds for six months and by that time my book would be out and we'd be on easy street.

After a day or two when I calmed down I studied Mr. Robinson's changes. My book was mostly about the war—what other theme did I have?—and this Mexican fellow from that border town in south Texas. I've said his name was De Leon but in the book he was called something else, which doesn't matter now because Mr. Robinson didn't like De Leon. . . .

In Naples De Leon got drunk every night just like any other GI, but that was when we first landed and he thought the fellows had forgotten he was not one of them but only a Mexican from a border town, where his people had never been accepted. Well he learned by degrees. He was a tall, thin fellow, skinny as a rail, with dark eyes and what in my book I called sensitive nostrils, and he was proud as a Spanish Don. At some insult he would draw himself up and there would be a contemptuous and angry look in his eyes and at other times he would be as timid as a child. In those days there was really much innocence about De Leon—something you don't often find in Americans. It was pathetic how hungry he was for friends. Once he started buddying around with a colored boy from a nearby service unit. That was in the early days. And then when we got to France De Leon found his pal—a lanky, taciturn guy from Nebraska, named John, who'd never seen a Mexican before. John taught him slang; how to deal with the French girls; and where to sell his cigarettes. De Leon was a fast learner; he even did John one better and fell for the I & E stuff they dished out to us; he learned to hate the Nazis, though down in that border town of his where he had been drafted, it wasn't the Nazis who had kept his people out of drug stores, off the buses, and segregated the boys and girls of his race in the classrooms of the public schools. De Leon was willing to learn anything if it meant acceptance. . . .

At Futa that day our company charged I saw him batter a German's skull to pulp. There was really no need; he could have used his bayonet as well. Afterwards I saw him go behind a tree. He stood with his eyes cast to the ground, his cheeks ashen, as if a sudden fever had come upon him. He was shaking all over. When he noticed me watching him, he straightened up and lighted a cigarette.

From the very start Mr. Robinson had objected to De Leon and in no uncertain terms had advised me to relegate him to a subordinate place in the novel. Finally of course I yielded to his arguments, but last spring when I read proof on the book I was conscious for the first time of the injury I had done De Leon, for in the process of rewriting I had made him nothing more than a phony. So I took out the phony De

Leon, borrowed in large part from the Mexicans of other writers I had
read, and restored the original of my first draft—a timid, sensitive, confused fellow, trying to hold his own in two worlds and not succeeding
in either. When Mr. Robinson got my corrected proofs he wrote me another of his friendly letters, pointing out the danger of changing proof
and advising me that with each change I delayed the date of publication of the book. By now my wife and I were down to our last hundred
bucks, so I decided not to fool around with De Leon any more. If Mr.
Robinson decided he should be a minor character, well and good with
me. . . .

No doubt it was a wise decision, because Tuesday my book comes out.
And, brother, it's going to mean a great deal in my life. Mr. Robinson
is an old hand at these things. He's planned a slick publicity campaign.
The idea is to sell fifteen thousand copies right here around Dallas. The
National Book Store is giving me an autograph party on the 24th; that
afternoon the book department of Loeb, Bach & Co. will be hosts for
a similar event. At night there will be a formal dinner at the hotel, with
the mayor presiding, and the next morning at ten I'll be at Chammon's
Book Mart to do some more autographing . . . There's also going to
be a spread in all the Texas newspapers, with particular emphasis going
to the East Texas dailies, because my novel in its final draft in large part
is set in the azalea country. When Mr. Robinson first traveled through
here last year, he fell in love with the countryside and said frankly he
wouldn't rest until he had a novel written about it. Frankly I don't know
how my novel came to be about the azalea country. I thought I was
writing a war novel, but as Mr. Robinson explained, the market has
been glutted with war books; people just won't read another one unless
it has a romantic touch, whereas the azalea country is something new.

Well, if it means some money I'll be satisfied, though in the long
run it's De Leon who'll suffer. I don't mind saying it was tough giving
up some of the incidents. For instance there was my account of the
night we landed in Southern France. The lieutenant in charge of our
platoon, a Yale boy about De Leon's age, and a little unsure of his
authority, didn't know how to carry out his written orders that our
platoon was to occupy the farm house on the hill. He had to be sure that
the surrounding field was clear of mines. But who to send? The whole
platoon waited in the valley while he tried to make up his mind what

to do. I remember watching him crack his knuckles and wipe his forehead with a brown handkerchief; it was very warm that moonlight night back in August, 1944. Suddenly the lieutenant's eye lighted on De Leon's friend from Nebraska. "You there," he called, and a sigh of relief went up from the rest of us. Having once called his name, the lieutenant's voice grew bolder. "Yeap, you John Coles," he said. John was so scared he could hardly move. "Me?" he called, and his voice was something more than a whisper. And then while we waited for John to get up the hill and find the mines, which would make the path safe for the rest of us, De Leon, holding his carbine in his hand, his bedroll strapped to his back, his helmet askew on his head, stepped forward. "I'll go," he volunteered, and as the lieutenant, taken by surprise, stared mutely at him, he insisted, "Please let me go."

Maybe he reasoned that being the only foreigner in our outfit, he had to demonstrate his bravery, to show us he wasn't afraid. Perhaps he was only thinking of sparing his friend, John. But he, the stranger among us, shouldn't have gone. And we, who remained silent and let him go for us, should have spoken as one man against it. The hell of it is that if he'd been killed, we wouldn't have minded. It was only much later that I came to realize this.

That same night he found the well, where the water was cold and clear and abundant. We couldn't get our fill of drinking it; but in the morning we spied the dead Germans, lying in a neat row at the bottom of the well, their green uniforms giving a murderous tint to the water. We looked at them in revulsion and afterwards none of us could touch our canteens, which the night before we had been so eager to fill, and yet De Leon paid no attention to our feelings. He filled his own canteen. "Good water," he remarked. "Very good water," and when he drank there was a shy, contemptuous smile on his face.

Mr. Robinson took this out of the book. Also much of the business of the PW camp, though John managed to survive in some of the chapters; in fact under Mr. Robinson's guidance he became something of a major character. Actually the only thing I remember about him at the PW camp is that he tried on two different occasions to escape. The monotony was killing us. Only De Leon seemed to hold up. During the long winter nights, when we were caged up in our barracks, he taught us sad Mexican songs and told us stories of saints he had learned at convent school. If it hadn't been for him both John and I would have gone crazy. As it was the three of us held together, and then in May of that year when the Russians started to advance and the German guards abandoned the camp, we were free to return to the American lines; and then our difficulties began. John came down with pneumonia, and De Leon and I were confronted with the choice of staying with him and so falling into the hands of the Russians or taking out without him towards the Czech border. There was no question in De Leon's mind about deserting his friend, and no matter how hard I argued that neither of us could do John the least bit of good, he was determined to stay with him. Finally by sheerest chance we found a discarded German jeep with a tank full of gas. Now we could take John along. All day we drove towards the border, while John grew worse; he lay with his head on De Leon's knee babbling about Nebraska and the farm. He died about dusk, though I don't think De Leon realized it, because all the way into Prague I could hear him singing to John . . . those sad Mexican songs he'd taught us.

Mr. Robinson says the time for morbid war books is over. So all this came out of the book. Also the part about De Leon's illness, when the army doctors gave him up. Later he surprised them by getting well and begging to be sent back to combat duty. Up until the very end De Leon thought he had some personal quarrel with the Nazis. . . . In the novel it's John who recovers. There is a scene at the station back home when his wife runs down the ramp and cries darling and a sweet-faced lady, who'd lost her own son, wipes her eyes and begins to understand why. . . . You know the scene—you've seen it in the movies. I didn't add a thing. . . .

When the army finally relinquished De Leon, he was a hardened veteran. We were discharged the same day. I came back to the Transcontinental Oil Company and he returned to the little border town he had left four years ago, a shy, virginal boy, who wore a St. Christopher medallion around his neck. His war, it seemed, wasn't over. He got mixed up in the segregation squabble, worked to get the boys and girls of his people accepted in the public schools on an equal footing with the American children, failed, started again with petitions, letters to the press, protest meetings. I remember hearing him talk over the radio; he sounded angry and determined, and when he talked about fair play, I could feel myself cringe. It was hard to believe he was the same boy I had known in the army. Well anyway one night a gang of hoodlums ambushed him. The papers said there were sixteen bullet holes in his body. His death made the headlines, and in three days he was forgotten.

But what De Leon did after the war had no place in my book, for as Mr. Robinson said, the market has been glutted with books on segregation and racial discrimination.

And yet I ask you, how could I forget De Leon or my debt to him? I can still hear his laughter—gentle, effacing, slightly apologetic during those early days of basic training. . . . I can see his medallion swaying on his chest as he ran the obstacle course for the first time. I remember how desperately he tried to get drunk with the boys . . . and the interminable nights at Ossheim, when he regaled us with stories of angels and saints. I owe it to him to bring him back. After all if I want to write about De Leon, it's not for Mr. Robinson to say I can't.

If my wife sees this, she'll say I'm carping. All right, she'll fret, if you can't listen to Mr. Robinson, who obviously is familiar with the reading tastes of the public—and not only that, he's taken the trouble to help you—then go ahead and write your book, so that nobody will buy it and it'll only gather dust in the Bureau of Copyright in Washington; a number will be stamped on it, and it'll be filed away and that will be the end of De Leon and his dreams of angels and home. . . .

It's like this. Mr. Robinson didn't force me into this writing game. I'm free and over twenty-one. I can do what I damn please. But wait a minute . . . I'm married, and my wife and I are hoping the book will make it possible for us to start a family. We're hoping it will be soon.

In the meantime after next week we're going to Mexico, and there I plan to start in earnest on my second novel. Mr. Robinson is sure he can get an advance from the publishers for me. He's been telling me I ought to do a costume novel about the Alamo. I might even work in the Alamo heroes—Bowie, Fannin, Crockett. "You got a fistful of personalities," he said. "That material has never been touched. It's all yours." Mr. Robinson can be very emphatic when the occasion demands it. He feels that my military experience will help me in the descriptions of battles and campaigns. The thing for me to do while I'm in Mexico is pick up a little Spanish. You see in a way he is conceding me De Leon. Perhaps I can work him in with Bowie, Fannin, and think up a few seduction scenes and throw in a lost treasure . . . and the point is to do it artistically in three or four hundred pages. . . . Who knows, it might turn out to be a Literary Guild book.

Outside the kids are making one hell of a racket. You realize I live on a street without lawns and the only place these kids have to play is on the street. Poor kids. . . . My children, when they come, will have a lawn of their own; they'll live in a fine Georgian house with lots of rooms. . . . No sir, my kids won't have to play in the street!

The shouts grow louder. I've already put my book aside for the afternoon, and for a moment I napped. I saw the Germans in the well, their green uniforms coloring the sweet-tasting water. I saw De Leon's proud smile as he alone of the men in the platoon drank. I heard him singing to dead John the night we pulled into Prague. I listened again: his voice was coming over the radio, scolding us about fair play . . . while I sat working on a story set in the azalea country. . . .

Suddenly I'm up with a start. It's too hot to nap. I should be planning my new novel, the one about the Alamo boys. If only it'll make me some money! It's got to. . . . That's all there is to it. As for De Leon, I think maybe I can use him later on—perhaps in a long short story. There are magazines that pay fancy prices for stories. Mr. Robinson, I'm sure, knows which ones they are. . . .

HARRY KIDD, JR.

HARRY LEE KIDD, JR., was born at Lebanon, Virginia, September 27, 1915. He came to Texas at the age of twelve, his family making its home at Mexia, in Limestone County. There Kidd learned to know rural East Texas, with its white farmers and Negro hands. In 1932 he was graduated from the Mexia High School. The following September he entered the University of Texas, from which he received the B.A. degree in 1935. He taught in and was principal of the high school at Anderson for several years. In August, 1938, he received the M.A. degree in English from the University of Texas, his thesis being "Vestiges of Calvinism in the Works of Edwin Arlington Robinson." In 1939 he joined the English faculty at Texas Agricultural and Mechanical College, where in 1945 he was made assistant professor, in 1950 associate professor.

Kidd did little writing until rather recently. Since 1945, however, he has written and produced many network radio shows and published in both big and little magazines. His story, "The Sound Prolong," published under the pseudonym "E. Leigh," was named to Martha Foley's "distinctive" list for 1946, as was "Don't Look Up—Don't Look Down," in 1947.

"Low Road Go Down," also a "distinctive" story, is part of an unpublished novel which would seem to deserve publication. In it Kidd avoids stereotypes and exhibits the paradox which marks the race problem in the rural South. Mister Jere would help Dee Dave out of trouble with "the law" or stake him to grits and fatback when necessary, but he would "hook him," too. Learning this fact—and that he must not ride with Dee Dave any more—is part of the boy Herb's initiation into manhood.

Low Road Go Down

De fahmuh, he say to de weevil:
"What you doin' in dat square?"
De boll-weevil say to de fahmuh:
"Gwine ter raise my fambly dere!"
He gotta hab' a home!
He gotta hab' a home!

D<small>EE</small> D<small>AVE</small> <small>WAS</small> <small>FEELING</small> pretty high, all right. It was Saturday morning, and on Saturday morning nobody ever felt too bad. Nobody ever picked longer than half a day Saturdays, not even in good cotton like Mister Jere's. Herb grinned, sitting on the seat of the spring-wagon behind the wobbling brown rumps of the sway-backed mules, listening to Dee Dave's soft rumble.

"No weevils in Mister Jere's cotton, Dee Dave! What you singing about, anyway?"

"Singin' fo' de payday, Mistuh Herb! Singin' fo' dem silvah dollahs gwine ter be a-jinglin' in mah britches 'fore de night git heah!"

Dee Dave laughed, his teeth white in dark, purply-red gums behind the thick black lips. He twitched the reins, and the mules turned slowly off the highway into the lane that went up past Gus Schreiber's place and on out to Mister Jere Thomas' river-bottom farm. The wagon rocked, leaving the smooth surface, and Clarissa and the children, lying in the flat-bed on quilts, bumped against the sides like so many sacks, boneless with sleep.

"Hey-oh, dere!" Dee Dave said, turning his head to look at them and laughing out loud. "Y'awl gwine drap outen de tail-end 'lessen you wakes up!"

Reprinted from the *Southwest Review*, Autumn, 1948; copyright 1948 by the *Southwest Review*; used by permission of the publisher and author.

Herb looked off across the half-dark fields to the horizon, where the robin's-egg blue of the early morning sky showed faint streaks of pink. He smelled the dry, pungent smell of dust and cotton, lint and weed-drift, rising from the fields and mingling with the faintly acid smell of the mules and the deeper, heavily fetid odor of Dee Dave, on the seat beside him. To Herb, it was a peculiar and a pleasant smell, and one not to forget.

Herb did not mind picking very much. It was hot work, yes. And sometimes, in the middle of the August afternoons, working in hundred-degree temperature or better, sweat pouring off his forehead and darkening his gray work shirt across his back where the broad strap of his cotton-sack fit tightly against the taut, bowed muscles, he wished he did not have it to do.

But mostly he liked the work. He liked riding with Dee Dave and his family in the spring-wagon—early, before the sun was up. He liked the smell of things, and the voices of the waking birds, just beginning to start the day off. He liked the odd, musty atmosphere around and among the broad, flat leaves of cotton, and the way the heat waves would come dancing up off them as the morning wore on. He liked to lean in the shade of the high-sided cotton-wagon, with his sack on the ground, heavy with cotton, sack strap knotted about the mouth to keep the cotton in, waiting for Mister Jere to weigh it on the scale slung over the propped wagon-tongue or maybe mounted on a crossbar there in the middle of the field.

Herb liked all those things, and more. But best of all he liked Saturdays—paydays.

"I got more'n fifteen dollars coming this noon, Dee Dave," Herb said, pulling his little red notebook out of his overall bib pocket. "Let's see here, now!"

He squinted at the figures in the dim light, screwing up his mouth as he tried to make them out.

"Let's see—Monday, two-sixty-two . . . Wednesday, two-forty-seven. Say, Dee—I got nothing less than two-forty-seven all the week!"

"Dat's good, all right. Hit sho' is!" Dee Dave frowned a little and scratched at the big crinkled wart on the lobe of his ear.

"Cain't figuah hit out nohow, Mistuh Herb. Heah is me and Clarissa and fo'five chillun—pickin' hard, evvy day in de week. An' come pay-

235

day we ain't got so much—fawty-fifty dollahs, maybe. Dat ain't so much —takin' in de all of us!"

"You got your weighing-book, ain't you Dee?" Herb asked. Like Dee Dave, he could not quite understand it, for he knew well enough Dee Dave was a four-hundred-pound hand, day in and day out. And Clarissa was mighty near as good. And the twins, Hop and Bubba, could outpick him any day, even if they were three or four years younger and a lot littler. They were used to hard work, and even on the hottest days they could go down their rows on their knees, picking one each and splitting the middle one, never missing a lick while he had to take time out and rest. They would laugh and joke and chunk green bolls at each other sometimes. But they could carry three rows to Herb's two, and lap him twice every hour or so. And then there was Hattie and Lena May too. Herb figured Dee Dave ought to be drawing more than just forty or fifty dollars, come the week-ends.

"How about it, Dee," he asked again, "you got your weighing-book, ain't you?"

Dee Dave grinned sheepishly. He was a good-natured nigger, Dee Dave, and he could not stay worried about anything more than a few minutes.

"Weighin'-book! Do' now, Lawd! What Ah need wif' a weighin'-book —an' ain't me nor nobody kin read what Mistuh Jere write down, nor what nobody else write down, fo' dat!"

That was true enough. Herb had forgotten that Dee Dave couldn't read or write. Neither could Clarissa. The older kids could read a little, but Dee Dave was boss man with them, and they would not have dared to open their mouths unless Dee Dave told them to.

"You ought to have a weighing-book, Dee," Herb told him. "You ought to know how much you-all pick every day!"

"Mistuh Jere, he know," Dee said. "He got hit all down on de big ledgeh—he done show me long time back!" He threw back his head and laughed at the joke on Mister Jere. "He-he-he! Mistuh Jere, he ain't know dat Ah cain't read what he got wrote down dere!"

"Maybe he do know hit! Maybe he makin' de fool outen you—you goin' on thinkin' you so smaht!" Clarissa, in the nest of cotton-sacks against the back of the seat, came suddenly to life.

"Maybe Mist' Jere he figuah you ain't know 'nough to ketch him iffen . . ."

"Shet yo' fool mouf, Clarissa!"

Dee Dave wasn't good-natured right that minute. He had worked for Mister Jere for a long time, off and on, and he trusted Mister Jere. He thought Mister Jere would take care of things for him, all right. And he didn't like for Clarissa to be talking that way in front of Herb, either. Herb was his friend, yes. But Herb was a white boy, too, and Dee Dave had lived a long time. He was strictly a "white man's nigger," and he aimed to see that his wife and children were the same.

"Shet up, now," he repeated angrily. "You ain't know nuthin'! Mistuh Jere he got hit all wrote down. Iffen you an' dem kids git yo'-sefs on out dere an' snatch dat cotton lak de way Ah kin do hit, dere'd be a heap mo' money—come Sattidy noon!"

He slapped the reins over the mules' rumps, and spat into the gray dust beside the wagon ruts.

"Ain't dat so, Mistuh Herb?"

Herb didn't know for sure whether it was so or not. He thought Dee Dave was likely right, though. Because, after all, why should Mister Jere want to cheat Dee out of a few dollars?

Mister Jere didn't need the money. He had plenty. He had this farm they had been working on these last couple weeks, and two more big ones—more than a thousand acres of good Texas blackland. He had a house in town and a house out on the river where he went for barbecues and fish-fries with the big shots from all over the state. He had horses and beef cattle and work stock and machines and tenant houses and hands. He even had his own stores, on his biggest place, stores that took care of all his three-and-four hands, and anybody else that he was willing to credit. So what did Mister Jere need with a dollar or two? Dee Dave was likely right.

Herb didn't think much more about it for awhile. Early morning, if you are in good cotton, is the time for work, not thinking. The dew is on the cotton then, and it weighs heavy. Lots of times a grower will keep his hands out of the field till the sun has been up an hour or so, to make sure they won't be weighing in any damp cotton.

But Mister Jere wasn't that way. He wanted that cotton out—out and ginned and baled and tagged and stacked in the compress ware-house. He wanted that cotton sold while it was worth good money—and he didn't care if it was wet or dry, very much, so long as plenty of it got in his cotton-wagons every day.

There were lots of hands already in the field by the time Herb got started. Maybe there wouldn't be so many on Monday—after the week-end and before Saturday's money was quite all gone. Or maybe a few would drop out on Thursday, after the big Wednesday night prayer-meeting out at Nigger Run Branch church. But everybody would always show up, Saturdays. Saturday was payday—and Mister Jere liked to pay off in silver dollars, right on the dot at noon.

Herb picked alongside Reece Jackson that morning. He and Reece were "nigger-picking it"—splitting a middle row and each taking an outside one, so they could company with each other. Reece was a town boy, too, only he had lived in town all his life instead of just a year, like Herb. He was a year older than Herb, but he was already two years in high school, for he got started early, while Herb hadn't had a chance at school till he was eight. Reece didn't pick every day. He just worked for spending-money, when he couldn't beg any out of his Old Man. And he could generally get his money without having to come to the patch after it. His father had a big grocery store downtown, and Reece had plenty, but he spent a good deal too, for a kid.

Once in a while, when he would feel like working a few days, Reece would ride out to Mister Jere's place on his bicycle. It was a nice bicycle —new, with a double-bar frame and good hard new tires on it. It had longhorn handlebars and a siren hooked onto the rear wheel, and Herb would look at it and wish he had one like it. Reece didn't seem to care much about it, though. He was feeling pretty frisky that summer, and he was beginning to think about getting hold of a jalopy like some of the older boys in high school ran around in.

"If I get one, Herb," he said, wiping his forehead with the back of his forearm, "I'll sell you my wheel cheap, if you want it."

"Wish I could buy it," Herb told him, grabbing automatically at the thick white fleece hanging from the sharp, five-pointed brown burrs. "Wish I could get hold of a good wheel! Maybe I can, if we stay here in this kind of cotton another week or so."

Dee Dave came up the row outside Herb, working the other way. Dee Dave was a fast hand, no doubt about that. He picked on his feet, bending till his body formed almost a right angle, his legs apart, straddling the thick, belt-high cotton in the center row of the three he was working. His eyes were half closed, for he was picking into the sun, but he didn't miss anything. His fingers looked like curved black hooks, tearing at the open bolls, filling themselves to overflowing. His arms moved like pistons—left, right, center—rhythmic and regular as if in response to some inner, metronomic cadence, filling the long sack trailing in the broken clods behind him with neat little balls of cotton, almost free of leaves or burrs.

"Heah dere," he said as he moved by Reece and Herb, "dis ain't gonna do! Y'awl gotta hurry—else'n Ah'm gwine lap you evvy time!" He grinned and moved on, picking without undue haste, yet forging steadily onward, leaving the stripped plants swaying behind him.

"Fast nigger," Reece commented, straightening up to watch Dee Dave. "Gits it clean, too, don't he?"

"Yeah. He's a good hand."

Herb did not much like to hear Reece call Dee Dave a nigger, just that way. Of course, he was a nigger, all right. But he had been mighty good to Herb, and Herb liked him. And nigger or no nigger, Dee Dave hadn't had to tell him about Mister Jere needing hands, nor ride him back and forth to town every day.

"I reckon he is," Reece agreed. "I'd hate to be a damn nigger fieldhand, myself." He sat down on his cotton-sack and pulled a pack of ready-rolls out of his pocket.

"Here," he said to Herb, sticking the pack out, "here—take one. There ain't no hurry, after all! Just watching that nigger work has done got me all pooped out!"

"I guess not," Herb said. "Might make me puke all over my cotton-sack. I ain't used to cigarettes."

Reece put the pack back in his shirt pocket. He didn't care. Maybe he would have kidded Herb a little if there had been a lot of boys around. But not in the patch. He figured Herb was telling him the truth. And he knew Herb was no baby, either; Herb was almost as big as he was, and Herb would weigh in more cotton every time. Reece took a few drags, just to show it was everyday stuff with him. He threw the half-smoked cigarette down, after a little, and slipped back into his strap.

Harry Kidd, Jr.

"Let's get going before that damn speedy nigger laps us twice," he said.

By the time the sun was well up, Herb was ready to weigh in. He had been working hard, and he figured he had nearly fifty pounds sacked, maybe more. He knotted the strap around the mouth of his sack and slung the sack over his shoulder, balancing the weight in the middle. Reece was ready too, and they walked up the ends of the rows toward the little rise where Mister Jere was waiting at the cotton-wagon.

All over the field the hands were coming in. Some were already there, up in the high wagon bed, slinging the cotton out of their sacks, holding on to the bottom left corner, where the weighing-boll is always wired on, and flipping the sacks empty. When they had all the cotton out, they would fling the sacks over the side of the wagon onto the ground, making sure they hit spread out flat, so Mister Jere could see that the cotton was all out.

Mister Jere didn't seem to pay any mind. Some growers kept a man on the wagon all day long, to do nothing but empty sacks out clean. Not Mister Jere. He hardly even bothered to look at the sacks as they came flying over the side of the wagon. But he didn't miss much, after all. He had a little clip-board tacked to the middle of the wagon tongue, and the big ledger lay on that. When he would read the weight of each man's sackful of cotton, he would walk over to the ledger and scratch with a pencil.

"Lonnie Dixon," he said, glancing around and talking extra loud, like he was announcing a rodeo, "Lonnie Dixon, seventy-one!" He made some figures on the ledger sheet, and Lonnie climbed up the wagon-side, his chocolate face split in a pleased grin.

"Sebbenty-one," Lonnie echoed. "Man—an' it ain't neah eight yet! Two-fifty 'fore Ah draws mah money at noon!"

Mister Jere smiled. He was a heavy-bodied, florid man with bristling reddish hair growing backward from a high forehead. He was very strong, and they told it on him that he had killed a nigger hand or two in his time, just hitting them with his fist. His sleeves were rolled up, and his arms were short, thick and powerful as they lifted the sacks effortlessly up to the wire hook on the scales. He was in a good humor, because his cotton crop was the best in several years. And the price was good, too, and the weather good for getting the crop out. Mister Jere was feeling mighty chipper.

He grinned at Reece Jackson and Herb, walking up to the scales with their sacks.

"Hey, boys!" he greeted them. "Got 'em filled up with wet cotton for me to buy offen you at a dollar a hundred, have you?"

He was just joking, though. He grabbed Reece's sack with one hand, flipped the wire around the weighing-boll over the hook, and picked up the little pee.

"Fifty-one only!" he said, pulling down the corner of his mouth and winking at Herb. "Reece—you are the sorriest hand in the field! Why don't you stay home?"

He grinned and reached into Reece's open shirt pocket and pulled out his cigarettes.

"One for the boss-man, hey?" he said, tapping the bottom of the package with his finger and catching the cigarette in his mouth as it jumped out of the package. It was a good trick, and Reece and Herb got a laugh out of it.

Dee Dave laughed too. He had come up with his sack, to weigh in, and he let the sack flop on the ground and stood watching Mister Jere fool around. Dee Dave pulled a sack almost twice as big as the one Herb had, and it was stuffed full. It looked to Herb like there would be three hundred pounds in that sack, just to see it there, bulging like an acorn-fed shoat. Dee Dave figured he had a good weight in it, too, and he was happy.

"Look at Mistuh Jere go!" he giggled. "Jes' looky theah—man, ain't many folks kin do lak dat!"

"Shore ain't, Dee," Mister Jere agreed. He flipped Reece's sack up over the side of the wagon with a quick turn of his wrist, and walked over to the ledger.

"What'd I say, Reece—fifty-one?"

"That's right," Reece told him. "Fifty-one only. But if I was fast as this nigger here, Mister Jere, I'd bust you picking your own cotton!"

"That ain't no lie, boy," Mister Jere said, writing in the big ledger. "That Dee Dave is one more cotton-snatching nigger—ain't you Dee?"

It made Herb feel funny to hear Reece and Mister Jere call Dee Dave a nigger to his face. But Dee Dave didn't seem much put out. He was proud of himself for picking so much cotton, and he liked for Mister Jere to say how good he was in front of the rest of the field hands that

241

were coming up, crowding in around the scales and dropping sacks off their shoulders to bounce in the dust beside the wagon wheels.

"Yassuh, dat Ah is!" Dee grinned and shuffled his feet. "Ah reckon ol' John Henery hissef mout haf ter stretch er gut ter keep in fronten me dis mawnin'!"

Mister Jere grinned and put Herb's sack up on the scales.

"Lawson," he sang out, "sixty-five flat!" He looked over at Reece and flipped a loose burr in his direction. "This here kid ain't more'n two-three times good a man as you, Reece!" he jibed.

He lifted Herb's sack from the hook and walked to the big ledger and wrote down the figure. Herb took his little book out of his pocket.

"Saturday, 3rd week, first weighing—65" he wrote. When he was through, he looked up. Mister Jere was watching him, leaning on the wagon-tongue. He was still grinning, and he winked at Reece when he spoke, but there was a little different note in his voice.

"What's the matter with you, boy?" he asked. "Ain't you willing to take my word for it?"

It made Herb a little nervous. He always kept his own records, all along, and he knew Mister Jere had seen him write in his book lots of times in the past three weeks. And on both Saturdays Mister Jere's figures were right on the money, too. Still, Herb liked to keep his own records. He figured maybe Mister Jere was just playing with him. Mister Jere was feeling mighty good, sure enough. Maybe he was just joking.

"Want to take a look, son?" Mister Jere asked, still looking at Herb. He sounded friendly enough, but Herb was somehow not quite certain what Mister Jere was thinking.

"No sir," he said. "Your figures are all right with me. I just like to keep my own score." Herb had a sudden happy thought. "I like to see if I can beat myself, every week," he lied.

"Damn good idea," Mister Jere said, walking back to the scales and motioning Dee Dave to lift the wired end of his sack up to the hook. "Damn good! Reece—why don't you do like that? Maybe you'd make more'n a dollar a week in my cotton patch!"

He was in a good humor again, Herb could see, if he'd ever been out of one. He threw Herb's sack up on the wagon, and Herb stepped up on the right front wheel and grabbed for the top. He hauled himself up over the high board side and tumbled onto the cotton in the bed. He got up and started emptying his sack, shaking out the little loose balls of cotton, sending them tumbling in fluffy heaps over the soft white masses already there.

On the ground, Mister Jere was weighing Dee Dave's cotton in. The sack was so full that it bowed the tongue of the wagon just a little, humping it a bit, just forward of the iron supporting rod that propped the tongue up in the air.

"Lordy!" Mister Jere exclaimed, picking up the big pee and letting his eyes roll around back in his head, showing out for the hands. "Lordy—better'n a hundred by eight-thirty! What'll this nigger snatch by noon?"

Dee Dave was tickled. He threw his shoulders back and grinned at all the hands. Mister Jere pushed the smallest pee forward on the tip of the scales. It went almost to the tip, well past the big hundred-pound pee. The scales quivered, and the beam arm moved gently up and down, up and down again. Mister Jere looked hard at the marker. Then he flipped the little pee back to the base of the scales and turned around. He spread his hands out wide, palms up, like a sideshow barker.

"Dee Dave Minton," he announced solemnly. "Dee Dave Minton—best cotton-nigger in Central Texas! One hundred and thirty-nine pounds!"

All the hands except Reece crowded around Dee Dave, laughing and feeling of his back muscles.

"Sho' man," Lonnie Dixon yelled, "one-thutty-nine on de fus' weigh-in! You is a six-hundehd niggah fo' true—effen hit wuz er week-day!"

Mister Jere went over to the big ledger. He started writing, and did not look up at Herb, leaning over the end of the wagon, watching the hands mill around Dee Dave. Herb didn't exactly mean to see what Mister Jere wrote on the blue ruled lines; he wasn't out to check on him. But he could see the ledger, plain enough, right there below him. He could even see his own name, down the column under the big scribbled dateline: "Lawson—first check—65."

And he couldn't help but see Mister Jere write Dee Dave's figure down. Only Mister Jere didn't write what he had said. He scratched hastily across the line: "D. Minton—first check—119." Herb's eyes widened, and he eased away from the end of the wagon, stepping gently over the soft cotton. For it wouldn't do, now, to have Mister Jere notice that he was up front, leaning over the end of the wagon.

But Mister Jere didn't notice; so that part was all right. Herb threw his emptied sack over the side of the wagon, and climbed over after it. He rested one foot on the top of the back wheel on the off side, and jumped to the ground. When he got back around, Dee Dave was wrestling with his bulging sack, pushing it up over the sideboards, and Mister Jere was already weighing in another sackful of cotton.

Herb didn't look at Mister Jere. He couldn't. He couldn't figure why Mister Jere would cheat Dee Dave out of a couple of sorry dimes. Mister Jere didn't need them, Herb knew that. But if he would cheat Dee Dave, he would cheat all his hands, most likely.

Walking back down the field with Reece, Herb tried to figure it out. Even now, after he had seen it, he found it hard to believe.

"Mister Jere hooked Dee Dave, just now," he told Reece all of a sudden, watching his face. "He hooked him for twenty pounds when he wrote down the weights!"

Reece stopped walking. He looked at Herb sharply, his eyes peering and without expression.

"Well now, Herb," he said slowly, "what about it? What you got to kick about? He never hooked you none, did he—you ain't no nigger!"

That was a new idea for Herb, and not a pleasant one either. But he had to admit Reece was right. Mister Jere had not hooked him, nor even tried to.

"No-o," he told Reece slowly, "he ain't hooked me." He looked across the field where Clarissa and the twins were finishing a row. "Reckon he hooks all his nigger hands, Reece?"

"Maybe. Looky here, Herb!" Reece spread his sack in the shade at the end of a row, sat down on it, and pulled a cigarette out of his pack. He lit it and flicked the dead match into the clods between the rows. Herb sensed that he was trying to find the words he wanted. Herb knew Reece liked him, and he liked Reece, too. But he didn't know what he ought to do about Mister Jere hooking Dee Dave and maybe all the rest of his hands, and he didn't know if Reece could tell him what he ought to do, either. He sat down beside Reece and kicked aimlessly at the broken clods.

"Looky here," Reece said finally, "you ride with them Minton niggers, don't you?"

"That's right," Herb told him, "every day."

"Are you going to tell 'em?"

That was what Herb was thinking right that minute. How could he tell Dee Dave that Mister Jere was hooking him? Dee Dave thought Mister Jere was his friend, and in a way Dee Dave was right. Mister Jere would go to bat for Dee Dave if he got in trouble with the law. He would stake Dee Dave for grits and salt pork if crops got so bad Dee Dave was plumb out of money. But he would hook Dee Dave, too —a little here and a little there—and he would hook Clarissa and Hop and Bubba and Lena May and Hattie and all the rest of the nigger hands. Herb knew it now. Inside him, he had known it all along, but this was the first time it had come up and hit him in the face, right out.

"I don't know," he told Reece. "I don't know. What would you do?"

Herb could figure pretty well what Reece would do, but now they had started talking about the thing, it was hard for him to think of anything to say. Reece didn't mind a bit, though, telling him what he would do.

"Me—hell fire, kid, it's just a nigger, ain't it? Besides—you want him to get hell beat outa himself? S'pose he was to go to Mister Jere and . . ."

"I know that," Herb said quickly. He felt a little sick. "No use in that."

Reece stood up and brushed himself off.

"Look Herb—I'm quitting this stuff today," he said. "Too hot to work. If you want to, you can borrow my wheel till school starts. And if you want to buy it, you can start paying on it any time you like. I'll make the price right for you."

"Reece is pretty smart," Herb thought, still sitting on the spread-out cotton-sack. "Smarter than I thought he was. He's put the sand in my well this time, all right!"

The choice had to be made: Herb could say yes and line up with Reece and Mister Jere and all the white folks, here and everywhere. Or maybe he could say no and line up with Dee Dave and laugh at fat Clarissa and the kids and smell the smell of the mules and the dusty wagon in the evening when the stars were beginning to shine and they were riding back to town, tired out and hungry, but feeling good with the goodness of a day's work back of them. He could line up that way, if he wanted to—line up with the fierce, sweet sadness that crept into Dee Dave's low, heavy voice when he would sing to himself, driving along home:

245

"High road go up,
   Low road go down.
De black man tremble
   When de boss come roun'.
Come anigh me, Lawd!
Come anigh me, Lawd!
Come anigh—come anigh!"

Only if he said no, though, Reece would mark him down for a nigger-lover and that would be enough. That would do for him, because there would not be a single white boy in town that would fool with a nigger-lover for two minutes. And he would be in high school in three more weeks, and it wouldn't be so good for him if the boys there got the idea he was a nigger-lover. It would be even worse than if Mister Jere had looked up a minute ago and seen him leaning over the end of the wagon. Herb knew that he had to make up his mind, and that he had to do it right that very minute.

He stood up and brushed the dust off Reece's sack and handed it to him, not looking him in the face.

"Thanks, Reece," Herb said. He walked beside Reece on down toward the rows they were going to start picking. "I'll take it. I can get out here faster—thataway!"

Reece glanced at Herb, looked away quickly. He was sorry about it all, but he liked Herb anyway, and he couldn't see why Herb would be bothered about a nigger, one way or the other.

"All right, Herb," he told him. "It's yours. And when we get done today, I'll pump you back to town, so's you can kind of get the feel of it!"

Herb didn't say anything. He walked on down to the end of his row, spread his sack, slipped into his strap, and moistened the tips of his fingers with spit. There was no need for him to say anything. For he knew, and Reece knew, that he would not be riding with Dee Dave any more.

THOMAS THOMPSON

THOMAS THOMPSON was born at Amarillo, January 27, 1909. He attended New Mexico Military Institute and Southern Methodist University. After graduation from the University of Southern California, he took a master's degree from Louisiana State University. During World War II he was a naval intelligence officer in the Pacific. He now lives in Amarillo, where he manages an investment business and serves as business editor of the *Globe-News*.

Thompson has written only a few stories, but they have been of high quality. "Good-bye, Old Man," part of a novel of which the manuscript was lost, was published in the *Southern Review* and placed on O'Brien's Roll of Honor for 1936 and given a three-star rating. The present work, "A Shore for the Sinking," also from the *Southern Review*, was chosen for reprinting in Brooks and Warren's anthology, *Understanding Fiction*. Like the stories by Anderson, Dobie, Goyen, Karchmer, and Kidd, it provides ammunition against those who say that Texas writers have spent all their time playing cowboy in a never-never land. Here is a successful city businessman, forced by the courage and resourcefulness of a woman and her daughter to make comparisons with his own womenfolk and to ask some questions about what-shall-it-profit-a-man.

A Shore for the Sinking

Rascoe was driving slowly, but before he could decipher the peeling street sign, he had almost passed Grant Avenue. He cramped his wheel and the back of his car slid around the corner. Stopping he looked back to make certain. These streets out here all looked alike, he told himself as he started forward again, slowly, with the heavy realization that he had about arrived at the place he was in no hurry to reach.

Grant Avenue was a shadeless, downhill street—a blind street. At its end rose a huge gas holder bulking over the rows of exposed bungalows like a drum over children's blocks. Here resided the poorest of the white collars with his five rooms of frail privacy, a garage for his car and a spot of yard for his children.

It was the noon hour, and the glare of the July sun had penetrated and become a part of everything. This was a job that had been rankling in Rascoe's mind for weeks. In defense of his purpose his mind darted to Veal.

Six months he had carried the chiseler and not a dime. The fellow had even stopped promising; he had stopped looking for work. One of these bag-eyed, say-nothing sort that put his own value on himself and sat at his window defying the public to get more than a hundred and twenty a month satisfaction out of him. Small wonder he got the sack. Too long a public employee—that was the trouble. Press him and he would lift the corner of his mouth and show his side teeth snarling: "Polotics, polotics!" And that was the end of it. You couldn't bully him or budge him. The man hadn't the steam, but born in him were the notions of one of these communist fellows in the East. A gone-to-bed communist—that was what he was!

Copyright 1938 by the *Southern Review;* reprinted by permission of the author and publishers.

248

A Shore for the Sinking

In front of the house stood the deputy's car, but there was no sign of a van or anything to haul their stuff away. . . . Well, this was silly sitting here. He gave the house a quick glance of distaste. It was one of the several monuments to his business foresight. In '28 he had invested some surplus earnings—oil royalties—in short term loans secured by city property that would always be good. A few years later, when H.O.L.C. came along, he had an opportunity to unload for bonds that were selling at eighty-one, but at that time he had a mind of his own, and now he had a dozen two-thousand-dollar houses, and H.O.L.C.'s were selling around 104. He despised the pettiness of this rent business. Fifteen here, eighteen there, once a month and twice a month. It was an endless business and it had become a sore spot with him; the more so, because all of his real estate-owning friends had been at him with their advice: Their warning about not turning soft and the little song they chanted at him about Taxes, Insurance and Depreciation.

Rascoe's hand reached for the door handle. There was little danger of his turning soft. He had been working up to this too long. This was as good a day as any for an eviction.

In the living room window hung a sign that said:

PIANO LESSONS
AND
TAP DANCING

Thinking of Veal, Rascoe gave a mirthless little laugh the traces of which deepened into a frown. He was reminded of Veal's family that he would have to face—a wife and a daughter the same as he had himself. He had never seen them because he had made a point of catching Veal away from his hole. But the time had come, and here he was, and as Budge Crawford said: Taxes, Insurance and Depreciation.

With this blithe little phrase lilting through his head he started up to the porch feeling nearly heartless, determined to be detached, warily incurious as to what was to become of them.

They were having their lunch, and it was not Veal that answered the door but his wife.

"Come in, Mr. Rascoe," she said pleasantly in a good voice, "we are just finishing our dinner."

The deputy was sitting in the only easy chair in the front room. His thumb was tucked under his gun belt. He nodded at Rascoe and shifted his tooth pick. Bereft of his rehearsed attitude, Rascoe felt stunned and guilty. It seemed somehow ironically natural that the fat old chiseler would have captured himself a fine woman. She was gracious—perhaps kindly—her house was immaculate, but the remarkable thing was that living with Veal had not destroyed the spirit she so obviously had. You felt the imprint of her personality all over the room: the bright little pictures, the cool dish of nasturtiums, the odor of the coffee—

But nothing was packed and that fool deputy had not said a word. Somehow Rascoe had a hopeful picture of him brandishing the eviction papers under Veal's nose. Veal raised his bright shoe button eyes from his plate and looked at Rascoe.

"Hydo," he said, chewing, like a fat old squirrel, Rascoe thought.

The prospect of being evicted did not seem to alter his appetite. In a way Rascoe envied him: no imagination, enough thick complacency to keep his mental fears fatted down.

Mrs. Veal passed the corn bread. She called to the daughter in the kitchen and said something quietly to Veal who grunted his reply. Rascoe did not hear what was said, did not want to—but about the woman's tone there was an echo, a forgotten quality of faith-for-the-sake-of-faith that had been lost in the women he knew.

The daughter—she was downright pretty—came in with the dessert. It was some sort of light crusted pie. She flashed a glance at Rascoe and hurried around to her father's elbow. "Daddy, here is your pie. Can't I bring you another cup of coffee?" she asked in a sprightly voice hovering over him like some bright bird.

Rascoe thought wryly of his own family. The two of them—his wife and daughter—seemed to be in some sort of pledged conspiracy to extort everything they could from him, to see that he never shirked in living up to his reputation as a good provider. At the same time, it never seemed to occur to them that they hadn't a perfectly legitimate right to criticize and be shocked at his method of doing it. Only this morning Winifred had said in her cool really disinterested voice:

"Joe, you're not going to actually throw them out, are you?"

"For cat sake, Winifred! What do you think that office I keep down town is, an eleemosynary institution?"

"An eleemosynary institution," repeated Kay after him, "that's what Daddy always says."

"Oh, be a sport, Joe," Winifred said putting on that voice that used to reach him so easily. "This is not the oil business."

"Yes, be a sport, Daddy."

It was a joke the way Winifred could scheme around to defend her emotional life. . . . Well, he thought, looking hard at the deputy, the fellow would have to do the talking. He gave him a harder look—harder and more enquiring.

Finally the fellow spoke up, rising bulkily and adjusting his gun belt. "These folks know a boy that's got a truck. He's goin' to haul their stuff off for them."

Rascoe nodded, relieved. There was nothing to do but wait. The daughter brought Veal his pipe, and while the women washed the dishes, Veal and the deputy sat smoking not saying a word. Rascoe's eyes wandering about the room rested on a handsome old cherry piano—a relic of better days. Rascoe's mind shunned the thought of better days. It was simpler just to consider them poor pay and be done with it.

Mrs. Veal came in with a smile—a strained smile, he guessed.

"Keep your seat, Mr. Rascoe. What part of town do you live in?"

Leave it to the women to make conversation under any circumstances. Better watch out.

"Adam's Park."

"Really. I used to teach music at Adam's Park High School. You know, you have to have your master's to teach in high school now."

Some one stepped up on the porch. Rascoe looked around, but it was not the boy with the truck. It was a neighbor woman squinting into the darkened interior.

"Come in, Mrs. Wyatt," said Mrs. Veal's voice.

The woman stepped inside saying, "Mr. Wyatt is home now for dinner. Him and Mr. Harper and Mr. Albright will be over to help Mr. Veal load as soon as the boy comes."

"That's so good of you, Mrs. Wyatt."

"Nothin', nothin' a-tall. You know, Minnie, the little thing, she's quite upset about your leavin'. She says it won't seem natural, her not comin' over here to her piano lessons."

"Bless her little heart. When we get settled, I want her to start them again. She has real talent, Mrs. Wyatt."

"Well, we could never afforded payin' lessons. The men folks will be over when the boy comes."

Thomas Thompson

The woman was unimpressive, but when her watery blue eyes looked him up and down, Rascoe flinched to his toes. Naturally, Veal's wife was the favorite of the neighborhood! Compared to this sort of thing the oil business was a clean high class way of making a living. You didn't take the roof off a man's head. You didn't move his family out on the street. At least, you didn't see yourself doing it. But what if he did let the fellow stay on a while? It would be only a brief respite; he was definitely down, and this would be a situation that would have to be faced sooner or later. Moreover, there was the restraining picture of his friends. It would tickle Budge Crawford to death to see him turn soft. What a damned idiot he was. Taxes, Insurance and—

A fruit company truck came to a fast stop behind Rascoe's car. A boy, whom Rascoe recognized as one of last year's high school football stars, leaped lightly out of the cab bursting with energy and muscle. He jumped on the back of the truck and tossed an empty banana crate on to the yard littering it with paper lining, straw and two blackened banana stalks. Snapping his fingers and swinging his arms he came up to the house. The daughter's small feet twinkled across the floor to meet him.

"Hy, Mary," he said grinning at the family and sweeping his eyes past Rascoe for something to put his hands on.

At first Rascoe was reassured to see some one strutting around with so much energy and confidence, but it was soon apparent that he didn't know how to take a hold and do a thing. He regarded it as a lark, and Rascoe could hear him saying: "Hey, boss, I've got to move my girl's family. How about the truck at noon?" When the other men came Mrs. Veal put him to work outside where he could do no harm.

The neighbor men all swept their eyes past Rascoe as the boy had done. It was the "working man" look; he had seen a lot of it around the oil fields and you did well not to shove at the barrier. Finding that he was invariably in the way, Rascoe went outside and sat on the porch rail. The deputy, however, laughed and joked, working right along with the others. He was accepted.

"Hey, there, Mrs. Veal, don't let that law carry those dishes. You know the story about the bull in the china closet."

"Pipe down, you. Lady what about this dish pan. There's a hole rusted in the bottom of it."

"Oh, daddy can fix that," said the daughter over her shoulder.

"Yes, Mr. Veal can fix that with his soldering kit."

As for Veal, who puttered around doing little or nothing, the men seemed not to resent his incompetence. They seemed hardly conscious of his presence. It was not he that Rascoe was putting out; it was his wife and daughter.

What made them stick by a man like that? What made them! It couldn't be the misshapen thing hiding in that thick rind of fat, that— It must be the memory of what he had been. No—perhaps an idea of what he should be. Women were damned fools.

Almost too soon Rascoe found himself standing in a house empty of furniture. There was only a broom and a waxing mop left. The daughter flitted between the truck and the bedroom where her mother was packing a few things in a battered suit case. Rascoe could not keep his eyes from her trim ankles and feet twinkling across the floor. It was she who taught the tap dancing. Twice the pep of his own daughter. Alert gray eyes and she hadn't a wheedling or pouty thing in her. Would his own family stick by him on a spot like this? Well, they would darned well have to, but he had a sneaking notion that they would do it whining. Winifred hadn't the guts. He had heard her and her cool-voiced bridge-playing friends talking it over. It was their figures, their hands, their afternoon naps, and the things they were used to, my dear. He was sick of the breed. Here was another kind and whether it was circumstances or God that made them that way, he didn't care. And it was they he was throwing out!

The men were going back to their homes. "No, thank you," Mrs. Veal said, declining further offers of assistance, "everything will be fine now. Good-bye, and thank you. Good-bye."

She came into the house. With alarm Rascoe watched her take the broom and begin to sweep the floor—the already clean floor.

"Mrs. Veal. Don't do that!"

"I beg your pardon."

"The floors, I mean. They look great. Never mind them."

"Mr. Rascoe, we couldn't think of leaving them this way. They were beautiful when we moved in—except for a few spots of grease where the stove was. There were just a few, but grease is grease. Mrs. Rascoe will tell you that, or does she do her own cooking? Mr. Veal took sand paper and tried to cut it out, but the stain was too deep. If you'll just step outside, we'll have your house clean for you in five minutes."

As he stepped on to the porch the girl slipped past him. She had rags over her shoes so as not to scar the darned floor.

Suddenly a hot film rushed over his eyes. He heard Budge Crawford's hoarse laugh—"Rascoe you've gone soft. Wait until the first of the year. Taxes, Insurance, Depreciation. You damned fool—"

Rascoe threw open the screen.

"Mrs. Veal," he said panic-stricken, "I've changed my mind."

"What do you mean, Mr. Rascoe?"

"I don't want you to move. You can tutor my daughter in music— teach her tap dancing."

The corners of her mouth quivered. Then she gave a little laugh. "I'm sorry, Mr. Rascoe. We've made our plans, and Mr. Veal doesn't like living so close to the gas holder. Mary, run to your father and get the key."

Rascoe had known it was no good as soon as he spoke. He should have propositioned Veal. Veal would have accepted calmly—calmly, and sat down on his fat tail.

The daughter brought the key and Rascoe put his hand out for it. She stood there looking at him with her red lower lip turned out. She held the key by the end of a string.

When she dropped it, Rascoe jerked as though he had caught a mouse.

"Thanks very much," she said in her sprightly cutting voice.

When the deputy had gone and when they had all piled into the cab of the truck, Rascoe locked his house. Why, he had acted green as a school boy. Getting in his car he started back to town glad to forget what he had learned.

JOHN W. WILSON

John W. Wilson was born November 2, 1920, near Navasota, in the Brazos River country of southeast Central Texas. Before entering Southern Methodist University in 1941, he was sports writer for the *Navasota Examiner* and correspondent for the *Houston Post*. At Southern Methodist and at Southwestern University, in Georgetown, he showed a special interest in folklore and in writing.

World War II interrupted Wilson's college training. Following in the footsteps of the writer with whom this book began, he with whom it closes became a "Fighting, Writing Marine." Wilson served as a platoon leader and company commander with the First Marine Division. He went through the whole of the Okinawa campaign, then moved on to North China for railroad guard duty during the Japanese repatriation program.

Home again, Wilson did further work in writing at Southern Methodist. In 1944 he published in the *New Mexico Quarterly Review* a story, "Thicker than Water," which was judged "distinctive" by Foley. Wilson was winner of first prize in the first *Dallas Times-Herald* Creative Writing Contest, with his book *High John the Conqueror* (1948), for which he signed a publication contract while still a graduate student. This deeply moving novel is the triangle drama of Cleveland Webster, a Brazos County Negro tenant farmer, his wife, and his white landlord. By the time of its publication Wilson had a second novel well under way and had published a number of excellent stories in the *Southwest Review, Prairie Schooner*, and other magazines. At the same time he taught English and helped run the publicity office at Southern Methodist.

But as Wilson wrote to the *Southwest Review*, "Nothing like a war to keep you from doing what you want to." For the Korean conflict he was recalled to active duty and served again with the First Marine Division.

Wilson returned to the United States in 1952. He now lives in Dallas with his wife and son and is presently engaged in public relations work and in writing two books: his interrupted second novel and a study of marine reservists in two wars.

John W. Wilson

"Grass Grow Again" returns to the Brazos bottoms to show in Munro Vance and his sons the spirit of the true farmer there and everywhere—his love of his land, his fidelity to it come flood or drought, his abiding confidence that it will sustain and enrich him. And I wonder if there is any better symbol to be found for the true spirit of the Texan.

Grass Grow Again

*In the autumn sometimes after a long and dry summer the
rain will come and fall to moisten the ground, and the grass will
spring up green again from its roots, refreshed and renewed
after pulling into itself in its thirst. Under the rain if it is a
soft rain and gentle, soaking the earth gradually without pelt-
ing hard and running off, the grass will spring new—young
again in autumn in the short days—and be green when the sun
shines. Before frost it comes out again to grow tall enough for
cutting in the fall, in the briefer sun between dawn and dark,
and autumn is a growing season.*

WE'RE ALMOST IN THE BOTTOMS NOW," my father told me. "There ought
to be some in here somewhere."

But the man said, "No."

"Not ara cow," he said. He had the longest face in the world and
the thinnest, and eyes so dark and deep-set they did not belong in
anything but the face of a hound dog. He had a great long black mustache and the ends of it were light reddish brown where it had got mixed
up with his chew. He had on a black hat, dusty on the crown and on
top of the brim, and he wore black boots on his feet. One foot was up
on the hub of the buggy wheel.

"Not ara cow," he said. "We had one but she died in the winter.
Had a bull yearlin but we butchered him in the spring. Things dry
around here; dry everwhere."

"Yes," my father replied. "Never saw the like. Grass is all burnt up.
Saw it dried up all the way out here from Beneden."

"You run the market, don't you?" the man asked. "Thought I knowed

Copyright 1951 by the *Southwest Review;* reprinted by permission of the author
and the *Southwest Review.*

who you was, but couldn't place you; we don't buy much meat."

"Yes," my father answered. "I run one of them. My name's Wedge."

"Proud to know you," the man said and put up his hand. They shook. "I'm a Vance—Munro Vance. This is all of us there is around here." He motioned behind him with his hand, toward the house.

The dogs were crawling back under the porch and the chickens had quit running around in the yard. A woman stood just inside the door wiping her hands on her apron. A boy about my own age was nearer the yard fence and a bigger one had looked around the corner of the house from the back and then was gone again.

We had been in the buggy nearly all day. It was before daylight when we left Beneden and about the only time we had got out was to sit by the side of the road under the tree and eat lunch out of the bucket. Both of us had the road dust all over us and I was so dry it felt like my throat had been hung out on a line. I kept punching at my father while they were talking, pushing at him a little in the back every now and then, and finally he turned.

"God damn it, Luke, what's the matter with you, boy?"

"Can I get a drink, Daddy? I'm thirsty and ours is all gone."

"Sho, you can get a drink," Munro Vance said. "Can draw up a cool bucket out of the well. Why don't you get down?"

He took his foot off the hub of the buggy wheel and turned toward the house.

"Tillman!" he shouted. "Tillman, why don't you go yonder to the well and draw up some water?"

He turned to us again. "Come on down. I can sholy offer you a drink."

We got down and my father pulled out his watch and looked at it.

"Much obliged. We'll take the water. Boy just plumb drained that jug today, and I'm a little dry myself."

"Sho been hot," Vance said, leading the way to the well. "Igod, it ain't been a breeze all day."

Tillman was at the well drawing up the bucket. He was almost the size of the man, but he did not have the mustache and he looked rounder in the face and his eyes were wider apart and not so shadowed by his eyebrows nor set so deep in their sockets. He wore the black hat, though, keeping his head covered even if he was walking around the yard barefooted.

"They lookin for cattle, Papa?" he asked as he lifted the bucket to the curb, dripping, and held it by the bail so that it would not turn over and spill out the water.

"Yes," Vance said, and motioned for us to drink.

My father took the bucket and held it down for me, tilting it so that I could get my lips to the brim. The bucket was nearly the size of a nail keg and was made of thick oak turned green by the moss that grew on it. The water was clear and cool and I could see the bottom of the bucket, also green with moss, as I drank, holding my mouth to the brim where the wood was worn above the strip of iron that banded it, and feeling the water spill down my chin and throat and into my open shirt. It felt good. I stopped to breathe and lifted my head, waiting for my father to drink. The water tasted slightly of rotten eggs, but I did not notice it until I had stopped drinking.

"We got one head of stock," Tillman said.

My father stopped drinking as he held the bucket up to his face. He kept the bucket up there and listened. The man turned on the bigger boy, looking at him as if he didn't know what he was talking about.

"What head of stock we got?" he demanded. "Igod, boy, you know as well as I do there ain't a thing on four legs on this place."

"Sho," Tillman said. "We got a head of stock but he's done butchered. Butchered him this morning."

Munro Vance kept looking at Tillman for a while and then he started laughing. He leaned sideways to spit and raked his finger across the hair of his mustache and bent over a little to laugh.

"Igod, boy, for a fact," he said, chuckling. "I'd say he was about a yearlin."

Tillman nodded and grinned and took the bucket back, pouring the rest of the water into the chicken trough that sat on the ground beside the well.

The mare was nickering out by the fence because she had smelled the water drawn up from the well and splashed into the chicken trough. My father went back to get her and lead her, still hitched to the buggy, around into the lot. There was a trough made out of an old iron washpot just inside the lot fence, and Tillman drew up a couple of buckets more of water and poured them in there for the mare. She plunged her head in and sank her mouth down in the water almost to the depth of her nostrils. She drank around the bit in her mouth, supping the water for a long time and making no sound but that of her swallowing. Then she raised her head and tried to work her tongue out and my father took the bit out of her mouth and let her sink her head back into the trough.

"Why don't you-all stay for supper?" Munro Vance invited. "It ain't far to sundown and we can offer you what we got."

"I'd about decided not to go much farther tonight," my father said. "Maybe you would let us stay here and I could sleep the boy out yonder in the barn. He's a little bit young yet to lay out on the ground and I was hoping we could put up somewhere he wouldn't have to."

Vance nodded.

"We ain't got much room in the house or I'd say come on in. But you can stay there and be welcome. You can unhitch your mare and turn her loose and supper will be ready in a little while."

The ends of his mustache twitched up when he finished talking and his eyes sparked bright where they were set deep under his brows. He turned his head to spit and chuckled as he wiped his lips.

"Well, I wouldn't want to put you out any, but we sure would appreciate it if we could stay," my father said. He was trying not to pay any attention to the talk about the butchered yearling, because the man already had told him they had butchered their last head in the spring.

The boy my size had followed us to the well. He did not speak to me, nor I to him, but we stood in the yard and looked at each other.

"That's Henry," Tillman said to me, and the boy grinned for a minute.

"I'll show you where to get some corn for the mare," Vance said, and all of us went through the gap to the lot where my father stood by the buggy. Tillman held the gap down for me to come through and Henry to follow.

My father backed the mare away from the watering trough and unhitched her.

"I'll be glad to pay you for the corn," he said. "I wasn't real sure whether we'd be out all night this time and didn't bring any."

Vance walked across the lot toward the crib door. "I won't charge you nothing; she won't eat that much." He laughed as he put his hand on the latch to the crib door and turned around to my father. "God knows, corn is the one thing we got plenty of this year."

"I know," my father laughed with him. "Looks like everybody made a good crop of it this year and there's nothing here to eat it up."

"We made thirty bushels an acre," Munro Vance said from inside the crib. The shucks on the floor rattled as he tromped through them. We followed him into the barn and the dust rose in the darkness to tickle our nostrils and carry into them the musty smell of the crib. "Can't get nothing for it; it ain't worth hauling to town."

"I tell you one thing," Tillman said from behind me. "We goin to eat hominy till the world looks level."

Munro Vance and my father laughed at that, and Henry and I laughed too. We felt the hard ear corn under our feet and then climbed up to sit on a higher pile of it. All of us began to shuck corn and to throw the shucks down onto the floor of the crib. Tillman shucked an ear and began to shell it into a bucket he held between his knees. The mare had her head inside the door and was lipping at the shucks to try to taste a clean one that was not too dry.

"It's about all we got," Vance said. "But I'm glad we got something. We get our meal ground and catch our meat and try to hold on." He shifted as he leaned to reach for another ear and the unshucked corn slid rustling down the pile. "That's why you don't see us none in town."

"I know," my father said. "Everybody's in the same shape. It looks like this country is just flat bound to ruin a man."

"You ever think of movin somewhere else?" Vance asked.

"Yes," my father said. "I've got part interest in a place back in Alabama. My brother's living on it. I said we ought to go back there, but my wife said no, she was raised here, so I said we'd try to hold on a little longer."

"That's what we tryin to do," Vance said.

He and my father gathered up the corn they had shucked and carried the ears outside for the mare. Henry and I had another ear apiece for her trough, and the mare ate. Tillman came out with his shelled corn in the bucket and began to feed the chickens.

Munro Vance squatted on his heels against the side of the barn, and my father lowered himself beside him while Henry and I stood and watched the chickens run to peck up the corn Tillman was scattering. Vance said nothing for a while and then he spit juice from his tobacco out onto the dirt of the lot and wiped at his mouth and laughed.

"We moved," he said. "We come in here from Arkansas. Been here pretty near long enough to raise that boy there; he was eight when we come. We didn't stay long back yonder, but my daddy's buried there. He's the only one there; he's the only Vance in that ground—all I know

261

he might be the only one in the whole damn state. We come here and we got this place."

My father didn't say a thing, and after a little while Vance chewed and spit again, and the ends of his black mustache rose as his lip curled when he laughed before going on. Henry and I sat and watched and Tillman fed the chickens.

"And that's about all," Vance said. "Got this place and it pretty near burnt out from under us already. Ground crackin so wide open I'm afraid to let this little one go down in the parsture. Little devil would fall in."

He had to straighten up and lean back this time, his teeth showing yellowish white under the mustache.

My father laughed, too, and shook his head, saying, "That's the truth. Wide open."

Henry's mother came to the back door of the house and called. "It'll be ready in a minute," she said.

We went to the back porch to wash up in water dipped into a basin out of the open-ended barrel that stood under the eave of the roof. The water in the barrel was low and it smelled the same rotten egg way the water in the well tasted. I understood why when Tillman carried water from the well to pour into the barrel.

"He has to tote it," Henry said. "He don't have to when it rains."

"If it wasn't so late I'd take you up the road after supper and show you something," Vance said. "You know where that little red clay hill is, got cedars growin on top of it."

"Yes," my father answered. "Red Top. The one they call Red Top?"

"Anh," Vance said. "We got us a little place there, about an acre of it, and got it laid out clean with a fence around it. Cedars growin in there."

"Yes?" my father said, curious, but not sounding too curious because he wanted Vance to go on and tell him. "It might make melons or sweet potatoes," he said, drying his hands. "It might do that."

"Nonh," Vance told him. "It ain't no count to grow anything. Not an inch of soil on it before you come to the clay."

Henry's mother came to the door again and said, "It's ready."

We went inside the house and sat down at the table. My father said "Good evening, ma'am," to Henry's mother, but she just nodded her head to answer him since she was too busy with the supper and the stove. There was no place for her at the table.

She put a plate of cornbread on the table and went back for another platter.

"Not any hominy tonight," Tillman said, and I could see Henry start to grin.

Their mother brought the second platter and started to put it down in the center of the table. The meat on the platter smelled good, and potatoes were arranged alongside the meat, with gravy over them making them brown. As she bent to lower the platter she stopped and looked at Vance.

He waved a hand toward my father and she put the platter down at our end of the table.

"Help yourself," Vance said. "Animal before you."

Tillman had been moving around in his seat and now he could not wait any longer. "A yearlin," he said. "Coon. We butchered him this morning."

They all began to laugh, Munro Vance leaning back in his chair at the far end of the table and tilting his head back to laugh up at the ceiling, Tillman and Henry laughing and reaching for cornbread while their mother stood over to one side and smiled.

"I sho had a race with him last night," Tillman said. "Run him till nearly midnight. Got him up a big old cottonwood down there . . ."

"That'll do," Vance told him. "Let's have supper now, and you can tell about that after while."

After supper we went out into the yard again and my father thanked Munro Vance for letting us eat.

"Glad to have you," Vance said, "and glad we had something to offer you. That boy and them dogs have made many a round; never did know I'd be dependin on them like that."

"I sho like to lost him," Tillman said. "Got him up that cottonwood and we settled down around it. Built a fire to wait him out and dogged if he didn't jump for it beyond the dogs and run again. We treed him in a little old persimmon that time and I shook him out and got a sack over him before the dogs could tear him up."

"Had to," Vance said. "Them dogs ruin more meat. Have to jump mighty fast to save it; but we learnin to jump fast. Everybody got it rough out here now; I reckon you know."

"I know," my father agreed. "Everywhere. I don't see how a man can hang on."

"We goin to," Vance told him quietly, his voice low and flat and echoless in the evening. "Parsture burnt out now, like it is everwhere. But we goin to stay here. I told you we got that acre of ground up yonder at Red Top. We got it laid out and it's bare now, not a thing on it but cedars."

He stopped talking and it was so quiet for a moment I could hear the mare nosing the bare cobs around in her trough at the barn. Then he half turned to face my father more directly and I could see them both silhouetted tall and dark against the sky.

"But we goin to fill it," Munro Vance said. "We goin to use it for a buryin ground and we goin to stay here. One way or another we goin to stay this time. Grass goin grow again, and we'll be here. Rain someday; God knows it uh rain so we wish it hadn't. You come out for a cow then and you'll find one. All you want. Grass goin grow. It ain't nothing wrong with the grass nor with the place, and we goin to be here."

"Yes," my father said. "Yes, by God, I'll come back then."

We slept that night in the barn with our blankets spread out over a level spot hollowed in the hay. The air cooled off, and the night was still, and I went to sleep almost immediately. I roused only once during the night, and that not for long, waking to hear the dogs barking and Tillman talking to them as they left the house.